IN TURBULENT
SKIES

IN TURBULENT SKIES

British Aviation Successes and Setbacks 1945–1975

PETER REESE

First published 2020

The History Press
97 St George's Place, Cheltenham,
Gloucestershire, GL50 3QB
www.thehistorypress.co.uk
© Peter Reese, 2020

British Library Cataloguing in Publication Data.
A catalogue record for this book is available from the British Library.

ISBN 978 0 7509 9302 9

Typesetting and origination by The History Press
Printed and bound in Great Britain by TJ International Ltd.

CONTENTS

ACKNOWLEDGEMENTS

This book owes an immense debt to both organisations and individuals. The bulk of the early writing took place within the ordered and welcoming walls of a library. For the most part this was the excellent National Aerospace Library at Farnborough with its ever-expanding collection of prime and published materials on aviation. There its dedicated librarians, Brian Riddle and Tony Pilmer, show insatiable enthusiasm for their subject and took infinite pains in fielding my endless queries. I also enjoyed the facilities of the one and only Prince Consort's Library under its librarian Diane Payne.

Further valuable assistance has come from the Farnborough Air Sciences Trust, with its remarkable photographic collection on Farnborough and British aviation as a whole, BAE Systems with the excellent photgraphs from their collection and the Royal Aeronautical Society (which sponsors the National Aerospace Library) and which in conjunction with the Mary Evans Picture Library has supplied me with so many further images; from the public lending libraries of Farnborough and Farnham and from the National Archives chiefly through its online services.

With regard to individuals, I am most indebted to Mike Stanberry for his painstaking reading of the whole book and most discerning critical comments; Paul Vickers, historian and author for inspiration with the title and invaluable work on the book's images; Shally Lopes for her much-valued computer skills and inspired interpretation of my long-hand script; Brian Riddle and Tony Pilmer in their additional invaluable capacities as copy editor and indexer; Tim Winter for his postcard illustrations; Sir Donald Spiers for his generously given expertise on aviation matters; Reg Milne and his wife Felicity for their hospitality and thorough briefing on the Royal Aircraft Establishment (RAE); Katrina Sudell for making available her father, Sir John Charnley's, personal life story and more besides; Arthur Webb for his inspiration and outstanding knowledge of the aeronautical industry; the Aerospace Library's dedicated team of volunteers, Rob Cooke, Rob Perry, Beryl James and David Potter for their valued friendship and active assistance; Dave Evans for his personal support to Barbara and myself; and my many good friends at FAST, most notably Richard Gardner, Graham Rood, David and Anne Wilson, Paul and Marie Collins and Veronica Graham-Green.

I also wish to acknowledge the vital support of The History Press, particularly my commissioning editor Amy Rigg, and Fenton Coulthurst.

Finally, as in so many past years I continue to pay tribute to my wife Barbara, who remains indefatigable and keeps everything going while her husband is absent in libraries and, when present, besieges her with aviation matters and depends on her ever-practical reactions to his early drafts.

As ever, I remain responsible for any errors and deficiencies.

Peter Reese
Ash Vale, Spring 2019

PROLOGUE

This is my third book about the development of British aviation with particular attention to the contributions of outstanding individuals. The first was concerned with the origins and development of manned flight in Britain, concluding with preparations for the First World War and the movement of the fledging Royal Flying Corps to France, where it was confidently expected to be expanded to meet its escalating commitments.

The second was about the interwar period (including the birth of civil aviation), which opened with the neglect and run down of military aviation during the 1920s and was followed by its rebuilding during the 1930s, when a new generation eventually succeeded in providing the modern aircraft needed for the coming war.

The present book about the thirty-year period following the Second World War portrays a reverse situation. It opens with British aviation at an historical high with continuing lofty ambitions – only for them to prove beyond its capabilities due to most formidable external competition, particularly from the United States.

It was not for lack of initiatives, nor without its successes, contingent as they might have been, but during the post-war years a succession of unforeseen reverses and miscalculations stacked the odds firmly against British aviation, with its core supporters unable to influence things in its favour as they had in the past.

Serious problems arose immediately after the war when the Brabazon Committee, which Winston Churchill was confident would identify new classes of civilian aircraft, came to a number of flawed decisions. These included favouring a grossly oversized airliner for the vital transatlantic route and advocating the use of interim turboprop engines rather than going straightaway for full jet propulsion. When the committee arguably got things right with the

Comet jet airliner – although it was envisaged primarily as a fast mail carrier – major structural weaknesses stopped it becoming a world leader.

During the early post-war years things appeared more favourable for military aircraft, although the government's diversion of capital from aeronautical research and development to domestic and social provisions not only brought about damaging cancellations but placed undue reliance on surviving aircraft programmes. While the Hawker Hunter interceptor and Canberra bomber were excellent aircraft, delays led to them acting as stand-ins rather than being at the forefront of technological development. The Hunter, for instance, lacked supersonic capability, while the Canberra's large orthodox wings appeared dated against other, swept-wing models. Although both surpassed themselves due to their outstanding designs, their successes helped conceal serious deficiencies in the continuity of military aircraft types.

Within the industry outdated industrial practices were soon apparent with the construction of Britain's V-bombers that highlighted the excessive numbers and varying strengths of British aircraft manufacturers at the time. Having them built by four different firms might have represented a safety-first policy but it brought about a situation where just one aeroplane, the Avro Vulcan, proved outstanding. Even so, whatever the underlying weaknesses some commentators in the self-congratulatory style of the day, considered the Hunter, Canberra and V-bombers (along with the Comet airliner before its later disasters) as heralding a new golden age for British aviation.

Such claims became increasingly difficult to support in the missile field when meeting with the greater urgency and higher investment levels of the American programme. The relatively long development cycle of the British IRBM Blue Streak, for instance, intended as a replacement for the V-bombers, put it behind its American counterpart and its growing vulnerability to Soviet missile strikes brought about its cancellation.

Major difficulties also became apparent in the fast-expanding field of civil aviation where, following the unfortunate Comet, the country's other aspiring airliners, the VC10, Trident and BAC 1-11 – designed primarily for British airline use and lacking rapid follow-up versions – failed to gain their anticipated foreign sales.

All such shortcomings were heightened by uncharacteristic timidity and lack of imagination that cost the industry clearly. In a country rightly proud of its originality and inventive capacity relatively little support was shown towards the production of unorthodox aircraft of V/STOL and rotary designs. The brilliant Hawker Harrier was long unappreciated by the RAF, with the Americans better appreciating its special abilities, and Britain's indigenous helicopter industry was hobbled by the most severe financial restrictions that enabled its US competitors to forge ahead, with UK helicopters having to be built under licence or produced in conjunction with the French.

With the immense pressures bearing down on UK budgets there was the greatest need to spend the funds wisely. Instead, some of British aviation's largest projects appeared to lack commercial soundness. Whatever its prestige, there were far fewer economic reasons for developing Concorde (whether in conjunction with France or not) than say supporting the development of BAC's advanced 3-11 aircraft. Such judgements moved into areas of financial unreality with Rolls-Royce's desperate attempts to sell its revolutionary bypass engine on adverse financial terms to the US, a state of affairs subsequently made worse by the government's decision to allow the company to descend into bankruptcy.

During the early post-war period there appeared to be fewer dedicated and fearless individuals than before. Arguably high taxation and controls on wealth creation played a part but with the current industry undertaking fewer, more costly and collaborative programmes there appeared less opportunity for home-based entrepreneurs.

Contrarily, during a time of declining military and political influence, lingering memories of one-time dominance, allied with a measure of over-confidence from winning the war, led to uncharacteristic weaknesses in decision-making.

Quintessentially this book identifies an exciting if ultimately tragic period of wasted opportunities, where want of confidence and botched decisions when facing unmatched competition deprived the most exciting and certainly the most romantic of Britain's industries of the successes – and their concomitant financial rewards – that initially seemed possible.

PART 1

CONTINUING
HIGH AMBITIONS

1

CIVIL FLIGHT AFTER THE WAR: STOPGAP AIRCRAFT

The Second World War checked what promised to be an exciting and expansionary time for British civil aviation, although just prior to the war Britain's aircraft industry lagged behind both the US and Germany in the development and production of saleable civil transport aircraft.[1] Journey times to other European capitals and to Empire destinations were coming down sharply, while flying across the Atlantic – if not yet in one bound – was increasing in frequency. As a result, flight was well on its way to becoming an accepted, if by no means regular, form of travel, with rapid growth certain.

Savoia-Marchetti S.73, a stylish Italian airliner. (Author's collection)

In Britain such progression was checked by the outbreak of the war when its civil aviation was still in flux. On 4 August 1939, one month before war was declared, Imperial and British Airways united to become the British Overseas Airways Corporation (BOAC), but it would be a further nine months before, on 1 April 1940, the new authority started operating. By this time, overriding military requirements had led to the RAF's takeover of Imperial's former headquarters at Croydon and the decision to stop building civilian airliners during the war, in stark contrast to the continued production and development of airliners in the US.

Remarkably, unlike the German Luftwaffe, the RAF had made no detailed plans prior to the war for using civilian aircraft to support its increasing transport requirements. In any case, the planes available were a mixed bag with many at the veteran stage, although just before the amalgamation attempts had been made to obtain new and better aircraft. By the end of 1938, Imperial Airways had introduced their first Empire flying boats, and in the case of land planes, Armstrong Whitworth Ensigns were coming into service along with (the far less robust) de Havilland Albatrosses.

British Airways had always been more fortunate in not having to buy British aircraft and they had purchased Fokker and Junkers aeroplanes before acquiring American Lockheed 10s and 14s, whose 200mph cruising speed brought even Eastern European destinations a morning's flight from London.[2]

The German Junkers Ju 52/3m, undoubtedly one of the best-known interwar aircraft. (Farnborough Air Sciences Trust)

On successive weekends in September 1938, the latter were used to fly Neville Chamberlain to Munich to engage in talks with Adolf Hitler over his proposed occupation of the German Sudetenland. Whatever the British airliners' capabilities, in view of the imminent war, Sir Francis Shelmerdine, the then Director of Civil Aviation, took the revolutionary step of recommending the compulsory chartering and employment of all civilian aircraft.

Consequently, when war was declared, domestic air services were immediately suspended with land-based aircraft moving to Whitchurch near Bristol and the flying boats to Poole. At Whitchurch the staff camouflaged the planes by hand-painting them using pots of green and brown paint.

Although some cross-water services to Scotland, across the Channel, and to neutral states were soon resumed, other civilian aircraft were brought into the so-called National Air Communication Scheme, which was intended to act as a surrogate transport service for the Royal Air Force.[3]

In November 1939, a number of aeroplanes were flown out to France, where some were destroyed by the advancing Germans. In 1940, for instance, four of the twelve Ensigns were lost and only four Lockheed 14s out of seven survived the year.

By the end of 1940 the British Purchasing Commission was buying up what planes it could in the US, including second-hand DC-2s and Lodestars, to reinforce both BOAC and the RAF's transport landplane fleet in the Near East and on the vital air route across Africa.[4]

With so many changes and aircraft losses, continuity among BOAC's senior management would have been of obvious advantage but Sir John Reith, its outstanding chairman and author of the airlines' amalgamation, left to join the War Cabinet as Minister of Information. He was succeeded by oil magnate the Honourable Clive Pearson, who although a gifted financier and air enthusiast who had masterminded the amalgamation of the internal airlines into British Airways, was essentially a shy man who lacked Reith's contentiousness.

Pearson selected ship-owner Walter Runciman to be his director general and brought with him his previous managing director at British Airways, Major Ronald McCrindle, together with the company's senior financial advisor, Gerard d'Erlanger. He quickly lost d'Erlanger, who assumed control of what came to be called the Air Transport Auxiliary, an organisation whose pilots, including women such as Amy Johnson, would ferry service aircraft from the factories to RAF squadrons.

From the outset, Pearson and his board faced major problems over aircraft capacity as they attempted to keep the traditional Empire routes open in the face of enemy action. These multiplied after attacks that caused repair facilities to be transferred from the UK to Durban, South Africa, with others established in Cairo, Egypt. From Durban, BOAC's flying boats were able to progress through the Middle East to Australia and New Zealand on the so-called Horseshoe Route. Converted Liberator bombers were brought into use to fly RAF crews across the Atlantic to Montreal, where they picked up new aircraft coming on line in the US and Canada.[5] Another important assignment was to fly between Scotland and Stockholm, to bring back indispensable Swedish ball-bearings.[6] These were dangerous times for in the Middle East BOAC's aircrews were often required to operate in extremely difficult conditions, such as having to fly a few feet from the ground to avoid enemy fighter interceptors in the Western Desert, or when flying to the relief of Malta.

Even so, to the dismay of some board members, during 1941 the Corporation's tasks were reduced when Churchill asked Pan American Airways to take over many of the arrangements for the delivery of military aircraft to the Middle East. Following the US's entry into the war, Pan American in turn relinquished its trans-Africa service to the United States Army Air Force, which commenced delivering supplies to its armed forces as well as those of China and Russia.

Whatever BOAC's best efforts, with no new British planes it suffered from a chronic shortage of aircraft, a situation highlighted in December 1942 when during a debate in the House of Commons. Robert Perkins, the one-time scourge of Imperial Airways, described BOAC's fleet in the following derogatory terms:

> This mixed contingent of aircraft consists partly of old crocks, five, six, seven years old, many of them ripe for the scrap heap. It consists partly of RAF throw-outs, crumbs from the rich man's table, machines which the RAF do not want, and partly owing to the generosity of our American friends, modern American machines.[7]

The modern American machines to which Perkins referred included the rugged all-metal Douglas Dakotas, which were delivered from 1942 onwards. In fact, BOAC not only had to share flying responsibilities with the Americans but had to watch the RAF's growing involvement in operating regular transport services, until on 11 March 1943 the House of Commons learned of the RAF's intention to establish its own Transport Command. The fast-expanding movement of personnel by air and the addition of other officials to the RAF's earlier VIP passengers made this an inevitable step. The beleaguered BOAC board hardly saw it this way, considering it a major threat to their existence and to British civil aviation as a whole.

Douglas DC-3 Dakota IV with RAF markings. A total of 1,928 Dakotas were received by the RAF during the war. (Farnborough Air Sciences Trust)

Short S.25 Sunderland III G-AGJO, named *Honduras*. (Farnborough Air Sciences Trust)

Acting on this belief, Clive Pearson sent a memorandum to Harold Balfour, the Under-Secretary of State for Air, in which he emphasised that BOAC should not be in a subservient position where RAF Transport Command was concerned, and sought his assurance that the Corporation should operate all the regular trunk services 'subject to political and military requirements'.

In fact, Pearson went much further, for when the minister's response did not appear to recognise 'the difficult conditions in which the Corporation has operated throughout its existence', the chairman, accompanied by his board members (with the exception of Gerard d'Erlanger, who was running the Air Transport Auxiliary) tendered their resignations on 19 March 1943.

This was a gross overreaction and an ill-advised one, since it was hardly likely to change the government's policy in their favour. In response it swiftly appointed a more malleable board with Lord Knollys, one-time Governor of Bermuda, as an 'amateur' chairman and Air Commodore Critchley, a veteran of the Great War and golf fanatic, as Director General. Despite his golf, Critchley saw that BOAC received extra aircraft and by the end of 1944 the airline had 44 flying boats and 111 land planes in service, including 52 Sunderlands.[8]

However inept Clive Pearson's tactics, he had already proved himself an unquestioned champion of British civil aviation and in a final riposte he and his fellow directors set their future hopes down in a White Paper emphasising especially the lack of provisions for long-term post-war matters.[9]

In fact, Pearson was mistaken about the absence of long-term planning, although things were unquestionably still in the early stages. Three committees had already met to consider the question of British civil aviation's revival after the war. Two sat as early as 1941, one under eminent aeronautical engineer Roy Fedden to consider future technological developments, while, under Sir Francis Shelmerdine, a government departmental committee discussed post-war policy in more general terms. In the following year an independent committee of senior industrialists with Peter Masefield as secretary also commenced looking at civil aviation's future.

Due to other more pressing priorities none were sure of bringing about major results. The situation was, however, about to change when the Prime Minister's attention was forcibly drawn to the problem. This occurred during 1942 when he decided to fly to Moscow and let Joseph Stalin know there was no chance of the UK and US opening a Second Front in Western Europe during the coming year. The only available aircraft was a Liberator bomber. Churchill was placed in its converted bomb bay, which was not only freezing cold but required him to wear an oxygen mask for much of the journey.

Consolidated B-24 Liberator heavy bomber, which saw war service from 1941 to 1945. (Farnborough Air Sciences Trust)

As a consequence, in December 1942, despite his other immense responsibilities, Churchill called together Sir Stafford Cripps, Minister for Aircraft Production, together with Lord Brabazon, (pioneer aviator and previous Minister of Aviation) whom Churchill had known since the earliest days of flight, to consider the future development of British civil aviation and its aeroplanes. Churchill meant business and under Brabazon as chairman, a committee of senior civil servants was formed to make specific recommendations for post-war civil transport aircraft for Great Britain and its Empire.

This moved with considerable urgency. It reported on 9 February 1943 following forty-eight days of investigation and (a month before Pearson and his fellow directors resigned from BOAC) it proposed the conversion of a number of military types into transport aircraft to compete with the current American airliners.[10] These included the Avro York based on the Lancaster bomber, the Short Hythe and Sandringham flying boats based on the Short Sunderland, the Vickers Warwick, which was a development of the Wellington bomber, and the Vickers Viking, also based on Wellington components.[11]

After studying the recommendations, the Cabinet authorised the setting up of a second Brabazon Committee, with more comprehensive, detailed terms of reference whose members would come from across the aviation industry.[12] Apart from Lord Brabazon, those selected included Sir William Hildred, the Director General of Civil Aviation (who served on the original committee), leading aircraft constructor Captain Geoffrey de Havilland, Major Ronald McCrindle, Alan Campbell-Orde and Major Roland H. Thomson from BOAC.

The Avro York's performance proved disappointing. (BAE Systems Heritage)

Brabazon described them approvingly as 'a useful mixed bag' who before coming to their conclusions would be required to hold discussions with the aircraft companies and Commonwealth countries.

In contrast to the initial committee's rapid decisions, the second sat for two and a half years before making its recommendations in December 1945. During this time, it met on sixty-two occasions and produced 151 papers. These confirmed the new aircraft identified by the earlier committee and authorised the construction of six new classes of aircraft, however, these were not expected to be completed until the later 1940s and 1950s. The importance placed on the future role of civil aviation and the assumption that Britain would unquestionably have a leading part to play in the post-war world was seen by the attendance of several Cabinet ministers, including Churchill, and senior civil servants from five government departments at a time when the war was reaching its climax.[13]

Churchill himself was concerned with the pressing requirement for interim aircraft to be brought rapidly into service, which he optimistically expected would hold their own against current American airliners both during the late stages of the war and in the immediate post-war years. To help see they were produced on time he chose Lord Beaverbrook who, following his vital achievements towards aircraft production at the beginning of the war, had resigned on grounds of exhaustion.

Churchill accepted his resignation providing he remained in the Cabinet with the sinecure post of Lord Privy Seal, where he would be available to carry out other special missions. On 28 September 1943, the Prime Minister instructed his prime troubleshooter to head a War Cabinet Committee to expedite the Brabazon Committee's proposals for stopgap aircraft and help formulate government policy for post-war civil air transport arrangements worldwide.

Beaverbrook wasted no time in appointing as its secretary the outstanding aviation journalist Peter Masefield, who had carried out the same task with one of the earlier committees. He also chose as its members influential figures from within the current government, including Archibald Sinclair, Secretary of State for Air; Sir Stafford Cripps, Minister of Aircraft Production; eminent scientist Lord Cherwell; Viscount Cranborne, Secretary of State for the Dominions; Lord Leathers, Minister of War Transport; Hugh Dalton, President of the Board of Trade; and Richard Law, Minister of State at the Foreign Office.

Following their first meeting on 11 November 1943, they became accustomed to assembling on a weekly basis. During the second meeting, Beaverbrook emphasised his belief in the need to use British aircraft (rather than American ones) on Empire trade routes after the war. Unfortunately, he was then forced to reveal that the interim Avro York that had been developed from the Lancaster bomber as a private venture under designer Roy Chadwick had in fact been found unsuitable for trans-ocean routes.

In the preceding February, the Secretary of State for Air had informed the House of Commons that the York was capable of flying at 235mph over a range of 2,700 miles and it was intended to produce forty planes a month towards a provisional total of 1,300 within three years. Following the withdrawal of Beaverbrook's support, just seventy-seven planes were built and by 7 October 1950. BOAC had withdrawn all its Yorks from service. Beaverbrook was quite correct about such a noisy and uncomfortable aircraft – reputedly Roy Chadwick's least successful design – which was not pressurised and whose large and rather ungainly body made it heavy on fuel and require a full 10,000ft runway to get airborne.

Beaverbrook heartened his committee by telling them about a better alternative, a civil version of the Lancaster IV with a pressurised cabin that he said would be flying within the year, so that 'in 18 months from now (by May 1945) it should be the equal of anything the Americans can set alongside it'.[14] This would be called the Tudor and he expected it to compete with the American Douglas C-54 Skymasters and Lockheed Constellations in load

The Avro Tudor 4 proved unsuitable for transatlantic service. (BAE Systems Heritage)

carrying. Unfortunately, like the York, the Tudor would meet with many serious problems, including one affecting its stability, which led to it being rejected outright by BOAC.[15]

During the harsh winter of 1943–44, while Beaverbrook was with Churchill in Marrakesh, Peter Masefield visited British aviation firms across Britain to learn about their plans for the aircraft that could be brought into service to give a breathing space before the Brabazon Committee's advanced models came on stream. He was, however, realistic enough to anticipate their likely shortcomings (which in fact proved worse than expected) when in competition with American airliners expressly designed for their tasks.

To produce successful aircraft of this nature, Masefield needed ready co-operation from an industry concerned with wartime production and which at this time he described as a largely sleeping giant. On a series of visits he found it difficult to transmit his own sense of urgency to firms that were still fully engaged in meeting recurring wartime orders. The vast Handley Page factory was, for instance, packed with Halifax heavy bombers and others were still continuing to churn out wartime aircraft as fast as they could. Masefield well understood that in such a situation they were far more likely to be concerned with immediate problems such as the dilution of labour due to conscription into the armed forces rather than trying to anticipate the challenge of future markets after the war. In fact, the companies that were persuaded to convert their aircraft for civilian purposes found it helped them safeguard their levels of employment and keep their production facilities going.

Masefield was delighted to discover a fellow spirit in the indomitable George Edwards, chief designer at Vickers, who proved willing to take high personal risks by flying the company's Viking aircraft in terrible weather conditions to eliminate serious design faults before authorising variants of what would become a most successful aircraft.

What did dismay Masefield was his discovery within BOAC of what he believed was a strong disposition to buy American aircraft. Masefield considered it unpatriotic and disloyal, although it was an understandable reaction against the earlier edict given to Imperial Airways about buying British aircraft when superior models existed elsewhere. The wish to buy American received further support when severe problems appeared with British interim aeroplanes.

Masefield's convictions about the need for British industry to produce civilian aircraft as soon as possible were understandably fully shared by his chief, Lord Beaverbrook, who after visiting the United States during 1943 wrote a secret memorandum about the crisis facing British civil aviation:

> The choice that must now be made, should be understood. It is between having or abandoning British Civil Aviation after the war. The Americans who will possess suitable aircraft will capture the traffic. And once their aircraft, ground organisation, repair services and equipment are installed, we will find it impossible to oust them. It may be argued that we should negotiate for American types of aircraft (but) were we to obtain these, any system we set up, would not be British aviation nor would we be permitted to secure our American type until the Americans had developed a better type for their own use.[16]

Understandably, whatever the efforts of Beaverbrook and his energetic secretary, the Americans were not obligingly standing still. During 1943 they held their First National Clinic on Domestic Aviation, during which they showed themselves aware of the vast numbers of civilian planes rendered obsolete by the latest technological developments, and above all the need to keep in the technological forefront themselves. As one of their delegates Bruce Urthus put it, 'Our only hope for ultimate salvation is in our ideas and motivations.'[17]

This was ominous when, apart from the serious shortcomings with the York and Tudor airliners, the majority of the other British interim aircraft were to reveal serious limitations. Another proposed long-range aircraft was

Avro 691 Lancastrian, another stopgap aircraft. (Farnborough Air Sciences Trust)

Handley Page Hermes 4. (Farnborough Air Sciences Trust)

Avro's 691 Lancastrian. Although noisy and uncomfortable, this rapid conversion of the Lancaster bomber would be used by BOAC for delivering the Royal Mail and to reopen the London to Sydney service when in May 1945 the first aircraft carried just nine passengers on the route. The Lancastrian was capable of flying for 4,000 miles at 230mph and however uneconomical it undoubtedly met an immediate need, albeit with an unimpressive safety record: of the twenty-three examples operated by BOAC, eight crashed or disappeared without trace within five years. In all, eighty-two were built and the type remained in service until 1952.

In the case of medium-range aircraft there was the Handley Page Halton derived from the Halifax C V111 Transport Aircraft with a capacity for ten passengers, a range of 2,530 miles and a speed of 320mph. Serious delays prevented it coming into service until 2 June 1947 and although twelve were taken up by BOAC it quickly proved unequal to its expected performance. Even so eighty civil registrations were allotted to other Halifax CV111s that were converted to near-Halton standard.

In 1945 came the Handley Page Hermes, which could carry up to fifty passengers in a pressurised cabin over a range of 2,000 miles at 270mph. Unfortunately, on 2 December 1945 its first prototype crashed during a maiden flight from Radlett and only twenty-nine aircraft would eventually be built. After being retired by BOAC the type remained in airline service until 1960.

The performance of shorter-range aircraft proved distinctly better. In the case of the Bristol 170 Freighter, the type's main use was in car-ferry operations – it could carry two cars, together with their passengers – although the Wayfarer passenger-only version could carry thirty-two passengers. In this role, it proved an undoubted success; from 1948 it enjoyed worldwide sales and a later version capable of carrying three cars was also produced. In all, 214 Bristol 170s were built and production continued until 1958.

The most successful of the shorter-range interim aircraft was the Vickers Viking. This was designed by Rex Pierson as a civil version of the Wellington bomber, although it had a metal fuselage rather than the original geodetic construction. Its success owed much to George Edwards, who, when he became Vickers chief designer, carried out several inspired design changes, including experimenting with the installation of Rolls-Royce Nene turbojets.[18]

The Viking was designed to carry twenty-seven passengers over 1,875 miles and its maiden flight took place at Wisley on 22 June 1945, following which, it entered service on 1 September 1946. After serious problems with ice build-up and elevator overbalance, successful modifications led to the plane becoming a solid performer for BEA, which operated eighty-three of the 163 produced.[19]

Bristol Freighter, inelegant but reliable. (Farnborough Air Sciences Trust)

Vickers Viking, Britain's first post-war airliner. (Farnborough Air Sciences Trust)

The type was not an immediate financial success, although it kept Weybridge solvent during a difficult period. During the plane's early stages, the company lost £1 million, which led Edwards to observe that 'this was unsurprising considering we sold them at £34,000 each all in, including the radio, seats and lavatories'.[20]

Vickers, however, went on to develop two further variants, the Valetta for carrying thirty to forty troops and the Varsity trainer. In all, 163 Vikings, 262 Valettas and 163 Varsitys were built, eventually making it an undoubtedly profitable venture.

The final aircraft in this category was the Armstrong Whitworth Apollo. This fell victim to other more successful designs, although its four Armstrong-Siddeley Mamba turboprop engines gave it an impressive top speed of 330mph and a range of almost 1,000 miles. The Apollo did not fly until 1949, by which time it was decided not to proceed.[21]

In addition were the relatively short-lived range of flying boats. Initially there was the long-range Short Shetland, which emerged after plans were announced in 1943 for an aircraft to carry up to seventy passengers plus eleven crew over a planned range of 2,750 miles at 240mph. However, after repeated delays, the first prototype was put into storage at Belfast.

In the medium range were the Hythe and Short Sandringham boats. The Hythe, an improved version of the Short Sunderland III, first flew in 1945 and twenty-nine were operated by BOAC. Accommodation was provided for twenty-four day passengers or sixteen sleeping berths, plus mail. From May 1946, the Hythe took part in the 12,000-mile journey to Sydney with a flying time of eighty hours in a total of five and a half days. While undoubtedly comfortable, such a leisurely pace proved of limited commercial value.

The Short Sandringham, a further conversion of the Sunderland III, offered an improved range of 2,440 miles, admittedly at a stately 175mph, and carried twenty-four passengers along with a crew of seven. Just nine Sandringhams entered service with BOAC, but during 1947 others were taken on by TEAL of New Zealand. By 1949, the Sandringham had been replaced by land-based planes.

It was not altogether surprising that the interim passenger aircraft should largely prove so disappointing. Their military forebears had never been designed with comfort in mind and the high mileage required of their civilian versions was only too likely to expose a number of further weaknesses. There were too the undoubted difficulties experienced in undertaking their development during the final stage of the war, which was not a good time for British Industry, including aviation.

Apart from the numbing twenty-four-hour shift system adopted by aircraft factories, its workforce faced other adverse elements, especially in winter where shortages of food, heating materials and disruptions to transport fell heavily on family employees, some of whose partners were away on wartime service and on whom news of battlefield casualties had such a serious effect.

In this context engineer John Brodie, writing about the design work on aero engines at de Hallivand at the end of the war, revealed first-hand the team's physical and mental state at that time:

> The war ended and we would have expected some let up. We had been working for nearly five years under almost inhuman pressure. In blacked out factories day and night merged, the days of the week had no identity, the hours of working were undefined.[22]

In spite of widespread exhaustion and the mixed record of the interim aircraft, as Winston Churchill understood so clearly, the Brabazon Committee's proposals for new types of civilian aircraft after the war offered a unique opportunity to compete against an ascendant American aviation industry.

There was no question about it being easy and it would not be achieved without unstinted commitment like that given earlier by Henry Royce or demanded by the great Roman Emperor Marcus Aurelius, who knew well that if only you could capture men's hearts they were ready to sacrifice food and sleep to the advancement of their chosen pursuit.[23]

Whatever the unquestioned difficulties, the expectations of Churchill and others depended on the foresight and practical inspiration of the Brabazon Committee's recommendations for new aircraft. However befitting, they could only succeed if they attracted sufficient orders both from Britain's national airlines and international ones, while their production schedules would need to equal the timing and cost of their American competitors.

How far the Brabazon recommendations achieved such hoped-for successes will be seen in the following chapter.

2

THE BRABAZON COMMITTEE:
FUTURE PLANS

The British government's attitude to civil aviation at the conclusion of the Second World War, with its Brabazon Committee tasked to predict the patterns of future aircraft, was markedly different from that after the First World War, when in 1920 Winston Churchill, the Secretary of State for Air believed the infant airlines should be left to stand on their own feet.

This greater sense of commitment was demonstrated on 1 April 1946 when Clement Attlee's incoming Labour administration declared the establishment of three nationalised state airlines: the British Overseas Airways Corporation (BOAC) responsible for air routes between Britain and other Commonwealth countries, the US and the Far East; British European Airways (BEA) for British domestic services and routes to the Continent; and British South American Airways (BSAA) for routes to South America (which, following a series of tragic accidents to its Tudor IV aircraft, merged with BOAC in 1949). BOAC was based in London at Heathrow, BEA at the nearby RAF base at Northolt and BSAA shared the Heathrow facility. The state monoliths were soon joined by a number of small private air companies, whose functions were limited by statute to charter flights and ambulance and rescue flying.

State subsidies were considered essential to take advantage of the anticipated build-up in European and world traffic (which from 500,000 in 1929 would, in fact, approach 30 million by 1949).[1] In 1945, the newly established Ministry of Civil Aviation published its blueprint for the future, justifying expenditure on the nationalised corporations by pointing out that although it was intended that air services should be made self-supporting as soon as possible, some measure of state aid was necessary 'to support essential but unremunerative services'.[2] The government also set sums aside to purchase the new classes of aircraft that the Brabazon Committee had identified would feature in post-war aviation: £21 million for BOAC aircraft, £9 million for BEA and £3 million for BSAA.[3]

This financial commitment assumed the Brabazon Committee's proposals would influence the design of virtually every post-war (transport) aircraft built by British manufacturers.[4] It was expected that such aircraft would gain worldwide orders; in 1945, the Ministry of Civil Aviation revealed its high hopes when it proudly stated that, 'Her Majesty's Government were taking all possible steps to accelerate the production of civil aircraft, both for the equipment of British airlines and for the export trade.'[5]

It also observed that because airline operations depended on technical progress 'for success or failure (they are) more dependent on the type of equipment used than on any other factor. Creative research and development, therefore is indispensable to advancement in an industry of which technical progress is the life blood.'[6]

Given British aviation's success in designing war-winning aircraft, the Ministry's anticipations for the development of successful civilian airliners seemed fully justified. Such high expectations partly help to explain the second Brabazon Committee's prolonged sequence of meetings over more than two and a half years before producing a list of proposals for the new types, along with their selected manufacturers, upon which work would proceed as soon as circumstances permitted. These were as follows:

Aircraft Type	Role	Constructor and name of the plane
1.	Transatlantic non-stop	Bristol Brabazon
1b.	Transatlantic non-stop	Bristol Brabazon II
2.	European transport	Airspeed Ambassador
2b.	European transport	Vickers Viceroy [later Viscount]
3.	Long-range Empire	Avro Tudor Bristol Britannia
4.	High-speed transport	DH Comet
5.	Feeder-line transport	Miles Marathon
6.	Light transport	DH Dove

The six classes, which included conventional piston-engined aircraft, turbo-prop and jet designs, ranged across the board, from the largest aircraft ever intended for commercial flight to small aircraft suitable for operating with commuter airlines. Whatever the committee's specifications, everything depended on the ability of its appointed designers and constructors and unsurpassed commitment from the workforce. Unfortunately, the latter was by no means guaranteed.

Following a tour of the industry during the winter of 1943–44, Peter Masefield harboured fears for the future because of what he considered was the British workforce's inclination for self-congratulation at the end of the war.[7] On returning from Washington in 1946, he expanded on this theme about an industry that 'had done an outstanding job in the war, but now appeared to be crippled by shortages of materials, electrical power cuts, petti-fogging arguments, small-minded political manoeuvring and a prevailing air of lethargy'.[8]

Masefield also feared that those responsible for the Brabazon Committee's recommendations did not appreciate the strong likelihood of failure, with some of its selected constructors unlikely to deliver the goods to a required standard or within a reasonable time frame. For him the only bright spots among the manufacturers at this time were de Havilland, with its many aircraft, engine, propeller and missile projects, and Vickers-Armstrong, with its profusion of dynamically managed programmes.[9]

Boeing Stratocruiser, proven and reliable. (WEZ VTEC licensed under CC by SA2.0)

The giant Bristol Brabazon. (Farnborough Air Sciences Trust)

Some of the difficulties identified by Masefield became evident with the proposals for the committee's Type 1 for non-stop transatlantic flights, which faced competition from the American Lockheed Constellation. This, together with the Boeing Stratocruiser, was already in service after some three and a half years of development, during which time some 1,700,000 drawing-office hours had been expended. [10]

The Type 1's specifications were for an epoch-making aircraft that came to be named after the committee's flamboyant chairman, who in the pre-war years had crossed the Atlantic on the *Queen Mary* and visualised a post-war world in which those who could afford it would be treated to the same level of comfort and luxury on that journey in an elegant airliner. [11]

The Brabazon was a Goliath weighing more than 100 tons with a 177ft-long pressurised cabin powered by eight Centaurus radial engines in coupled pairs (designed by Roy Fedden) that was scheduled to fly at some 250mph at 25,000ft over a range of some 5,500 miles. Despite its prodigious size, it was proposed to carry up to just 100 passengers in unquestionable comfort, or less than half that number when provided with commodious sleeping berths.

In 1942, Bristol Aeroplane Company designed a heavy bomber with a range of 5,000 miles and although it was not produced this led to the company's selection as builders of the Brabazon. On its Filton site, a new hall for the plane's construction and assembly would become the largest hangar in the world, at some 1,054ft wide and occupying 7½ acres. A crane system was installed in its roof capable of moving a 12-ton load around the interior, by means of which it was hoped to assemble as many as eight Brabazon airframes at a time.

The massive plane also required the construction of a vast new runway some 8,250ft long and 300ft wide, in the course of which the village of Charlton was swept away.[12] All this took place during the freak bad winter of 1946–47 that brought serious delays, while major problems were being experienced with the plane itself from what proved to be inadequate wing loading and engine power. In addition, the very size of its fuselage and wings resulted in unexpected range reductions and severe cost penalties.

Due to its vast size, Bill Pegg, who became chief test pilot at Bristol in December 1945 and aimed to fly the aircraft at the Farnborough Air Show of 1949, went out to the US to gain experience by flying the giant B-36 bomber, the so-called 'Peacemaker'. The Brabazon's subsequent first flight (as an empty shell), which took place on 4 September 1949, went relatively well, although the plane was unquestionably slow.

At Farnborough, the already obsolete aircraft succeeded in impressing the crowds of spectators, although more for its vast size than its unspectacular performance. Whatever its virtues, BOAC was already losing interest in what it saw as an uneconomic white elephant (whose construction cost £13 million) and the programmes for both model 1 and 1b (which was scheduled to be powered by eight British Proteus gas turbines) were subsequently cancelled.

Britain was thinking big at this time and in 1946 the massive Princess flying boat was added to the Brabazon programme. However, BOAC would soon decide the days of the flying boat were over. In any case, after the Princess's first flight in 1952 its Proteus turboprop engines experienced serious problems and it was retained as an experimental project only.

The Brabazon's problems came fully to roost during its protracted construction period, when fast-growing passenger demands for transatlantic flight were making capacity the most important factor, and the prospect of jet propulsion with its reduced noise and vibration, along with shorter journey times, rendered the underpowered Brabazon's luxury and huge dimensions unnecessary. By 1949, cheap excursion fares had already been introduced on the London to New York run.[13]

Even so, had its designers revised the seating arrangements and gone for gas turbine propulsion from the start – and had there been no serious delays with its proposed Proteus engines – it might conceivably have been another story. The sad outcome was that in 1945 (four years before the Brabazon's first flight) BOAC decided to purchase the double-decked, piston-powered, Boeing Stratocruiser (with sleeping accommodation and a range of

Saunders-Roe Princess flying boat. (Farnborough Air Sciences Trust)

Convair XC-99, the world's largest plane at the time. (Author's collection)

3,800 miles) for its transatlantic service. Although not jet powered, this smaller but still roomy aeroplane had, at 340mph, a significantly higher cruising speed than the Brabazon. With no other orders on the books, the high hopes for the giant aircraft came to an ignominious end.

The committee's Type 2 was for a European transport to replace the legendary American Douglas DC-3 on short-haul routes. Airspeed (whose majority shareholder was the de Havilland company) designed a high-wing aircraft powered by two Bristol Hercules engines, capable of carrying thirty-six passengers over 800 miles at 300mph. This was named the Ambassador and it made its first flight on 10 July 1947, becoming airborne at the same time as its main American rival the Convair CV-240.

Although it was considered a far better aircraft than the Convair, its constructors experienced difficulties with its all-metal construction and it took a further four years before, on 1 March 1952, it entered scheduled service.[14] As a consequence, the Ambassador could neither compete with the Convair nor the somewhat later American Martin 2-0-2A, which, despite experiencing delays, came into service on 1 September 1950.

When, in trying to regain the initiative, the Ambassador's passenger capacity was raised to forty-seven and its cruising speed to 255mph (over a range of 1,000 miles), its cost rose to a heady £225,000. As a result, only twenty-three aircraft were sold, twenty of which were to BEA, while the Americans sold 368 Convairs.

The committee's European transport aircraft Type 2b was confidently expected to be a popular model and it attracted two competing aircraft, Armstrong Whitworth's Apollo and the Vickers Viceroy, a situation freely accepted by the committee. The rivalry was soon resolved because, although two Apollos flew, their Mamba engines experienced major technical problems and they were abandoned, leaving the field to Vickers.

While initially inferior to the Apollo, under the dynamic leadership of designer George Edwards the private-venture Viceroy was proceeded with, and equipped with four Rolls-Royce Dart turboprop engines that offered both improved payload and higher wing loading. In 1947, after India's independence the country no longer had a viceroy and the type was renamed the Viscount. This pressurised aeroplane proved to be one of the milestones of British civil air transport: technically superior to the Convair, its engines gave greater smoothness in flight along with a 30mph speed advantage. From 1950 onwards, it proved most successful commercially with sales of 445 totalling £217 million, of which £147 million came from overseas.

Vickers Viscount, the first taurbo-prop-powered aeroplane in passenger service. (Farnborough Air Sciences Trust)

Bristol Britannia turboprop airliner. (Farnborough Air Sciences Trust)

The Brabazon Type 3 was for a long-range Empire aircraft that in Britain was believed to be the most important class of all. For the purpose, Avro produced its four-engined 693 Tudor. Two prototypes were ordered but following repeated problems it was cancelled in 1947, making it the only Brabazon class without a projected aircraft.

The requirement was eventually met by a post-war addition to the Brabazon programme, Bristol's 175 Britannia, which was propelled by four Proteus turboprop engines and designed to carry ninety-one tourist-class passengers over a range of 4,500 miles. Unfortunately, development was prolonged due to continuing problems with the engines and, although in July 1949 BOAC signed a contract for twenty-five and its first flight occurred in 1952, it did not come into service until February 1957. By then, its earlier lead had been lost and it had become too close to the pure jet era. There were only eighty-two sales for what has been called 'one of the safest and most reliable transport aeroplanes ever produced', most of which were to BOAC.[15]

The committee's Type 4 specification was for a high-speed transport, particularly for airmail, where the Ministry of Supply opted for the technologically advanced jet-propelled DH.106 Comet. De Hallivand sensibly developed it into a passenger aircraft, and its immense early successes and subsequent catastrophic failures from metal fatigue are recounted more fully in Chapter 5.

Types 5 and 6 were for smaller aeroplanes suitable for 'feeder-line' and light transport purposes. Type 5 was for a land plane to fly within the UK whose specification was met by a twenty-seat, high-wing design by the Miles Aircraft Company. Miles called it the Marathon and its four engines of 333hp each gave it a speed of 210mph, over a range of 960 miles. Its prototype flew in May 1946, but prior to its production the Miles company experienced major financial difficulties, which led to it being taken over by Handley Page.

Both BEA and BOAC rejected the Marathon because they considered it too large for short-haul flights within Britain and it never sold in the United States. Although the RAF purchased twenty as crew trainers, only forty-three in all were built.

Fortunately, the situation was quite different for the smaller de Havilland Dove. This was scheduled to carry between eight and eleven passengers at a speed of 140 knots over a maximum of 650 nautical miles, for which its original Gypsy Queen 305hp engines were subsequently uprated. The Dove's first flight took place at Hatfield on 25 September 1945. Despite two early crashes, its subsequent trials went relatively smoothly and it entered service in November 1946. Early sales were affected by its high price of £20,000 but they grew steadily and eventually a total of 582 Doves were built, making it the most numerous British-built transport, serving a host of countries worldwide, even penetrating the difficult North American market.[16]

At Churchill's urging, the Brabazon Committee's attempts to create a British air-transport industry by anticipating the pattern of future air-transport needs, ranging from massive airliners to small feeder aeroplanes, was unparalleled and was justly seen as a tremendous act of optimism and vision.[17] In reality, the results proved bitterly disappointing.

Even so, the committee could hardly be held responsible for fundamental weaknesses in British aerospace after the war. With the notable exception of its transatlantic behemoth (and the massive Princess flying boat) the range, and proposed dimensions of its classes of aircraft proved reasonable. In any event, with the Comet there were always opportunities for stretched versions and adaptations, and although the Brabazon Type 3, for instance, was conceived by the need to traverse the Empire routes, it was also suitable enough for longer European flights.

De Havilland Dove, the very popular successor to the Dragon Rapide. (Farnborough Air Sciences Trust)

Where the Brabazon Committee was undoubtedly culpable was in its projected means of propulsion by proposing a mixture of piston-engined, turboprop and pure jet designs. Had it only championed pure jet or geared or turboprop propulsion, it could have stolen a significant march over American civil aircraft manufacturers. It was also open to strong criticism in its choice of constructors, some of whom lacked the technical ability and capital resources to take full advantage of the opportunities offered.

Bristol, for instance, found the building of the Brabazon overtaxed its technical resources and it appeared unable to react quickly enough to the serious difficulties it confronted. Technical failures similarly doomed the future of the Avro Tudor, while the relatively small Miles Aircraft Company actually went broke during the production of the Marathon. Apart from these issues, most manufacturers seemed incapable of keeping to scheduled timings, which pointed to constitutional weaknesses among many of them.

At the time there were more construction companies in Britain than in the US and while amalgamations were urgently needed the post-war Labour government stopped short of forcing them upon the industry. In such a situation it was never possible for the Brabazon Committee to confine its appointments to the two dominant manufacturers, de Havilland and Vickers, although Vickers might well have accepted additional responsibilities.

It could never be disputed that the second Brabazon Committee took an overlong time to reach its decisions. However much this could have helped to set the tone for some manufacturers' subsequent drawn-out construction programmes is impossible to say, but a separate committee under Lord Beaverbrook that was intent in producing interim aircraft moved with notably more speed. While the Brabazon Committee might have lacked some urgency there were many prominent individuals in both government and industry who appeared unaware of the fiercely competitive nature of the post-war world.

One was S. Scott Hall, Director General of Technical Development at the Ministry of Supply and an active author, who during early 1953 wrote in the aviation publication *Aeronautics* about the Brabazon Committee's formula for developing civil aircraft. He emphasised the prodigious amount of work during its sixty meetings, resulting in 150 papers on the aerodynamics of the proposed aircraft together with their engine systems, as if this guaranteed success.

Scott Hall, for instance, believed the committee's work provided a striking illustration of collaboration between government and industry that offered tremendous potential for the future. Adopting military terms, he wrote that he believed Britain should press on with the development of new civil designs if it was to hold the position it had won. He did not make clear what this advantageous position actually was, although he undoubtedly believed the aviation industry's chief need at that time was to satisfy an ever growing (and inevitable) list of buyers. To meet their demands he approved decisions to give top priority to models such as the Comet, Viscount and Brabazon that he believed should materially help the aircraft industry.[18]

Although Scott Hall wrote before the significance of metal fatigue with the Comet 1 had become fully apparent and before interminable delays that prevented the Britannia coming into service, he was quite sure there would be unlimited numbers of customers queuing up to buy British planes.

Such overblown expectations from a senior representative at the Ministry of Supply appeared to support Peter Masefield's conviction that a degree of overconfidence prevented some of the numerous aircraft constructors performing adequately.[19] Aviation commentator Peter J. Lyth took a somewhat different view by attributing such delusion down to mental exhaustion after a long and hard war.[20]

Whatever the causes, in spite of the unquestioned talent within the industry, most constructors appointed by the Brabazon Committee proved far slower in moving from the prototype stage to their planes' first flights and in tackling and correcting design faults than their American rivals – with de Hallivand a notable and possibly dangerous exception. In some cases this could be attributed to using obsolete methods such as outdated jigs, rather than through deficient management practices.

Yet one notable critic of aircraft design, veteran designer F.H. Robertson, was unimpressed, for instance, by the sketchy design work for the Brabazon, sometimes wondering whether any was done at all and concluding that the only thing that appeared to have been right about it was the percentage fuel weight.[21] Broadening his criticism, he believed that with better preliminary design the troubles that beset other recent aircraft could also have be foreseen.[22]

Beyond any technical shortcomings of its own, British aviation undoubtedly suffered from varied government initiatives. At the end of the Second World War, for instance, it became an area for intervention and support, notably through its nationalisation of the civil airlines and grants for its civil aviation programmes amounting to £40.65 million.[23]

Although determined critic Peter Lyth did not go so far as to condemn nationalisation as such, he argued against the manner of its post-war implementation, seeing the 1946 Bill establishing the national airlines as a case of dogma over sound commercial strategy in that it did not go far enough and exhibited a curious lack of clarity about long-term objectives for either the air-transport business or the aircraft-manufacturing industry.[24]

Lyth pointed out, for instance, that by making BOAC responsible for long-haul services and BEA for short- and medium-haul ones, the government made the road to profitability unnecessarily hard for both airlines and more important still prejudiced the aircraft procurement process in such a way as to make it difficult for British manufacturers to build a world-class airliner.[25] With their internal routes in mind, BEA ordered aircraft that were small and ordered them in such small quantities that it was difficult for manufacturers to market them elsewhere in the world – especially in America. As a result, Lyth considered much public investment was used to purchase aircraft without enough thought for their full commercial viability. What was more, Lyth pointed out that although the 1946 Nationalisation Act was designed to encourage the air corporations to buy the products of British aircraft constructors, the government made no attempt to encourage the weaker companies to amalgamate and improve the quality of their aircraft.

Lyth noted that with the absence of strong government pressure (which did not come until the later 1950s) it was understandable that the industry should be in no undue haste to amalgamate its airframe constructors and engine makers, and that as a result its individual firms would remain fiercely independent. Had they not survived serious threats after the First World War and were not some, such as Handley Page, still run by founders whose family interests tended to predominate?

In Britain, apart from such powerful forces of inertia and long tradition, there existed another powerful force in the form of the Society of British Aircraft Manufacturers, which had been expressly established in 1916 by George Holt Thomas to defend the interests of its member firms. The minutes of its management committee provide rare insights into its aims and methods during the later stages of the Second World War and beyond. These show its parochial tendencies and suspicion of intellectuals, along with its unwavering belief that it should have a voice in any new arrangements for post-war aviation research and development. It proved ambivalent about the Brabazon proposals, and apparently believed there was a danger that they would develop into something rather academic instead of bringing about an organisation that would be of direct benefit to the industry and to aircraft and engine design.

In any case, it was convinced the chief developments that had taken place with aircraft and engines had been despite government action rather than because of it and therefore 'the industry (i.e. themselves) should be consulted on these matters'.[26]

The society argued against the committee's proposals for specific firms to carry out its design and construction work because it cut out all competition and therefore did not appear to be in the best interests of the British air transport industry.[27] Its arguments that all firms should be given the chance to participate – although democratic – was nonsensical where the large programmes were concerned. The SBAC defended its own right to observe on everything that was offered to its members, including the work of the Air Ministry's Airworthiness Inspection Department where it believed the charges made (upon firms) in relation to the services rendered were excessive.[28] It wanted to have it all ways, for regardless of its support for the continued independence of the separate firms, the SBAC considered the cost of development of civil aircraft was likely to be so high, that financial assistance (for the industry) from the Ministry of Supply would be essential.[29]

A combination of truculence on the part of individual firms against amalgamation and a powerful defensively minded SBAC wedded to the status quo both held back the rationalisation of the British aircraft industry and affected its capability to carry out the Brabazon Committee's proposals.

Across the Atlantic constructors were especially fortunate because of the remarkable progress by American airlines during the 1930s and early 1940s, both within the United States and overseas, and because of their long-haul experience gained with their armed forces during the Second World War, where American four-engined monoplanes, Douglas DC-4s and Lockheed Constellations, were brought into service equipped with powerful engines and modern nose-wheel undercarriages.

What was more, the American domestic market that had increased eightfold between 1930 and 1939, continued to operate during the war, where, by 1945, traffic on the US domestic airlines had increased to 60 per cent of the world total. During this time, they had achieved improved regularity and comfort, along with a better safety record, where an average of five passenger fatalities per 100 million passenger miles in 1940 were reduced to about one and a half per year.[30]

Whatever the Brabazon Committee's best efforts, a ballooning domestic market served to give American constructors massive advantages over their British competitors. While in the 1950s air transport in Europe also grew at a phenomenal pace, the majority of its passengers came to be carried by American planes. In order to compete, British constructors had to build and introduce new and superior types of aircraft such as the turboprop Vickers Viscount and de Havilland's Comet airliner, the world's first long-haul jet. Along with superior inventiveness, they needed to reduce the length of time prior to going into production and curb the vestiges of earlier British propensities of flying by grace and by God, while hoping the Americans would not come up with a world-beater of their own.

In such circumstances, the Brabazon Committee needed an outstanding chairman to help the British aviation industry perform out of its skin. What it got was John Theodore Moore-Brabazon, two years from his 60th birthday, a noted early motorist, balloonist, aviator and politician who in May 1907 had become the first Englishman to make a flight in a heavier-than-air aeroplane, lasting for just over a minute, that qualified him for the first aviator's certificate awarded by the Royal Aero Club.[31]

Following an air crash in which his friend Charles Rolls was killed, his wife persuaded him to abandon flying, but this resolution ended with the outbreak of the First World War when he joined the Royal Flying Corps and served on the Western Front. During this time he pioneered aerial photography, rose to the rank of lieutenant colonel and was awarded the Military Cross.

In 1918, he became Conservative MP for Chatham, a seat he held until 1929, where his high confidence and gift of humour led him to being appointed Parliamentary Private Secretary to Winston Churchill, the current Secretary of State for War and Air.[32] During the interwar years 'Brab' strongly supported Churchill's calls for rearmament and unsurprisingly on Churchill's return to power he became Minister of Transport in the wartime coalition. Brab's tenure of office ended prematurely, when at a private lunch party in 1942 he was unwise enough to express his approval of the Germans and Russians slaughtering each other while Britain got on with manufacturing armaments for the knockout blow. This was leaked to the press and Churchill was compelled to dismiss him, although the offer of a peerage followed rapidly. While his parliamentary career was over, Brab was an obvious candidate to head future committees on post-war civil reconstruction, including an important and exceedingly difficult one on post-war aircraft design. In many ways he seemed the ideal choice.

Churchill, who was generally a good picker of men, had known Brab over a good number of years and was well aware of the fierce competitive instincts and rare enthusiasms behind his languid public image. On the other hand, his latest biographer Kenneth More (who lacked Churchill's personal acquaintance) writing in the Oxford DNB, is of the opinion that, 'It is unlikely that (he) would have achieved Cabinet rank, except in a wartime administration led by Churchill.'[33]

However different their assessments, Brab's problem as a politician was that whatever his judgemental powers, his adventuring and sporting image predominated. A witty Irishman he enjoyed being funny, something his friend, Lord Hugh Cecil warned him against at an early stage of his parliamentary career.[34] To Brab however, the greatest crime in life was being a bore and he became renowned as an excellent after-dinner speaker and an equable and humorous committee chairman, who emphasised his insouciance by brandishing a long cigarette holder. Together with his deserved reputation for humour there was his unashamed and indefatigable participation in sports: in addition to his early driving and flying, he was a scratch golfer, a yachtsman with the Royal Yacht Squadron and a tobogganing enthusiast who continued to ride the Cresta Run until his 70th birthday.

Such activities undoubtedly went against him. On one occasion, when he had done good work at the London docks during the General Strike, he was greeted by Stanley Baldwin with the words 'Hullo Brab, what have you been doing with yourself during the General Strike, playing golf?'[35]

Churchill gave him the massive responsibility 'of preventing the US from extending its air transport lead in the post-war world that it had established in 1939'.[36] By supporting the immense Class 1 aircraft named after him Brabazon showed his soaring imagination and regard for the grand gesture, but whether he fully appreciated the imperative need for it to be powered by turboprop or pure jet engines is less certain. Despite his expertise about the mechanics of vintage cars and early aircraft, his later aerodynamic knowledge did not appear that deeply rooted.[37]

In 1962, as a self-proclaimed champion for air safety, he was still criticising the world's airlines for sacrificing safety for speed and earning power with their passenger planes' high take-off and landing speed. Whether or not he fully appreciated the significance of technical advances, he predicted that at the end of the century, 'We shall be killing 10,000 passengers a year, with a crash every other day.'[38] Quite apart from such wild forecasts, as a long-time member of the Safety Board and Chairman of the Air Registration Board, responsible for issuing certificates of airworthiness, he still campaigned against the use of 'inflammable petrol rather than paraffin for aero fuels'.[39]

In spite of Brab's repeated emphasis on safety, it came second to his enthusiasm for a great imaginative project such as the Comet airliner. At the Court of Inquiry on the Comet disaster, he proved somewhat ingenuous when speaking as chairman of the Air Registration Board:

You know and I know, the cause of the accident: it is due to the adventurous pioneering spirit of our race. It has been like that in the past, it is like that in the present and I hope it will be in the future.

Of course, we gave hostages to fate – but I can't believe that this court or our country will censure us because we ventured. When we gave a certificate of air worthiness to these machines, they were airworthy. True they deteriorated in a way no one on earth at that time could foretell … It is metallurgy and aeronautics that is in the dock. If you grounded every aeroplane that had an unexplained accident you would scarcely have a machine in the air today … we saw nothing in that accident [off Elba] which justified grounding it.[40]

In his strong advocacy for the Comet, one can see Brab's delight in the plane's hugely exciting developments. With him, emotions were never far from the surface, something that became more pronounced as he aged. For instance, he voiced his concerns about the unfair criticism of aviation in May 1942 during the thirtieth Wilbur Wright lecture which he delivered to the Royal Aeronautical Society. He told his audience that history showed 'that the birth of flight was of clean parents but due to the First World War, it was landed with the mark of Cain and ever since it has been tied to the apron strings of Mars'.[41]

While his style was always arresting, his propositions were not above questioning, for during the same address, he made an amazing reference to the British Army. He told his startled audience that, 'The situation in the Army is that they have no policy at all, no equipment and no technicians. They work on the charity of the Air Force who co-operate with them.'[42]

Brabazon's emotive approach and occasional exaggerations are well documented but whatever the abilities of the chairman and members of the Brabazon Committee, they must have felt like prisoners of their age. As a Cabinet paper on Civil Aircraft Requirements during 1946 rightly concluded, 'Not all the designs in this period of change and new technologies can hope to prove outstanding successes.'[43]

But Brab and his committee members had perforce to lay down guidelines for a number of superior aeroplanes, including at least one world-beater, to have any chance of countering the American challenge for worldwide dominance.

Whatever the chances against this happening – and it should not be forgotten that the Comet could have tilted the balance towards British Aviation forever – it will never stop some aerial enthusiasts, including his latest biographer, from being highly aware of his deficiencies and wondering that if Churchill had appointed someone with no more than half Brab's wit but twice his technical knowhow, untrammelled by memories of very early flight and never involved in cosy relationships with constructors who were not up to the mark, someone single-minded in keeping his committee members fully focused, then a fair share of the civil aviation market would have stood more chance of being won back for Britain.

In reality, such expectations were always exceedingly optimistic, due among other things to the large scale of America's civil aviation requirements, seemingly compulsive tinkering by different British governments and the insular policies of the state-owned airlines.[44] Yet with the mercurial Brab responsible for civil aviation's future blueprint, a more modest outcome was only to be expected.

3

GREAT ALL-ROUNDERS: THE HAWKER HUNTER AND ENGLISH ELECTRIC CANBERRA

Following the Second World War, the reputation of Britain's military aviation stood high with its interceptors having single-handedly broken the German Luftwaffe's early attacks on the country, while during the subsequent air war, despite the USAF's signal responsibility for day bombing, the RAF continued to conduct widespread operations, including frequent and massive night-bombing raids.

During 1940, the superlative Rolls-Royce Merlin engine had given Britain the edge over her opponents and it powered other wartime aircraft, including the four-engined Lancaster bomber with its unrivalled bomb loads, the ultra-fast de Havilland Mosquito and the American Mustang fighter, which it transformed into a long-range escort fighter.

Over the course of the war, while the Merlin's capability would be massively increased from 1941 onwards, Frank Whittle's jet engine was developed and during 1945 small numbers of the jet-powered Gloster Meteor entered RAF service. The Meteor was followed by de Havilland's twin-boom Vampire jet fighter, with its Goblin engine designed by Frank Halford, 2,250 of which were built and adopted by air forces worldwide.[1]

In 1945 British expertise in jet propulsion compared favourably with any others for although the Americans had a workable jet aircraft in the Bell Airacomet their Lockheed Shooting Star single-seater fighter that first flew on 8 January 1944 was powered by Halford's Goblin built in the US under licence.[2] At this stage the Soviets also lagged behind.

Gloster Meteor, Britain's first jet fighter. (Farnborough Air Sciences Trust)

De Havilland DH.100 Vampire twin-boom jet interceptor. (Farnborough Air Sciences Trust)

This was to change during the early post-war years when, despite the deteriorating international situation, priority was given to bringing about the recovery of war-torn and austerity Britain before supporting advanced technological programmes required for the armed services.

This policy's baleful effect on British military aviation became apparent with the cancellation of programme E.24/43 for an experimental supersonic jet aircraft capable of reaching a speed of 1,000mph at a height exceeding 50,000ft.[3] Work being undertaken by the Miles Aircraft Company was well advanced with the M.52 prototype's first flight confidently expected to take place during the summer of 1946.[4] If it had proved successful, it was bound to have extended Britain's technological lead in military aviation.

However, in February 1946, Miles not only received an order to cancel but another to destroy the jigs used in the construction process. No prior warning was given and the company was forbidden to announce it until the following September. It was a decision that continues to provoke anger and bafflement to the present day, and less than a decade afterwards a government White Paper considering the supply of military aircraft acknowledged that although 'it is easy to be wise after the event it is clear now that this decision seriously delayed the progress of aeronautical research in the UK'.[5] In reality, it set back the British supersonic effort for five years at least and affected the entire industry for more than a decade.

This proved all the more serious when both the Soviet Union and the US were determined to develop their aviation expertise in jet propulsion and rocketry. Towards the end of the war they became heavily involved in what has been referred to as the systematic and legalised looting of German ideas and technology. In 1944 both countries sent specialist missions to Germany to follow up their occupying troops and by VE Day the number of scientists involved exceeded 600. In contrast, Britain sent three teams totalling twenty-seven people in all, apparently without the benefit of the slightest back-up or interest from London.[6] As a result the two superpowers gained clear benefits, with the US acquiring the expertise of Herr Braun and other scientists for its space programme and jet aircraft development, while the Soviet Union took scientists forcibly to Russia to help with a number of research programmes, including the development of swept-wing jet aircraft.

The British, in contrast, seemed content to carry out restricted knowledge-gathering. Aviation correspondent Bill Gunston, for one, had no doubt the UK came off third or fourth-best in combing through German resources, largely because he believed the newly elected government and the aircraft industry were utterly disinterested. Despite the exhibitions of capital German aircraft and equipment staged in London and Farnborough, he felt there was 'never the slightest idea that anyone might learn anything from them'.[7] In 1945, for instance, he maintained the German 'axial engines and swept or delta wings were considered to be outlandish rubbish, far removed from reality'.[8]

Some measure of disinterest and undue sense of superiority from winning the war was understandable, if not excusable, but during the early post-war years certain British politicians actively helped to change the balance against their own country by giving assistance to the Soviet development of their first operational swept-wing fighter – the MiG-15. Although in 1945 Soviet engineers had taken everything they could salvage from the Junkers and BMW gas-turbine programmes, they still lacked a reliable centrifugal turbojet engine for a high-performance fighter and they approached Sir Stafford Cripps, then President of the Board of Trade. After ignoring warnings, in September 1946 he directed Rolls-Royce to sell them ten Derwent and ten Nene engines with the prospect of more to follow in the next year, making fifty-five in all. The Soviets paid £255,177 15s 5d, reputedly 'saving themselves five years of hard development'.[9]

This was far from the whole story, for although the Soviets had no agreement to manufacture Rolls-Royce engines nor spares, they went ahead and incorporated improvements that they licensed to France and the US before subsequently supplying them free to other countries, including China. It has been estimated that, working on a 10 per cent royalty, the Soviet government still owes Rolls-Royce £75 million over the sale.[10]

The irresponsibility of Cripps's decision was underlined in March 1946 when Winston Churchill re-emphasised the world's new strategic balance during his famous speech in Fulton, Missouri, USA, in which he talked about a separation between Western and Eastern Europe through an iron curtain coming down from Stetin in the Baltic to Trieste in the Adriatic. Even so, it was not until the Communist takeover of Czechoslovakia some two years later and the Soviet blockade of West Berlin in 1948 in which the Western Allies had to fly in all necessary supplies, including coal, that such politicians became convinced about Soviet hostility.

The British government's lack of appreciation of Soviet threats and its conviction that the RAF could, for the most part, rely on its interceptors came to roost during the Korean War in which the only British fighters in the conflict were piston-powered Royal Navy Sea Furies that were outclassed by Russian MiG-15s that had first flown in 1947 and US Sabres that entered service in 1949. In Korea, British technological inferiority could legitimately be compared with the situation in France a decade before, when the Fairey Battles of the RAF were outclassed by German Me 109s.

Three North American Sabres in formation. (Chino Air show 2014 by Airwolfhound, licensed under CC by SA2.0)

The difference in 1950, however, was that although the RAF was the West's second most powerful air force, it had no superior aircraft to support its Meteors. As an equipment-led service it was vital to keep its aeroplanes up-to-date but although in 1947 contracts had been issued for advanced single- and two-seater fighters, they were cancelled three months later.

In the same year, Hawkers submitted a brochure for the P.1081, an interim swept-wing jet fighter sorely needed by the RAF, but after the prototype crashed on the South Downs on 3 April 1951, resulting in the death of its pilot, Squadron Leader Wade, it was not proceeded with and reliance was placed on two other advanced fighters, the Hunter and the Swift.[11] Following the earlier vacillation, these proved too late for the Korean War, with the Hunter not entering service until 1954 and the Swift proving a failure as a fighter. The delay proved costly when the government bridged the fighter gap before the Hunter came into service by procuring 430 American Sabres, despite the need to pay for them in scarce US dollars.

The fast-moving political events of the 1950s were to wreck any long-term British procurement policies. Following the earlier cancellations of advanced defence projects the Labour government's late realisation about the dangers of communism, followed by the invasion of South Korea by the communist north, led them to commit to an overambitious rearmament programme. As a consequence, on Churchill's return to office in 1951 amid a sterling crisis, he attempted to cut back on defence expenditure that had been due to rise steeply from £200 million a year in the late 1940s to a projected £670 million in 1954, with planned increases of 55 per cent in manpower for the aircraft industry.[12] Due to the strong likelihood that this would choke off the nation's attempted economic recovery, on 30 October 1951 it was decreed that all defence departments should reduce their expenditure and investigative committees were appointed.

In 1956 the findings of a select committee on finance, which had examined the air estimates to gauge whether or not the government was getting full value for its money over its Hunter programme, were published.

It identified certain long-established shortcomings and although it acknowledged that British aviation had produced some of the finest military aircraft in the world together with engines and various electronic devices[13] it concluded – predictably enough – that up to that time, 'the programme for the supply of military aircraft had both been ambitious and expensive – if not in some ways over ambitious – and (in the current world) it was essential for all future projects [to] be scrutinised much more carefully than before, to ensure that only the most essential are carried out'.[14]

To a finance committee this meant a closer consideration of contracts between the government and industrial firms, something it acknowledged was far from easy with the build-up following the Korean War, followed by equally rapid reductions.

Even so, the committee commented adversely on the traditional system of competitive tendering by multiple numbers of firms, leading to excessive numbers of proposed military aircraft being unsuccessful and to essentially similar projects being adopted.[15] It regretted that unsuccessful projects had not been stopped by the Ministry of Supply soon enough, although it acknowledged that it was undeniably difficult to cancel at the right moment with the undue length of time taken by the British aviation industry to develop an aircraft or a piece of equipment.[16] It believed this trend was encouraged by the Treasury paying the firms' costs, plus a percentage for profit, resulting in inefficiency and not giving the greatest incentive for firms completing projects as quickly as possible.[17]

There was general criticism about the excessive numbers of aviation constructors, with one of its witnesses, the redoubtable Lord Hives of Rolls-Royce, observing that as far as jet engines went 'the same engines could be used for more types of aircraft', although the strongest comment from both committee members and witnesses were about the small numbers of military planes being ordered at the time by the Ministry of Supply.[18][19]

The tragedy for the industry was that with Britain engaged in massive national reconstruction the committee could give no assurance about increasing defence orders to provide a better platform for overseas sales, nor propose the root-and-branch reforms needed to meet formidable US competition.

Such criticism of government policy was by no means limited to the committee. Arthur Reed, air correspondent for *The Times*, placed most responsibility for the failures of post-war British aviation on successive governments, which he said had failed to support legitimate spending to retain the technological dominance it had enjoyed during the war.

Aviation author Francis Mason went even further, accusing the British socialist administration immediately after the war of creating a technological wilderness, that was to remain fallow for nigh on twenty years, while other nations reaped the benefits of carefully planned continuity of effort.

Mason believed, for instance, that it was the lack of research funding between 1945 and 1948 that deprived the RAF of an up-to-date jet fighter with which to play its part in the Korean War.[20]

Whatever the merits of such observations, due to the earlier cancellations and the impending failure of the Supermarine Swift it was imperative for the Hawker Hunter to succeed for, with the exception of Gloster's Javelin, which was due to follow in 1956, it was the only new British fighter on the horizon.

Project work had begun in 1947 for a single-seat interceptor fighter powered by what would become the Rolls-Royce Avon axial-flow engine or an Armstrong-Siddeley Sapphire engine to give it a capability of flying at Mach 0.94 (620mph) at 36,000ft for use against Russian Tu-16 bombers. In 1948, the tenders were won by Hawker's specification for the P.1067, which would be equipped with four 30mm Aden guns. So urgently was the fighter needed that the Churchill administration granted it super priority, thus giving it precedence for the acquisition of both production materials and components.

There was never any intention that the Hunter would be supersonic but in spite of the relative lack of knowledge in Britain about high-speed flight problems, designer Sydney Camm decided to give its large mid-fuselage wings a sweep back of 42½ degrees in the fashion of the American Sabres and Russian MiGs, which with an elliptical fuselage and curved fin helped to create an aircraft that has been called the most beautiful fighter ever built.

By the end of 1948, work started on mock-ups through the time-honoured method of assembling jigs for the purpose, although it was subjected to novel wind tunnel tests, following which its tailplane was moved down the fin. By April 1949, the Hunter had taken on its final proportions with production planned for 200 Rolls-Royce Avon-powered aircraft at Kingston, with similar numbers of Armstrong Siddeley Sapphire-powered examples to be built at Armstrong Whitworth's factory at Coventry. Assembly commenced in December 1949 and its first flight under Squadron Leader Neville Duke took place at Boscombe Down on 20 July 1951, before the first production aeroplane flew from Dunsfold on 6 May 1953. The RAF considered the plane so necessary that, after the flight of the first prototype, orders were placed for 350 aircraft, rising to 600 by the end of the year.

The first two marques suffered serious problems that Francis Mason characteristically attributed to 'parsimonious attitudes towards military procurement and research funding during the late 1940s'.[21] Farnborough, for instance, had been starved of funds to pursue in-depth examinations of captured German aircraft such as the Messerschmitt Me 262, which the Americans found gave them a priceless short cut to transonic aerodynamic technology.[22] Two of its major problems were with engine surging during gun firing and the plane's critically short endurance time.

Fortunately, Camm's robust design gave the plane the capacity to accommodate technological advances as well as ever-increasing demands for adaptability without recourse to radical alteration of its overall airframe envelope.[23] Production continued while substantial modifications were carried out with the introduction of the surge-free Avon RA21 engine that transformed its performance, while its earlier short endurance time was solved by introducing 100-gallon drop tanks.

Modifications were to continue throughout its life and the Hunter F.6 with its 10,000lb thrust engine was virtually a new aeroplane (if still within its classic airframe) that was regarded as one of the world's finest all-round fighters. That said, it was still not capable of level flight at supersonic speed. (In 1952, the Hawker team began work on the P.1083, a genuinely supersonic version of the Hunter, but this was cancelled following cutbacks after the Korean War.)

While the Hunter must always be considered as something of an interim aircraft compared with the American supersonic F-100 Super Sabre and the Soviet MiG-19, it proved very robust and manoeuvrable, with the RAF able to keep it in service far longer than it had ever expected. In fact, it would continue to perform successfully into the 1960s both as an interceptor and in the ground-attack role, before graduating to training and demonstration duties.

The swept-wing MiG-15. (Charlie Golf Photography, licensed under CC by ND 2.0)

An indication of its undoubted success were the 2,500 aircraft produced over its lifetime, many of which were exported to air forces throughout the world. More than a fifth of these were refurbished machines that became available in the early 1960s[24] and which proved an attractive proposition by offering customers a stout combat aircraft with a life of 3,000 hours. Such refurbishment was only made possible by the interchangeability that Camm had built into the design from the beginning.

Fortunately for British aviation at this time, the design characteristics of strength and adaptability so evident in Camm's Hunter fighter were also achieved by a less-renowned designer with a quite different aeroplane, English Electric's Canberra bomber. Test pilot Roland Beamont would make the remarkable declaration about it that, 'A relatively small number (of aeroplanes) have proved to be so successful in combining performance, utility and maintainability with ease of operation and popularity with aircrew as to make them historically famous.'[25]

The Canberra's genesis preceded the Hunter's, when in 1944, English Electric, along with other longer-established aircraft manufacturers such as Avro, Handley Page and Vickers, was shortlisted to commence design studies on the country's first jet bombers.

The company chose 'Teddy' Petter, former chief designer at Westland Aircraft, to form a small design team for the project. The team included Freddie Page as Petter's right-hand man with others like Don Crowe and his colleague Ray Creasey who went on to enjoy outstanding later successes with the Lightning, Jaguar and Tornado.

Petter saw the Canberra as a fast light bomber to replace the wartime Mosquito whose crew of three would fly at up to 50,000ft and operate at up to Mach 0.88, close to the speeds of current jet fighters. In 1945 he agreed that a Rolls-Royce axial-flow jet engine giving 6,500lb thrust (shortly to be called the Avon) should power it. He decided to bury its two engines in orthodox wings for he believed a swept construction would reduce its manoeuvrability and any greater speed would be beyond the thrust of the proposed engine. As Freddy Page put it, somewhat confusingly, the team's aim was for a plane that was 'the extreme in adventurous conventionalism'.[26]

English Electric Canberra, an outstanding performer. (Farnborough Air Sciences Trust)

To help develop the design, Petter recruited Wing Commander Roland Beamont who during the previous seven years had completed three tours of fighter operations, including the Battle of Britain, followed by experience with the Meteor IV at Gloster. Appointed in May 1947, Beamont was to prove an outstanding test pilot as well as being one of the Canberra's greatest champions.

By the end of 1948, the prototype of the first major aircraft from English Electric's Warton factory was almost complete and featured a large wing and symmetrical fuselage of stressed skin, semi-monocoque construction, whose pilot and co-pilot enjoyed a pressurised cockpit and ejection seats. It was 15ft 7in high, with its wing of 64ft slightly exceeded by its body length of 65ft 6in.

On 2 May 1949, painted in so-called 'Petter blue' and with Beamont at the controls, Britain's first bomber designed round an axial-flow jet engine was rolled out.[27] Taxiing began on 8 May, followed by its first flight on 13 May (two years before the Hunter). As it was Friday the 13th, Petter told Beamont he could delay by a day but he opted to fly. Spectators were barred from the immediate vicinity but the take-off proved faultless and, except for a possible 'overbalance of the rudder', the flight was completed without incident. Beamont recalled his moment of realisation:

> that this was indeed a remarkable aircraft with firm sure characteristics which seemed to almost invite the pilot to fly itself quietly home; it was with a sense of real pleasure that he felt its precise responses, as the final turn was rolled out on to the approach with only gentle guidance required (from himself).[28]

After testing, which led to some modifications of the elevators and rudder horn, progress was rapid and during thirty-six flights between 6 July and 31 August, all the required manoeuvres were carried out up to a height of 42,000ft, with outstanding manoeuvrability achieved throughout.

On 22 August, roll-off loops and full loops were performed, and on 4 September 1949 the prototype was flown to Farnborough for the annual air show. There its initial demonstration was aborted when one engine stopped due to confusion over the amount of fuel carried. Another aircraft was called forward and the intervening display included the initial public appearance of the world's first jet airliner: the de Havilland Comet. As the Canberra was relegated to last on the programme, Beamont was able to put it through a full range of manoeuvres that amazed the spectators, although unbeknown to them during one of them an instrument pack actually fell out of the bomb bay.

His demonstration moved *Aviation Week* to write that:

The biggest military surprise of the show was the English Electric, sky blue, Canberra jet bomber. US observers were not impressed with the Canberra's straight wing and somewhat conventional configuration on the ground. But in the air, the combination of test pilot Roly Beamont and the 15,000lb thrust from the two axial Avons made the Canberra behave in spectacular fashion.

Its speed range from 500mph to less than 100mph was ably demonstrated by Beamont, who followed his high-speed passes on the deck with an approach using full flaps, gear down and bomb bay doors open that slowed the Canberra to less than 100mph. At this speed, he rocked the big bomber violently with the ailerons to show the full control available as it approached stalling speed.

Beamont whipped the bomber designed to carry a 10,000lb bomb load around the deck like a fighter, flying it through a series of slow rolls, high speed turns at remarkable rates of climb. The Canberra was originally designed for radar bombing at around 50,000 feet but Beamont's demonstration convinced many Britishers that the new bomber may prove to be another Mosquito in its versatility at everything from low-level attack through night fighting to high attitude bombing.[29]

After continued development during the spring of 1951, the aircraft was cleared for RAF service and its importance quickly became apparent because the Vickers Valiant, the first of the projected V-bombers, was not expected to enter service until 1955, with the Avro Vulcan two years later and the Handley Page Victor one year later still. As a result, English Electric's 'compromise bomber' acquired a strategic role, during which it showed itself capable of outperforming the principal fighters still in service and climbed to heights above their ceiling.

The Canberra doubled the speed of the UK's bomber forces and between 1951 and 1958 set a series of world records, including flying from Northern Ireland to Gander and back, covering 4,144 miles in ten hours three minutes at an average speed of 411.99mph. It became the RAF's bombing mainstay for high-, medium- and low-level operations, and by 1954 the number of squadrons equipped with it in the United Kingdom reached fifty-five. It carried out photo-reconnaissance duties in Germany and a number were even fitted out to carry American theatre nuclear weapons.

Its ultimate triumph came about when, following a brilliant flying display by Beamont at Andrews Air Force Base in Washington that concluded with him bursting the nose wheel tyres due to heavy sanding of the concrete runway, the Americans contracted to build their own version, called the B-57. Its maiden flight took place on 20 July 1953 and during three and a half years a total of 403 B-57s were produced in six different versions. They were in action until 1969 in Vietnam, where they proved the best night interdiction aircraft of the war.

With the build-up of the V-bomber force, the Canberra squadrons in the UK were reduced and the last three were due to be stood down at the end of 1961. However, following the cancellation of TSR2 along with other defence cuts, the type was kept on as a tactical strike aircraft until the end of the 1970s.

In all a total of 1,376 Canberras were built in Britain, the US and Australia, 823 of which were for the RAF. Due to its sound airframe, it was capable of major modifications, particularly with the 403 USAF models, while other modernisation prolonged the type's life. Amazingly, a squadron of RAF Canberra PR.9s were still acting in the reconnaissance role during the early 1990s.[30] Beamont himself believed the aircraft achieved its remarkable acrobatic performances at air shows and during operations because such a docile and vice-less aircraft with its exceptional twin Avon engines could be flown to the limits of its performance and manoeuvrability and at far lower speeds than the minimum for contemporary jet fighters.

In spite of the stop-go policies and cancellations of hi-tech aircraft, the exceptional performance of the Hawker Hunter multi-purpose fighter and the eminently versatile English Electric Canberra bomber led some politicians and aerospace commentators to view the 1950s as a golden age. *The Aeroplane* wrote unconditionally, 'There can be no doubt that what Lord Alexander called the Elizabethan age is dawning in the skies of British Aviation.'[31] Such claims were made possible by the two outstanding British chief designers and their teams – and the entry in the civilian field of a jet airliner to be named Comet.

As for the chief designers' profiles, while Sydney Camm was already a legendary figure renowned for developing a series of outstanding aircraft, including the Hawker Hart and Hurricane, while driving his design teams hard, Canberra's brilliant, if undoubtedly eccentric designer, Teddy Petter, was far less well known. Yet whatever his outstanding work with the Canberra, his other achievements surely warrant him a deserved place in British Aviation's gallery of world-ranking designers.

Petter's family owned the aircraft constructor Westlands and following Cambridge, where he gained a first-class degree in the Mechanical Sciences tripos (with a gold medal in aerodynamics), his father took him into the firm as a graduate trainee. This did not prevent the then managing director, Robert

Westland Lysander. (Jim Spouge, licensed under CC by SA 2.0)

Bruce, ignoring his presence and it was only after Bruce's resignation that his father appointed him as a technical director when still only 26. While undeniably aloof and overbearing, Petter learned from Bruce the necessity of maintaining close contact with his draughtsmen and aerodynamicists by spending time at their boards and desks.

His first major design came with an unorthodox high-wing army co-operation plane, the Lysander, with a short take-off and landing capability, that has been described as looking like a splay-footed butterfly.[32] This entered service in 1938 and became the main product of the Westland works; out of a total of 1,670 aircraft built, 1,368 were delivered to the RAF, where the type became renowned for its use in clandestine operations.

During this time, Westlands was taken over by John Brown Shipbuilders and Petter acquired a new managing director in Eric Mensforth. Their clashes were predictable, for Petter had the greatest difficulty with working under other people.[33] His next design was unfortunate in its timing. Although in February 1937 the British government signed a contract for his Whirlwind, a two-engined, all-metal fighter, that mounted four cannon (like German fighters late on in the Second World War) and outperformed both the Spitfire and

Me 109 in speed and rate of climb up to 20,000ft, delays in production – for which Petter blamed Mensworth – meant it missed the Battle of Britain.[34] In any event, it was reckoned that the time and materials needed to produce the Whirlwind were equal to those for two Spitfires and it was never produced in any numbers. Petter declared it the most radically new aeroplane that had never gone into mass service.

He next designed an impressive high-level fighter, the F4/40, called the Welkin. This derivative of the Whirlwind was not needed because high-level attacks by the Luftwaffe never materialised. It did, however, make valuable contributions to the technology required for high-altitude operations, including the development of a fully automated, pressurised cabin system.

After yet another clash with Mensforth, Petter consulted Sir Wilfrid Freeman, chief executive at the Ministry of Aircraft Production, who advised him to join English Electric. This he did, taking with him the rights of a jet bomber on which he was working at that time. This was, of course, the Canberra, for which he assembled a design team that would lead to BAC Warton subsequently becoming the technical headquarters of military aircraft for the whole of Britain.[35]

In addition to the Canberra, at English Electric Petter instigated design studies for the F23/49 Lightning, the first and only wholly British aircraft that could reach supersonic speed in level flight. While it was remarkably advanced for its time, Petter also intended it to be both simple and strong.[36] It had a small frontal area, which he achieved by the novel means of mounting two reheated Rolls-Royce Avon engines one above the other in the fuselage. Its stubby wings were swept at 60 degrees to minimise wave drag and it had a swept-back, all-moving tailplane mounted below the wing plane. Apart from being twice as fast as the Hunter, it had an integrated weapons system with its radar enabling the pilot to search above and below the horizon for its target, which, when located, was sought by a missile that automatically locked on to it.

When the Lightning entered RAF service in May 1960 it put Britain in the forefront of interceptor technology, although any chance of a follow-up version had been ended by Duncan Sandys' 1957 White Paper on future fighter needs.[37]

In February 1950 Petter had moved from English Electric to become deputy managing director and technical director at Folland Aircraft. Here he planned the conformation of his beautiful Gnat lightweight fighter, which was designed to compete with contemporary fighters although it was about a quarter of their production cost.[38] This, his last design, was in accordance with his belief that fighters were becoming too large, too heavy and difficult to keep serviced.

English Electric Lightning, Britain's first supersonic jet fighter. (Farnborough Air Sciences Trust)

Petter's design was full of clever weight-saving ideas, although his insistence on it retaining high-pressure tyres led to it being rejected by both NATO and the RAF. Nonetheless, it came to be ordered in substantial numbers by the Indian government. This exciting little fighter finally found favour when it was used by the Red Arrows' demonstration team, in whose skilled hands its powers of manoeuvrability and close control entranced audiences world-wide.[39] Through such types Petter exerted a novel and powerful influence on British military aviation.

The contributions made by Camm's Hunter and Petter's Canberra to British aerial defence in the early post-war period can hardly be exaggerated. Both planes were to some degree compromise designs; Canberra with its large straight wing and the Hunter, swept wing or not, unable to fly supersonically. In the case of the Canberra, its moderate wing loading and high power-to-weight ratio made it able to outperform contemporary fighters in terms of both altitude and manoeuvrability, and although the Hunter was never as fast as the MiG-19 or Super Sabre, it proved a highly robust and adaptable interceptor.

Both aircraft had highly successful careers with the RAF and were sold to other air forces, with the ultra-critical Americans contracting to build their own version of Canberra that would distinguish itself in action over Vietnam.

With their outstanding durability both aircraft were not only capable of performing a variety of roles but were retained by the RAF long after their anticipated life term. The cancellation of TSR2, for instance, caused Canberra to be used in a strategic and tactical strike role twenty years after entering service, while the Hunter acted as both interceptor and ground attacker well into the 1960s.

In such ways, the Hunter and Canberra helped to disguise serious deficiencies caused by the absence of more advanced aircraft and the cancellation of their own intended replacements.

However successful, the methods used by their constructors were startlingly different. Camm favoured progressive families of aircraft while Petter was said to wipe the slate clean after each aircraft to start on a completely new concept. Sir George Edwards said of Petter that he always brought people up with a jolt in his public utterances because he said what he thought and what he thought was seldom what anyone else thought.[40] Neither (although revered) were easy to work with, Camm with his theatrical rejections of technical drawings that did not come up to standard and Petter with his stubbornness and overbearing attitude, although capable of recognising others' strong views and supporting them.

Both, however, sought excellence that with Petter came through a conscious striving to balance a sense of aesthetics with engineering efficiency and with Camm in his ceaseless hunt for a beautiful aircraft that performed well.

Both were unafraid to court controversy throughout their careers, Petter with his unorthodox but extremely fast Lightning and his lightweight Gnat fighter and Camm with his Harrier, which despite many doubters at home came to be so highly appreciated by the Americans. Both were men of their time who believed in having small design teams that worked intensively on specific projects, something that would become impossible with the far larger teams associated with future collaborative projects.

In their contrasting ways, Camm and Petter can be said to have exemplified what still distinguished British aviation up to the 1960s: its continuing aura of romance and regard for unashamed characters, its originality of design, allied to an underlying conviction about risks being part of things, and above all its faith in British superiority. During the early post-war years they operated in a country struggling for a new sense of identity whose aspirations favoured security, rather than adventure, and whose existence was dominated by economic limitations where it was bound to suffer disappointments and major setbacks, particularly when competing with the United States that unashamedly viewed aviation as vital in projecting its massive presence worldwide.

However sombre the future, those who viewed the 1950s as a golden age due to aeroplanes such as the Hunter and Canberra were also bound to celebrate the V-bombers, Britain's last and most powerful heavy warplanes, bearing the country's fearsome nuclear weapons.

4

THE V-BOMBERS:
POWER AND PRESENCE

In 1945, the detonation of atom bombs whose explosive power was equivalent to that delivered by 1,000 wartime heavy bombers changed the practice of strategic bombing for ever.

When a single American B-29 bombed the Japanese city of Hiroshima, 75,000 people died with as many maimed and 5½ square miles of its built-up areas were devastated. Such concentrated destruction along with its deadly collateral effects helped bring about the speedy surrender of Japan and proved a rapid game changer for the US and her allies.

In Britain the reaction of the newly elected Labour government was that for the country to retain its national security and status as a world power, it should develop its own atomic weapons. Despite American refusal at the end of the war to share its nuclear information, the British scientists who had already played an important part in the earlier Manhattan Project had a good knowledge of the technologies required and the country's first atom bomb would actually be detonated on 3 October 1952, with a thermonuclear one following five years later.

In the meantime, with the prime emphasis on bringing about the nation's economic recovery, it was decided that the RAF's bombing capabilities during the early post-war years could continue to be discharged by well-tried and relatively inexpensive means. The agreed solution was to replace its wartime Lancasters with Lincoln bombers, piston-engined, unpressurised planes capable of carrying a 14,000lb bomb load over a range of 2,250 miles, 440 of which entered RAF service.

Avro Lincoln, a bomber of Second World War design. (Farnborough Air Sciences Trust)

No one, however, could view the Lincoln as anything more than a stopgap, for apart from its other serious deficiencies, including inadequate speed, it was incapable of carrying the projected British deterrent. Britain's first atomic bomb weighed more than 10,000lb and the Air Staff's profile of aircraft for this purpose was for types with four jet engines capable of flying at more than 500mph (compared with the Lincoln's 220mph) at an altitude of 50,000ft over a range of 3,350 miles. They were required to be highly manoeuvrable with an all-weather and orthodox bombing capability and able to use electronic counter-measure (ECM) equipment against hostile missiles and anti-aircraft systems.

At a time when effective high-altitude surface-to-air missiles still seemed a long way off they, like the RAF's wartime Mosquito bombers, were expected to reach their targets, without having to engage opposing planes, by using their speed to outrun rudimentary air-to-air missiles. (In contrast, the American nuclear bombers retained their rear gunners for the next thirty years.[1])

These requirements were contained in specification B35/46 produced in 1946 and in January 1947, when the British aviation industry was in the remarkable position of still having more aircraft firms than the US, all six of its major military aircraft manufacturers were invited to make submissions by 31 May 1947 for the new bomber contract.[2] Those involved were English Electric, Bristol Aeroplane Co., Vickers-Armstrongs, Short Brothers, Avro and Handley Page.

With such revolutionary aircraft, it was anticipated that prolonged wind-tunnel and scale-model testing would be needed, something that seemed quite reasonable due to the expected long interval before the production of British atomic bombs. Working on this reasoning, it was thought the V-bombers would not go into service until the late 1950s. Even so, commentator Bill Gunston painted a vivid, if not depressing, picture of the companies' harassed designers trying 'to create splendid jet bombers in soggy wooden huts in the rain, while wondering how their shapes would behave in a transonic wind tunnel – if there existed such a thing (there didn't because the ones in Germany were pinched by our allies)'.[3]

In British fashion, the firms took quite different design routes. Two quickly left the contest: English Electric's submission of a somewhat larger version of its Canberra medium bomber was soon rejected, and while the Bristol Aeroplane Co. initially submitted plans for Type 176, a high-speed research aircraft, it subsequently decided to put their resources into Type 175, its Britannia turboprop civil airliner.

In the case of the four remaining companies, the submissions from Vickers and Short were undoubtedly less radical than those from Avro and Handley Page. Even so, all involved advanced aeronautics beyond the competence of current Air Ministry officials to supervise, and it was decided that the designs should be considered by an Advanced Bomber Project Group, made up from a team of structural engineers and leading aero-dynamicists under 35-year-old Welshman Morien Morgan, based at the Royal Aircraft Establishment (RAE) at Farnborough.

The Vickers proposal was for an aircraft that it believed would bridge the gap between the Lincoln and the most advanced proposals by Avro and Handley Page. The firm's redoubtable chief designer, George Edwards, was so confident about his team's prowess that he guaranteed the plane would be produced by 1953 following the prototype's flight two years before. Vickers decided

Vickers Valiant, a quantum leap in technology. (Farnborough Air Sciences Trust)

its plane's wings should have a sweep of 20 degrees for their outer sections with four Rolls-Royce Avon engines buried inside them, giving a speed of 567mph. Tail surfaces were to be swept back with a high tailplane, while its undercarriage featured two large pairs of wheels retracting in tandem outwards into the wing section.

The first prototype was duly flown by Vickers' chief test pilot 'Mutt' Summers on 18 May 1951 and in the following June, after receiving a production order for the first twenty-five aircraft, the type was named the Valiant. In spite of a fire in its port wing that led to the loss of the prototype and the death of its second pilot, Brian Foster, development went ahead relatively smoothly. The first pre-production version appeared in December 1953, although by now there was no longer any chance of George Edwards fulfilling his promise of bringing it into service within the same year. In any case, at a time of high international tension and with the prospect of a major conflict between the West and the Soviet Union, the British government briefly gave priority to remotely piloted vehicles. This programme was soon cancelled due to the Air Ministry's preference for manned bombers equipped if necessary with stand-off weapons.

The RAF's first Valiant squadron was formed on 1 January 1955, with a second following in July of the following year. Sixteen months later it was involved in long-awaited aeroplane trials, at Maralinga in Australia, for a

British atomic weapon, where a device called Blue Danube was detonated on 11 October 1956. This was followed by the release of Britain's first thermo-nuclear (hydrogen) device on 15 May 1957, near Malden Island in the Pacific, also carried by a Valiant. It was detonated at 10,000ft, thereby giving the aircraft approximately fifty seconds in which to get away. Its pilot, Group Captain Kenneth Hubbard, described the deadly beauty of its cloud with the stem:

> a cauldron mass of orange as the fireball had developed and the hot gases risen into the atmosphere, progressively forming a foaming white canopy which can only be compared with the top of a mushroom. This top must have reached an altitude of approximately 60,000 feet, with ice caps forming.[4]

By July 1957, production of the Valiant was already being run down as the much superior Avro Vulcan entered service with Bomber Command.[5] The Valiant's role as part of Britain's nuclear deterrent was further reduced when two squadrons were converted into inflight refuelling tankers to extend the other V-bombers' operational range. Even so, the Valiant's retirement as a nuclear bomber resulted from external events, the most notable of which was the surprise shooting down of an American U-2 high altitude spy plane (piloted by CIA pilot Francis Gary Powers) by a Soviet air-to-air missile at above 60,000ft. This highlighted the V-Force's vulnerability and the Valiant's in particular, because its operational ceiling was below the others. Although the V bombers were switched to a low-level nuclear strike role, in December 1964 fatigue fissures were discovered in the Valiant's main spar. Within two months the fleet was grounded and finally scrapped the following year.

While less advanced than the Vulcan and the Victor bombers, the Valiant spearheaded the V-Force's early work and within its technical limitations proved to be a sound and versatile aircraft that was streets ahead of the Lincoln.

The second 'less advanced' aircraft was Short Brothers' SA.4 Sperrin bomber, whose contribution was negligible compared with the Valiant's. It was the least imaginative of the company submissions and its unswept wings illustrated Short's decision to trade performance for speed of production. To help accommodate a large bomb bay it had a clumsy, slab-sided fuselage, and although its five-man crew shared a pressurised cabin, only the pilot had an ejector seat. The Sperrin's four Rolls-Royce Avon engines were mounted in pairs one above the other in single nacelles within its non-dihedral wing. Despite its relative ungainliness, they gave it a speed of just over 500mph and the 6,170 gallons of fuel carried in wing and fuselage tanks provided a range of 3,600 miles.

Successive developmental problems delayed the first flight, which did not take place until 10 August 1951, by which time the Valiant prototype had been flying for three months. This led the less-developed Sperrin to be judged superfluous – even as an interim bomber – although its prototype came to be used as a test bed for a large turbo-jet engine being produced by de Havilland.[6] Work on this was abandoned following the 1957 Defence White Paper and in 1958 the Sperrin prototype was scrapped, too. The limitations apparent in the Valiant and Sperrin meant the main responsibility for carrying and delivering Britain's nuclear weapons fell on the more advanced Vulcans and Victors.

The importance of this role was highlighted in a paper about global strategy produced in 1952 by the British Services' Chiefs of Staff. This described a British bomber force designed to complement the role of the USF with a capacity to attack targets vital to the Soviet Union but of no direct threat to the United States, thus marking what it described as 'the start of the official deterrent role of the Royal Air Force'.[7] Such a strategy was expected to help reduce what was seen as overblown defence expenditure following the Korean War, which had largely been spent on conventional forces. The financial viability of the V-bombers was underlined when the British Government voted a comparatively modest outlay of some £275 million on a strategic bombing force of 220 advanced planes, costing approximately £1,250,000 each, among which the Vulcan would prove outstanding.

Although unfairly branded 'airy-fairy' by the Valiant's designer George Edwards, this most distinctive delta-winged aircraft, conceived by renowned Avro designer Roy Chadwick was generally recognised to be some way in advance of the Vickers' and Short's specifications. Sadly, Chadwick's participation ended with his tragic death when Avro's Tudor 2 prototype, in which he was travelling, crashed. He was succeeded as technical director for the Vulcan by Bill Farren. The plane's design team was headed by Stuart Duncan Davies, who had always favoured the delta-wing concept.

On 27 November 1947 Avro was authorised to build a prototype for a large delta aircraft with a wing swept back 52 degrees with its tail surfaces limited to a swept fin and rudder and its engines, undercarriage, fuel and bomb load, enclosed within a wing that was 7ft thick at its root end. It was designed to hold four superlative Bristol Olympus turbojets, with up to 20,000lb thrust giving it a maximum speed of 645mph, and each main undercarriage leg made up of eight-wheel bogies retracting forward. It had two pairs of rotating flap airbrakes above and below the wing sections, supplemented by a 24ft diameter braking parachute to assist in landing. Its five-man crew were to be carried in a pressurised cabin where the pilot and co-pilot were provided with

Avro Vulcan, a robust, high performer. (Farnborough Air Sciences Trust)

Martin-Baker ejection seats while the others seated immediately behind them would have to bail out by parachute. In the first instance, the prototype had Rolls-Royce Avon engines, giving a much reduced 6,500lb thrust, although Avro's chief test pilot Roly Falk still astonished the crowds at the 1952 Farnborough Air Show when setting 'the great white delta wheeling in a blue sky'.[7]

The first production Vulcan flew on 4 February 1955, when it experienced serious buffeting. This was soon cured by installing a 'kink' to the wings' leading edge and the first operational aircraft was delivered in July 1957 to the RAF's 83 Squadron. Forty-five B.1s were produced, followed by eighty-nine B.2s. The aeroplane entered service two months after the Valiant had released the first British megaton bomb off Christmas Island and within a year the Vulcan carried such bombs itself.

The Vulcan's hand-picked crews were soon fully aware of their special responsibilities. With Britain's nuclear deterrent concentrated at just ten major air bases, its squadrons were required to adopt a quick reaction alert role. This meant that at times of international tension the aircraft, with their crews aboard, were lined up for operational readiness. Upon receiving a signal, they were required to get airborne within five minutes to escape any nuclear strike against their airfield, an interval that was steadily reduced with repeated practice.

It was the Vulcan B.2, powered by its 16,000–20,000lb thrust engines, which gained the plane its reputation as an awesome all-round performer. With the subsequent installation of a nose probe, it could be refuelled in flight and, providing it was within range of a tanker base, was capable of reaching targets anywhere in the world. Additional defence measures included a much-enlarged tail cone accommodating an improved radar warning receiver, together with chaff dispensers (whose metal strips baffled opposing radar) positioned beneath the engines.

The notable robustness of the Vulcan's airframe proved a distinct advantage over the other V-bombers; along with carrying the Yellow Sun free-fall 2 megaton bomb and the WE.177 lay down nuclear weapon, it proved capable of mounting the Avro Blue Steel stand-off missile, with its megaton warhead. Another adaptation enabled it to carry the larger and longer-range American Skybolt air-launched ballistic missile, although this never took place.

The V-Force reached its operational peak in February 1964 with Vulcans providing the largest component. Of the 159 aircraft, there were seventy Vulcans, fifty Valiants and thirty-nine Victors in sixteen squadrons, although by this time the effectiveness of Russian high-altitude air defences forced the force to train for low-level operations.[8]

As already mentioned, the Vulcan's durability made it markedly superior to the Valiant, which developed serious fatigue faults, and to the Victor, whose chapter of early misfortunes are described later. A dramatic instance of the Vulcan's continuing viability came fourteen years after it had relinquished its deterrent role and some twenty-seven years after its first flight. On 30 April 1982 the ageing but still sound aircraft found itself in the limelight once more when, during the Falklands War, it made a non-stop flight of 7,700 miles from Ascension Island to bomb Port Stanley Airfield with twenty-one conventional 1,000lb bombs. This ambitious operation needed a back-up Vulcan and eleven Victor tankers, which refuelled the attacking Vulcan five times on the outward flight and once on its return. (The Victors were themselves refuelled ten times between them.)[9] At the time this was the longest point-to-point bombing raid by the air force of any nation and a fitting climax for a remarkable aircraft. The Vulcan would complete a further four Black Buck missions before the end of hostilities.

The Handley Page Victor was the last of the V-bombers to enter service and following the cessation of its strategic role it assumed tanker responsibilities that continued until 1993, well after its famous manufacturer had gone out of business. The plane was designed in 1948 by Reginald Spencer Stafford in conjunction with Handley Page's chief aerodynamicist, Godfrey Lee, one of the few Englishmen who had visited German research establishments for information about their work, including swept-wing construction.

In the first instance, it was decided to construct a 40 per cent scale research aircraft, incorporating a unique wing that combined three progressive angles of leading edge sweep, amounting to 48½ degrees on the inboard section, 37½ degrees on the semi-span and 26½ degrees on the outboard section.[10] This crescent wing was said to combine in one aerofoil the virtues of a swept-back thick wing and an unswept thin wing, with the added advantage that by varying the wing's thickness, the different sweeps could give a constant airflow. Its construction was a remarkable achievement when such necessarily complicated calculations were carried out without the benefit of computers.

Apart from its wing, the main aircraft – where its five-man crew were situated on one level, with ejection seats for the two pilots – was distinguishable by its very smooth pointed nose with the windscreen glass and Perspex panels forming part of an unbroken aerodynamic skin shape,[11] while to the rear a small, swept, single-piece, all-moving tailplane was mounted high on the swept fin and rudder.[12]

Handley Page Victor, renowned for its massive bomb bay. (Farnborough Air Sciences Trust)

By such means the characteristic profile of the Victor was born, although on 26 August 1951 the programme met with a serious setback when the HP.88 research aircraft broke up in the air, killing the pilot. Fortunately for the aircraft, the Ministry of Civil Aviation's Air Accidents Investigation Branch found this was not due to faults in the design or construction of the wings but to a servo control failure to the tailplane.

By now, two prototypes were being built with four Armstrong Siddeley Sapphire engines enclosed in the wing roots. With more than 17,500lb thrust, these made the Victor marginally the fastest of the V-bombers, while its body design, including an enormous bomb compartment some 5ft longer than the Vulcan's and with nearly twice its capacity, rendered it capable of carrying a 22,000lb Grand Slam bomb or its nuclear equivalent.

Further delays occurred to the aeroplane's development when, in June 1952, an economy-minded Ministry of Supply decided that because its home runway at Radlett was too short, the prototype should be dismantled and transported in trucks to Boscombe Down with its very long runway. While it was being reassembled, leaking hydraulic fluid caused a fire to break out in a small compartment at the rear of the aircraft. This brought about the death of electrician Eddie Eyles and led to an inevitable enquiry.[13] By the end of 1953 the first Victor prototype was flying but on 5 February 1954 tragedy struck again when during pressure tests, the whole tailplane came away due to tail flutter and in the subsequent crash the pilot was killed. This was cured and the second prototype made its maiden flight on 11 September 1954 before appearing at the Farnborough Air Show that very afternoon.

The plane's halting progress before entering full production attracted the opposition of the Treasury, which favoured standardisation based on the Vulcan. This was successfully opposed by the Air Ministry, in case (as with the Supermarine Swift) serious and fundamental deficiencies should arise after the Vulcan entered service with potentially disastrous results for Britain's deterrent capability. It was April 1958 when the first RAF squadron was equipped with the Victor B.1 just as the Yellow Sun megaton nuclear weapon was reaching the RAF. In the event, the Vulcan was given priority to carry it.

Sixteen months later, on 20 August 1959, the Victor faced yet another crisis when its first Mark 2 aeroplane was lost in mysterious circumstances off the Pembrokeshire coast. Following extensive salvage operations, it was found that the accident had been caused by a wing tip static head coming adrift – something that was easily rectified.

Even so, by February 1962 when the Mark 2 reached RAF squadrons the whole future of the V-Force was coming under scrutiny and with the

Victor some two years behind the Vulcan, it was to suffer the heavier cut backs with twenty-eight aircraft cancelled and only thirty-four delivered, some of which were given non-strategic tasks. A proportion were equipped with cameras and reconnaissance radar, although the early grounding of the Valiants due to fatigue cracks led to every available Victor being put on tanker duties. A final reverse occurred in 1968, when all the retrofit Victors were phased out of service due to their parent company's financial difficulties and compulsory winding up on 27 February 1970, although this did not prevent standard Victors from continuing their in-flight refuelling services for Strike Command until, with their numbers diminishing, they were joined by VC10 and TriStar aircraft.

Despite its earlier curtailments and severe setbacks, the Victor proved itself a valuable member of the V-Force. Not only could it carry much the heaviest bomb load but in its tanker role it was ultimately the longest-serving marque.

By any standard, as worthy successors to the RAF's wartime Bomber Command, the V-bombers marked a glorious if relatively short phase in British military aviation that matched up to Trenchard's earlier dreams. They not only represented a giant technological advance over the propeller-driven Lincolns but with the Vulcan and to a somewhat lesser extent the Victor, the British aviation industry created world-beating aircraft. Despite adverse conditions during the immediate post-war years with near national insolvency and massive industrial upheaval, by working in close conjunction with gifted scientists from the Royal Aircraft Establishment at Farnborough, their designers succeeded in producing striking-looking, high-performance aircraft, capable of flying at unrivalled speeds and carrying the large and heavy devices that made up the country's deterrent.

Even so the initial decision to invite bidding from all six firms made it virtually certain that progress would be uneven and there would be serious delays and cancellations. As a result, a request had to be made for eight squadrons of American B-29s to fill the gap before the V-bombers entered service, which in the event were returned to the US some eighteen months before the first Valiant squadrons became operational.

Despite such self-induced complications, three genuine V-bombers were produced. Yet, however superior to their piston-driven forebears in terms of speed and manoeuvrability, rapid developments in Soviet radar and missile technology soon compelled them to make major modifications in material and tactical respects.

They were to carry air-launched ballistic missiles and, with their terrain-following radar, adopt low-level flying practices. The Vulcan, for instance, was

Britain's three V-bombers. (Farnborough Air Sciences Trust)

adapted to carry British-made British Blue Steel ballistic missiles equipped with nuclear warheads that after being released at 50,000ft would rise to 70,000ft and head towards their target at a speed of Mach 2.5. However, due to their limited range of some 130 nautical miles, it was planned to replace them from 1965 onwards with longer-range American Skybolt missiles. The Vulcan was modified to carry them before recurring problems with the missile led the Americans to offer Britain its submarine-launched Polaris missile system.

With Polaris the strategic responsibilities of the RAF's fearsome but relatively short-lived V-bombers were set to end, with the change officially taking place on 30 June 1969 – when the Royal Navy's third nuclear submarine, HMS *Renown*, became operational – just fourteen years after the forming of the RAF's first Valiant squadron. In spite of Polaris's dependence on the submarine's manned launching platform, this more than any other single occurrence appeared to bring into reality Duncan Sandys, forecast of the nation's core defence responsibilities passing from manned aircraft to missiles.

At Farnborough, on Sunday, 11 October 2015, some forty-six years after the Vulcans gave up their deterrence role and more than thirty years since their brilliant cameo campaign in the Falklands War, the author was privileged to watch the last Vulcan, XH558, make its final show overflight and landing. The aircraft was named *The Spirit of Great Britain* and its restoration had been supported by thousands of contributions countrywide.

Standing on the promontory next to the Cody pavilion we watched the great delta aircraft circle that same patch of sky from where Britain's first manned flight took place more than a century before. We found ourselves enveloped in the thunderous sound and smoke trails coming from its unreformed jets as pilot Mark Withers dipped his wings in greeting and circled the aerodrome before lining up for his final pass prior to landing. The plane was so low that we could make out the pilots' features and so large that it temporarily masked the sun. By unspoken agreement cameras were left to dangle around their owners' necks as everyone relished the very power and daunting presence of the historic plane. Although missiles might have assumed the deterrent role, like early aviation enthusiast Antoine de Saint-Exupéry we knew they could never replicate the mystery 'of metal turned to living flesh in a pilot's hands'.[14]

As the great plane settled over the runway we lost sight of it before its brake parachute blossomed and we heard the changed engine notes of reverse thrust. It was safely down and following our scattered applause there came an awkward pause before we realised it was all over and we commenced chattering while moving towards our cars.

The general consensus was that if Cody's ungainly large craft was the Alpha of Britain's massive planes, Vulcan XH558 surely represented the Omega of the British heavy bomber. As Farnborough had witnessed the first (and only) flight of British Army Aeroplane No. 1 it was felt appropriate that it too should have witnessed the Vulcan's last show flight.

PART 2

EXPECTATIONS DENIED

5

COMET: THE LEAD THAT WAS LOST

If British aviation was to continue as the world leader, it went without saying that it needed to construct and market world-leading civilian and military aeroplanes. The civilian aeroplanes were expected to come from the types defined by the Brabazon Committee, whose most advanced project was for a high-speed mail carrier, powered by jet engines, capable of flying the Atlantic with a ton of mail and just six passengers.

Before the end of the war, it was decided that it should be designed and built by de Havilland, a firm already responsible for so many notable aircraft whose founder Geoffrey de Havilland had already designed both the B.E.2, the early mainstay of the Royal Flying Corps in the First World War, and the DH.4, reputedly the best day bomber of that war. During the interwar period, his company had gone on to produce the famous DH Gypsy Moth family and the DH.88 a twin-engined, low-wing monoplane, called the Comet, which in 1933 won the £10,000 prize for the MacPherson Robertson Air Race from Britain to Australia. For the Second World War the company designed its revolutionary all wooden, ultra-fast Mosquito bomber, while immediately afterwards came the Vampire twin-boom jet fighter.

Despite widespread doubts among some of the Brabazon Committee members concerning jet propulsion, following his Vampire, it was only to be expected that Geoffrey de Havilland should strongly support the construction of a jet-powered civilian aeroplane to forge ahead of the American piston-engined models. It was also no surprise that the company should discard the Brabazon Committee's mail-carrying concept in favour of an airliner.

De Havilland's Chief Designer R.E. Bishop considered several unorthodox aeroplanes for the purpose, including one with twin booms and three turbojet engines, and even a rear-engined canard, before in 1944 proposing a tailless 40-degree swept-wing jet airliner, powered by four de Havilland

De Havilland DH.89 Dragon Rapide, a notably successful light transport plane. (Author's collection)

Ghost engines and capable of carrying twenty-four passengers. While the Ministry of Aviation accepted Bishop's design, in view of its radical nature they required the construction of a smaller research aircraft to see how things turned out. This aircraft, with no horizontal tail surfaces, became known as the DH.108 Swallow.

The wisdom of specifying an experimental aircraft quickly became evident when during testing de Havilland's eldest son, Geoffrey, was killed following a high-speed dive from 10,000ft.[1] Geoffrey's death following that of their youngest son, John, in an air collision during 1943, proved the heaviest of blows to Geoffrey de Havilland and his wife. However exciting the Swallow's performance, serious question marks over its controllability at high speeds led to the design being abandoned in favour of a more conventional aircraft that was expected to be brought into service far more quickly. The revised specification was for a streamlined and graceful aeroplane at an all-up weight of just 100,000lb, with wings swept to some 20 degrees and powered by four de Havilland Ghost jet engines buried in them. With its anticipated high-speed capability, Geoffrey de Havilland decided to name it Comet after the firm's 1934 racer.

De Havilland DH.108 Swallow research aircraft, very fast but unstable. (Farnborough Air Sciences Trust)

De Havilland DH.88 Comet, winner of the 1934 MacRobertson Air Race. (BAE Systems Heritage)

De Havilland DH.98 Mosquito, the Second World War's great all-rounder. (BAE Systems Heritage)

Although the American Boeing and Douglas companies were yet to have such a model on their drawing boards, in view of their renowned competitive instincts it was decided that speed of construction was vital and the first two DH.106 Comet aircraft – like the company's earlier Mosquito – should go straight into production off the drawing board.

De Havilland's managing director, Wilfred Nixon, summarised the problem: 'Had we built and tested a prototype first, the aircraft would have been out of date before it could be delivered to the airlines, and we should miss the market altogether.'[2] With the Comet, it was intended that the prototype would go straight into airline service.

Time was also precious for financial reasons; de Havilland had already received orders for fourteen such aircraft, eight from BOAC and six from British South American Airways, at a fixed cost of £450,000 apiece. Although this was still far below de Havilland's financial break-even point, they represented a valuable contribution towards their construction costs. The company also heaped additional pressure on itself by agreeing to fixed delivery dates and guaranteed performance figures, which it announced before design work was complete.

In such circumstances, it was understandable that to avoid undue, time-consuming enquiries, the firm should press on with its design work under a cloak of self-imposed secrecy while trying to eliminate as many faults as possible at the laboratory stage. Even so, with a pioneering aircraft designed to fly at great heights and at unrivalled speed, the company needed to pay particular attention to the requirement for a long fatigue life for both its airframe and components by conducting a series of comprehensive tests under the most adverse conditions, including many that continued to destruction.[3]

The jet engines' unrivalled appetite for fuel brought another challenge, namely a pressing requirement to find ways of lightening the plane, because every pound of structure lowered the plane's potential payload by the same amount. BOAC had, in fact, already estimated that with the Comet every pound of payload would be worth £50 a year. Whatever reductions were sought, more than a million parts were expected to go into each aircraft, most of which were made separately by de Havilland or its sub-contractors.

One option was to go for the smallest possible diameter of fuselage while still accommodating two passengers on each side of the aisle in reasonable comfort. Another was to use Redux adhesive rather than orthodox – and heavier – rivets to bond the Comet's wings and fuselage and fix the alloy skin covering the cabin area to the plane's skeleton. This skin had already been reduced to a gauge no thicker than a postcard, known in the trade as twenty-two gauge.[4] De Havilland had previously used Redux on both its small Dove transport and Hornet fighters, and it did away with the risk of rivet holes leaking air from a pressurised cabin. Whatever its advantages, the possibility of cabin failure was so serious that to achieve great strength it was decided to build the fuselage on the lines of a submarine. This was considered vital for at 40,000ft the temperature of the outside air was as low as minus 70 degrees Celsius and the cabin's differential pressure was nearly double that of existing aeroplanes.

However daunting the requirements, the firm planned to fly their first commercial aircraft just six months after the prototype's appearance rather than the usual passage of years. In fact, the first production batch flew twelve months after the prototype, slower than expected but in a remarkably short time considering the new materials and applications required in the construction process. These included glass cloth moulding that required tailoring, then impregnating, with Nuron resin, following which it could be built up in laminations to the correct thickness.[5]

Although the Redux bonding method had already been used, the extent of its employment on the Comet was unrivalled. This required applying heat and pressure to the parts that were to be bonded, which had to fit together perfectly and have equal pressure exerted on them throughout. It was a process needing specially designed tools and its attendant difficulties and potential dangers were highlighted when 'some of the construction workers complained that the alloys being used were too stiff to roll into the shape of the fuselage without using excessive force and thereby imposing extra stress on the fuselage skin … the primary alloy DTD 564/L73 was proving difficult to work and some material was showing signs of stress cracking.'[6] The technique of attaching window frames to the fuselage skin was also novel 'in that they were assembled in situ where the necessary pressure and heat were applied'.[7]

Apart from such problems with the fuselage, the Comet's wings were to become integral fuel tanks. During the process, they were filled with 2,000 gallons of paraffin, when any weeps were remedied. To seal them a Bostik protection fluid was used whose toxic fumes required special breathing apparatus for the men involved.

Along with such new production techniques, unparalleled methods were adopted to test the length of the aircraft's working life before metal fatigue became evident. Structures were tested by being placed under a stress loading of 20.5psi, two and a half times greater than that expected in ordinary service. This also applied to the aircraft's doors and hatches, while its windows and surrounding structures were subjected to extensive test-loading up to ten times the projected operating load factor.[8]

When testing components to destruction, de Havilland adopted a new method that involved placing a fuselage section in a water tank where the point of failure could be more easily traced. At the point of failure, however, it was estimated that the structure would have already undergone the equivalent of at least ten years' flying. The manufacturers also constructed a compression chamber that was large enough to take a complete fuselage pressure cabin. This was subjected to an extensive range of temperatures peaking at minus 70 degrees Celsius at a simulated altitude of 70,000ft. During such trials, no major changes to the metal employed in the fuselage were observed.[9]

Following such extensive tests, de Havilland believed that if any disaster befell the Comet, it was likely to be caused by fire rather than from material fatigue.

However thorough and pervasive such testing might be, there was still no doubt that the Comet's future success depended on its speed of development. In this respect, de Havilland's achievements were particularly impressive. Fewer than three years elapsed between the Ministry of Supply's order in September 1946 for two prototypes (and fourteen aircraft) with the first prototype being rolled out of its hangar for engine runs in April 1949. This compared with a 'normal' interval of some seven years.

Unsurprisingly, there were some penalties for potential early customers. Although all models were equipped with four-wheel bogie undercarriage, BOAC and BSAA, who had placed orders for Comet 1s, had to accept they would be powered by de Havilland Ghost engines rather than the projected more powerful Rolls-Royce Avons.

De Havilland DH.106 Comet jet airliner, an initial winner. (Farnborough Air Sciences Trust)

The headlong pace of construction continued with prototype Comet G-ALVG (referred to as Victor George from its last two serial numbers) making its first flight on 27 July 1949 and, in the absence of mechanical and other defects, being due to move on to a series of overseas flights during October. These were particularly important as they were expected to lead to new orders.

The second prototype followed in 1950. On 24 May 1951 BOAC borrowed a Ministry of Supply prototype for a projected overseas publicity flight. The corporation's first production Comet was delivered on 31 December 1951 and after being awarded its full passenger-carrying certificate of airworthiness, on 2 May 1952 Comet G-ALYP (Yoke Peter) left London Airport for Johannesburg with the first fare-paying passengers to fly by jet.[10] The rewards of such extreme endeavours came with the Comet entering service years ahead of its nearest rival, the American Boeing 707, construction of which was not even approved until 22 April 1952.

From the beginning the Comet proved outstanding, effortlessly setting new records for journey times and, contrary to dire financial forecasts due to its unrivalled fuel consumption, it made a profit of £600 on each trip. Such was the pride in its achievements so far, that in July 1952, the Lord Privy Seal, Viscount Swinton, proudly told the House of Lords:

> We have got such a lead in civil jet aviation and the Comet has established such a reputation, that we may not only get the orders which airlines all over the world may want to place in the next three or four years, but we may have collared the market for a generation. This is one of the greatest chances we have ever had.[11]

For five and a half months the run of successes continued unabated with the Comet's services fully subscribed and extended to Tokyo.

It was then the disasters commenced. On the night of 26 October 1952, a major crash occurred during take-off from Rome. The plane did not build up enough power and its pilot, Captain R.E.H. Foote aborted the take-off. Happily, while the plane was extensively damaged, all its passengers emerged unhurt. Although 36-year-old Captain Foote had been awarded a Distinguished Flying Cross for his wartime service and was a most experienced pilot, there seemed to be no question of the plane being to blame. The Chief Inspector of Accidents concluded that, 'The accident was due to an error of judgement by the Captain in not appreciating the excessive nose up attitude during take-off.' The unfortunate Foote was transferred to the pilot's version of Siberia, flying York Freighters carrying smelly animals.

The accident at Rome was followed on 3 March 1953 by an identical incident at Karachi airport with Canadian Pacific's Comet – *The Empress of Hawaii*
– in which it failed to take-off and, after skidding into a 22ft bank, burst into
flames at the expense of all eleven of its passengers. The official enquiry echoed
the Rome report by blaming the pilot, Captain Pentland, who 'had limited
experience of Comets but elected to take-off at night'.[12] In fact, de Havilland
itself took the crashes seriously enough to reshape the leading edge of the
Comet's wings, thereby eliminating the take-off problems by reducing stalling
speed and increasing lift off power.

Unfortunately the news was to get even worse. On the afternoon of 2 May
1953 Comet Yoke Victor, homeward bound from Singapore, crashed six and a
half minutes after leaving Calcutta with no survivors among the thirty-seven
passengers and crew of six. The wreckage was spread over an area of 8 miles
and a sightseer believed it had flown into a most violent storm. The Court
of Inquiry convened by the Indian government ruled out sabotage and once
again placed responsibility on the pilot, giving its opinion that 'the crash had
been caused by overstraining the plane, either as a direct result of the storm
or through over-control or loss of control by the pilot. As a result, it suffered
structural failure in the air which caused fire.'[13] The court recommended that
the wreckage be taken back to Britain for a detailed examination. This time
de Havilland responded cautiously, stating that until a detailed examination of
the wreckage by the Royal Aircraft Establishment at Farnborough had been
completed it was impossible to determine any sequence of structural failure.

Meanwhile, despite another relatively minor mishap, the prototype for
the Comet 2 gained new publicity through its record-breaking flights to
Khartoum and the South Atlantic. The future looked brighter than ever; by
the end of 1953 de Havilland had delivered all twenty-one Comet 1s and
1As, thirty-five Comet 2s were on order and eleven long-range Comet 3s
had been ordered.[14]

Such fast-increasing expectations ended tragically when, on the morning
of 10 January 1954, Comet G-ALYP – Yoke Peter – left Rome for London
and while still close to Elba its pilot Captain Alan Gibson was enquiring
about an in-flight weather report when his conversation broke off. Italian
fishermen watched in horror as a series of explosions flared across the sky and
aircraft wreckage spiralled into the sea midway between Elba and the island of
Montecristo, 16 miles to the south.

In London, Sir Miles Thomas, Chairman of BOAC, straightway held a number
of conferences and a statement was issued that 'as a measure of prudence the
normal Comet passenger services were being temporarily suspended to enable

minute and unhurried technical examination of every aircraft in the Comet fleet to be carried out at London Airport'.[15] Sabotage was not ruled out and as Yoke Peter had flown only 3,681 hours over 1,200 flights, and as de Havilland's fatigue tests during construction had shown fatigue life to be in the order of at least 18,000 flights, this was not considered likely. In fact, the company vigorously discounted the suggestion put forward by Sir Victor Tait, Deputy Chief Executive BOAC, that metal fatigue in the fuselage could have been the cause.[16]

A group of specialist engineers and technicians were assembled under Charles Abell, the Deputy Director of BOAC who was in charge of engineering operations, to examine all seven planes of the British Comet fleet. As a consequence, nearly fifty modifications were recommended. These were announced on 4 February 1954 and they included fitting armour-plated shields between the engines and fuel tanks, reinforcing fuel pipes and installing smoke detectors. However sensible the proposals, their general nature suggested the experts were far from certain about the main cause of the latest crash.

After carrying out the proposed changes, the Comet re-entered service on 23 March 1954. Any assurance concerning their effectiveness ended just sixteen days later when news reached London that Comet Yoke Yoke, which had undergone the recommended modifications, crashed off the coast of Sicily on a flight between Rome and Cairo. All Comets were grounded again after having flown more than 10 million miles. This time it was clear that an

exhaustive and impartial investigation was needed to preserve the reputation of both de Havilland and British aviation as a whole. Sir Arnold Hall, the director of the Royal Aircraft Establishment at Farnborough, was instructed to investigate the two recent disasters and told his enquiry should take precedence over all the RAE's other activities with no money spared in conducting it.

Sir Arnold Hall. (Farnborough Air Sciences Trust)

This resulted in a series of brilliant deductions, some of which were dependent on the work of the Royal Navy divers who recovered much of Comet Yoke Peter some 70 fathoms down on the Mediterranean sea bed. There was no hope of any similar recovery for Yoke Yoke, the bulk of which had come to rest some 3,500ft down, close to the island of Stromboli.

This time the attention of the investigators was directed towards possible fatigue in the pressure cabin. The reason was obvious: in both cases the aircraft suffered a disaster when it was reaching the top of its climb when pressure inside the cabin was reaching its maximum.

As for the likely results of metal fatigue: with the Comet flying 6 miles high, if the cabin skin had burst it was estimated that the outrushing air would have been equivalent to the explosion of a 500lb bomb.[17] Such a likely occurrence was corroborated by the findings of Italian professor Antonio Fomari from the University of Pisa, who carried out a post-mortem on the victims of Yoke Peter and concluded that although none had drowned, they had died quickly 'by violent movement and explosive decompression'.[18] Most had fractured their skulls a split second before death, although the professor believed that after their long drop from the aeroplane other severe injuries to their limbs and abdomens were most likely to have been caused on impact with the sea.

Sir Arnold Hall's own investigation at Farnborough involved an exhaustive test programme upon the three Comets sent him by BOAC. To this end he decided to examine Yoke Sugar for fire hazards, conduct flight trials on Able Victor and test Yoke Uncle to the point of destruction. Such investigations were to be complemented by a microscopic examination of the wreckage salvaged from Elba, which was sent to Farnborough and built up on a wooden skeleton to take on the exact proportions of the original aircraft. Brilliant salvage work enabled nearly two-thirds of the fuselage wreckage to be wired to the skeleton and this indicated that the cabin must have burst, with the split passing through a point where holes had been drilled to stop a small crack in a reinforcing plate near its rear automatic direction finding window on the roof.[19]

In the case of the tests made on the first two Comets, those conducted on Yoke Sugar for fire hazards proved negative, but although Able Victor came out of the daily flight trials well, it was concluded that the hot air produced by the two engines nearest to the fuselage was likely to produce fatigue close to the tail.

As expected, the most protracted tests were conducted on the third aircraft, Yoke Uncle, which were to continue to the point of destruction. To enable the outcome to be observed more accurately, Sir Arnold Hall (like de Havilland) decided to use water rather than air pressure. A giant tank was constructed at the RAE to hold the plane and after it was filled the plane made 3,060 'simulated flights', achieved by raising and lowering the pressure. The cabin structure finally failed at the corner of one of the windows where there was a drilled crack. With the pressure tests agreeing with the conclusions reached from the salvaged wreckage about fatal weakness at the corner of a window, this was confirmed as the undoubted cause of Yoke Peter's crash.

The water tests marked the climax of an inquiry costing more than £2 million; the RAE's report totalling 380 pages of transcript was produced within five months of the crash and was presented to the government's Comet Inquiry conducted by Judge Lord Cohen, a Lord of Appeal in Ordinary. Cohen's subsequent deliberations took a further twenty-two days, stretching over six weeks, involving sixty-eight witnesses.[20] On its conclusion a final transcript of 1,600 pages was made, containing 800,000 words.

On 12 February 1955, Lord Cohen published his report on an enquiry that had earned the full respect of interested observers, including American designers who closely followed the Comet's misfortunes and their aftermath. The New York Herald Tribune, for instance, gave 'Full marks to Britain for its brutally honest and frank enquiry into the Comet,' with Time Magazine acknowledging that, 'British science has told the world without excuse or cover up what happened to Britain's proudest airliner, the ill-starred jet, Comet.'[21]

Re-reading the report some sixty years later, one's overriding impression is that the chairman was not disposed to apportion blame. Although Lord Cohen fully accepted the findings that the Elba crash was due to structural failure of Yoke Peter's pressure cabin in the region of the ADF window brought about by fatigue, he concluded that the accident was not due to the wrongful act or negligence of any party or of any person in the employment of any party.[22]

The obvious question raised by Lord Cohen's verdict was that if everyone was blameless, why did the disasters happen at all? In fairness, his further conclusions were rather more circumspect. In the case of de Havilland, he said he was satisfied that in the then state of knowledge they 'cannot be blamed for not making greater use of strain gauges than they actually did or for believing that the static test that they proposed to apply would, if successful, give the necessary assurance against the risk of fatigue during the working life of the aircraft'.[23]

However, he also included a memorandum by assessors working for the inquiry that concluded that during the design of the Comet de Havilland did not make use of its calculations to arrive at a close estimate of the stress distribution near the corners of the cabin windows.[24] What was more, they reported that when the company was carrying out its tests 'the panels (about

3ft square, including a window) were supported on the face of a stiff steel pressure box, and not in conditions truly representative of those that existed near the window on the pressure cabin itself'.[25] The report went on to say:

> The test sections of the cabin differed from the cabin fitted to the aircraft in several respects ... In the first place, each was incomplete and incapable of sustained pressure if it had not been fitted with a stiff bulkhead at the open end or ends ... Moreover, the windows of special interest in this Inquiry which were in the front test section, were rather near the bulkhead mentioned, so that the stresses in the skin around them might have been appreciably different from those in similar places in the complete cabin.[26]

While acknowledging that the drilling of cracks would have been appropriate if the stresses had been as low as de Havilland thought, Lord Cohen concluded that the stress on the skin at the edge of the window near the corner was far higher than had been suspected by de Havilland and was probably 40,000lb/sq in under the normal pressure difference.[27]

Such observations clearly raised questions about whether de Havilland's inspectors were as curious and thorough as they might have been. Nonetheless, Lord Cohen attached no blame to anyone for permitting the resumption of air services after the first enquiry, despite the continuing uncertainty about the causes of the crashes. Notwithstanding, he thought it essential that, in the future, manufacturers should be aware of and should make full use of such facilities as the research establishments that the Ministry of Supply could offer.[28]

Despite its critical elements, Lord Cohen's report exonerated the government, the Air Registration Board and de Havilland from blame. It brought about a situation that, while de Havilland could in no way be jubilant, after a period of great pressure and uncertainty its reputation had been saved and following the depth of the investigation it now knew what techniques needed revising to make the Comet both safe and successful. Above all, the investigations pointed to the need for new design standards for airframes and pressure cabins. Henceforth, the spectre of metal fatigue would be ever present with pressure-cabin cutouts, together with the imperative need for heavier skinning and smaller windows.

Such knowledge was, of course, also available to the Americans, who were now making relentless strides with their Boeing 707. The direst penalties for de Havilland from the Comet disasters came in the loss of vital time in which to consolidate the company's lead over the Americans and by throwing into confusion the question of when and what planes built by the company would

De Havilland Comet 4, never sold in the numbers it deserved. (BAE Systems Heritage)

be flying again. The Comet Series 1 was, to all intents and purposes, written off, although the Royal Air Force undertook to use modified Series 2 Comets for Transport Command and BOAC, which had later Comets on order, showed its confidence by considering raising its order to twenty. Even so, compared with the previous headlong progress there was a strong note of caution, if not over-caution, in the air. The Chairman of BOAC, Sir Miles Thomas, declared, 'We shall make haste slowly and satisfy ourselves fully before offering the new Comets for passenger service. They will be flown for more than 2,000 hours before being put into passenger service.'

The decisions announced by BOAC dealt a hammer blow to the Comet's fortunes. It decided not to go for the reskinned and modified Comet 2 that became available some two years after the first Comets had been withdrawn from service, or even the Comet 3 (as a result of which only one was registered), but to wait a further two years for the Comet 4, by which time American competition had not only caught up but surged ahead.

The Comet 4 was a larger aircraft with an all-up weight of 152,500lb, compared with the 107,000lb of the Comet 1, and was intended to carry between sixty and eighty-one passengers in far greater safety. Its fuselage skin was increased in thickness and made of alloy L72 and fibreglass, increasing its strength by 22 per cent.[29] The cabin's skin was also thickened with reinforcement applied to the door, hatch and windows.

Boeing 707, an outstanding aircraft by any standard. (Royal Aeronautical Society/ National Aerospace Library)

Yet by now the majority of de Havilland's large customers had moved to other manufacturers and the Americans had taken advantage of the Comet's non-production to overtake it and capture the worldwide sales market. After such unlimited promise a total of just over seventy Comet 4s of all versions were manufactured – nineteen Comet 4Bs and 4Cs were handed over to BOAC from late 1958 onwards, fourteen went to BEA, twenty-six to the RAF and others were taken by small airlines such as Olympic, Aerolineas Argentinas and Mexicana. They were not only faster than the previous series but equipped with the latest fail-safe techniques that complied with the more stringent standards set by the Air Registration Board.

While Geoffrey de Havilland hoped the Series 4 would be followed by the Comet 5, with which the firm intended to compete against the transatlantic airliners being produced by Boeing and Douglas, BOAC delivered a further rebuff by favouring the British VC10 instead.[30]

In retrospect, had things not gone wrong with the Comet 1 the world's large players would surely have signed up for an aircraft of unrivalled beauty and speed that was years ahead of the field. Once committed they were likely to have retained their loyalty for British airliners rather than American ones. As it was, the Boeing 707 left the ground just one month after progress on Comet was halted. Although like the Comet, it had originally been designed as a tanker, the company went on to make a prototype for an airliner carrying 139 passengers at 600mph before in March 1955 the company's great break came when the USF agreed to buy it. The position improved further when, faced with competition from the Douglas DC-8, Boeing reduced the 707's price from $2 million to $1.8 million, at which Pan American placed an order for thirty long-range versions. They called it the Intercontinental and it provoked a flood of orders from across the world.

In contrast, following the Comet disasters attempts by British manufacturers to sell civilian airliners (some of which like the VC10 were undoubtedly very good aeroplanes, if over-tailored to British needs) proved highly disappointing.

In spite of de Havilland's exoneration by Lord Cohen, the irredeemable damage to British prospects owed something to the company's omissions as well as its actions.

In spite of some inevitable delay, if only it had decided on the more powerful Rolls-Royce Avon engines, for instance, it would not have needed (among other weight-saving measures) to use such a spectacularly thin gauge of metal to cover the Comet's cabin. Had de Havilland also allowed experts from Boscombe Down to assess the pioneering aircraft, rather than carrying out all their tests in-house, whatever the time lost in taking further safety measures, the company's design flair was still most likely to have brought Comet out well before the Boeing 707. In this case the nation's airlines would have been able to purchase a dominant British plane for sound business reasons rather than because of government edicts about buying British.

Whatever the particular instances, it has to be acknowledged that the Comet's initial failings owed something to the company's ethics, its unmistakable sense of elitism and strong self-confidence on what it had already achieved and what it could achieve in future under its outstanding founder, who had already lost two sons in his all-out quest for success.

At the Comet Inquiry, a traditionally uncritical Lord Brabazon observed that the technological achievements of the plane were allied with terrible dangers that were either unknown or not considered seriously enough by the company. In this regard, at a later interview, David Davies, chief test pilot of the Air Registration Board, who flew both Comet 1 and 2 prototypes, went further, maintaining that de Havilland chief designer R.E. Bishop just did not listen to any pilots, including Davies, when they suggested modifications.[31]

Along with the problems of moving into new technological territory, the company's urge to seize an unparalleled opportunity along with a fatal touch of arrogance, brought terrible penalties for British aviation in the shape of the Comet crashes, and more serious still with them a loss of confidence by would-be purchasers of British civil aircraft that the Americans were only too happy to exploit – and continue exploiting.

6

SANDYS DEFENCE REVIEW: FROM AIRCRAFT TO MISSILES

Unlike the decade following the Great War, when military aviation was not considered that seriously and the RAF had to operate with its wartime equipment, that following the Second World War was notably different. The onset of the Cold War with open conflict in Korea and Soviet threats to Europe required new tactical interceptors and bombers, while the UK deterrent required larger, more powerful and faster aircraft from which to launch it.

Even so, in the UK following exceptional wartime expenditure and postwar spending towards national revival, including a massive house-building programme and major health and welfare reforms, defence budgets – including those for the RAF – were much affected by repeated and serious financial crises.

In the early post-war years attempts were made to bring defence costs down to some 7 per cent of the country's gross national product (GNP) although they were still higher than those of other NATO nations (with the exception of France, which was heavily committed to its Algerian operations) and considerably higher than the United States, whose defence costs during 1949 and 1950 stood at 5.1 per cent and 5.5 per cent of its GNP.

Despite this, following the outbreak of the Korean War Britain's defence spending again rose sharply with the Attlee government rashly increasing it to a massive £4,700 million during the years 1951–54, equivalent in 1951 to 8.9 per cent of GNP, and to a massive 11.2 per cent in both 1952 and 1953, decisions only made possible by US loans to relieve the country's shortage of dollars.[1] The new obligations, including the building of extra aircraft, resulted in a sharp rise in the number of civilians employed in the aviation industry, thereby reducing the levels of those available for other metal-using industries with much-needed export programmes.

Sir John Slessor speaking at a dinner on 31 May 1951 to commemorate the tenth anniversary of jet-powered flight. (Royal Aeronautical Society/National Aerospace Library)

Such expenditure was clearly unsustainable and in 1952 the Service Chiefs of Staff were heavily influenced by Marshal of the Royal Air Force, Sir John Slessor, whose doctrine of nuclear deterrence was thought by defence analyst Michael Howard to have provided the basis of all such thinking until the end of the Cold War.[2] Slessor opted for deterrence with the RAF's projected V-bombers carrying nuclear weapons able to threaten targets in the Soviet Union that posed a threat to Britain but not to the US.

In reality, the anticipated reductions in defence spending through this strategy were thwarted by the UK's continuing commitment to the build-up of NATO's conventional forces against a possible Soviet invasion of Europe. Serious weaknesses in the UK's conventional forces for operations beyond the Soviet theatre also became evident during the 1956 Suez Crisis, where the three months spent attempting to assemble a task force to counter Egypt's nationalisation of the Suez Canal brought diplomatic disaster for both Britain and France.

The results were profound. British anger at the debacle, together with the continuing need to reduce public expenditure, led to the most thorough

Duncan Sandys, Minister of Aviation, and Peter Masefield, President of the Royal Aeronautical Society during 1959–60, discussing the 1959 White Paper on Defence. (Royal Aeronautical Society/National Aerospace Library)

consideration of future defence strategy since the war. This was undertaken through the Defence Review of 1957, most commonly named after Duncan Sandys, Prime Minister Macmillan's Defence Minister at the time. In conducting his review Sandys was given powers to decide on all matters of policy affecting the size, shape and organisation of the armed forces and their equipment.[3] Predictably, his findings would have immense effects on the armed services and on the RAF in particular.

Much of the White Paper was written by Sandys himself and it opened with the declaration that Britain's defence policy must be radically revised. 'This,' he wrote, 'has become necessary on economical, international and Military grounds.'[4] Sandys drew attention to the undoubted fact that Britain's position and influence in the world depended first and foremost upon the health of her internal economy and the success of her export trade, 'Without these, military power is of no avail and in any case cannot in the long run be supported …' and he concluded that 'it is an inescapable necessity that defence expenditure, along with government expenditure of all kinds, should be reduced to a level which does not place an excessive burden on the economy'.[5]

To this end Sandys pointed out that defence instruments were changing, with increasingly formidable weapons succeeding one another, including rocket weapons and hydrogen bombs. During the Second World War, Sandys had been selected by his father-in-law, Winston Churchill, to carry out a study of German missiles and rockets and the best ways of defending against them, which had affected him immensely. This was evident in the startling prediction in his White Paper that in a few years' time '[t]here will be missiles steered by electronic brains capable of delivering megaton warheads over a range of 5,000 miles or more'.[6] He added that human pilots would only be needed for transport aircraft.

Sandys believed such weapons would change the whole basis of world strategy and would, for instance, replace RAF fighter planes, because it was unlikely that Britain would ever be involved in a major war without the United States.[7] In such circumstances, its forces would not need to be fully balanced nor self-sufficient, with the RAF, for instance, not able to provide protection against a nuclear attack. To Sandys, British military policy would depend largely on the nuclear power of the United States, although Britain already had its own atomic bombs and a megaton weapon shortly to be tested 'that could in the first place be delivered by the British V-bombers which in due course (will) be supplemented and later replaced by ballistic rockets'.[8]

Sandys was fully conscious that British defence expenditure was almost twice as high as the average NATO member (except for the US) and believed that necessary reductions in its conventional forces could be achieved by reducing British military commitments in the Middle East, South-East Asia and its colonies and protected territories overseas. In their place he proposed the creation of a central reserve capable of rapid reaction, thus avoiding the protracted and unsuccessful build-up that had taken place prior to Suez.

Much the largest of Sandys' proposed savings was expected to come from the ending of National Service, which he considered an expensive and inefficient method of raising manpower. In its place he envisaged compact numbers of regular forces trained to the highest standards and equipped with the newest weapons, which in the case of air defence meant moving towards megaton bombs, ballistic rockets and missile systems at the expense of manned interceptors. By such means, Sandys aimed to reduce the projected defence spending for 1957–58 from £1,700 million to £1,424 million, while releasing several hundred thousand men for productive employment, including many badly needed scientists and technicians that he anticipated would come from the aviation industry.

Although a halving of forces' manpower from the current 700,000 was fully expected to bring about economies, Sandys acknowledged that, as individuals, regular servicemen and women equipped with modern weapons would cost far more than conscripts. This required additional economies by adopting a defence posture more in keeping with a medium-sized power, 'including some pruning of the research and development programme'.[9][10] This decision was bound to fall hardest on the two equipment-led services, with the RAF the most likely loser.

Predictably, Sandys' proposals met with strong opposition from MPs on both sides of the House of Commons and from many influential figures in the armed services, including Sir Gerald Templer, Chief of the Imperial General Staff, who at one point reputedly came to blows with the Defence Minister. This was said to have been partly due to Sandys' uncompromising attitude and his attempts to combine the administration of the three defence services into a single integrated department. Although the latter proposals were not implemented at this time, his White Paper undoubtedly threatened service establishments that were arguably still overblown since the war.

Lord Mountbatten inspecting a Hovercraft test model in 1959 with constructor Sam Hughes. (Royal Aeronautical Society/National Aerospace Library)

In fairness, his proposals hardly came as a surprise for all three services were anticipating cutbacks with the end of the Korean War. In 1956 the Army produced a report by Sir Richard Hull, Deputy Chief of the Imperial General Staff (DCIGS), proposing an all regular Army, including a strategic reserve, which involved the ending of National Service.[11] In such circumstances, Sandys' White Paper was concerned with how Hull's proposals would be implemented rather than introducing entirely new ones.

In the case of the Royal Navy, its priorities had already changed from the earlier emphasis on battleships and fighting the Soviets in the Atlantic to projecting power east of Suez. However, partly due to Sandys' good working relationship with the Navy's First Sea Lord, Lord Mountbatten, a major expansion of the fleet's amphibious capabilities was agreed upon, followed in November 1957 by Sandys' relaxation of the Navy's manpower ceiling from 80,000 to 88,000.[12]

In contrast, the RAF found itself at a distinct disadvantage. It had produced no report equivalent to the Army's and could make no strategic changes to compare with the Royal Navy's. Moreover, however able and committed to his service's needs, Sir Dermot Boyle lacked the clout of Mountbatten and the bloody-mindedness of Sir Gerald Templar.

In any case, his relations with Duncan Sandys were bound to be more confrontational due to the Defence Minister's direct threats to his traditional aircraft and the demoralising effect this was bound to have on his service. This was evident when Sandys' enthusiasm for missiles brought about the rapid cancellation of two major fighter projects, the Saunders-Roe SR.177 rocket-assisted fighter (which was to be procured for both the RAF and the Royal Navy) and the P.1083, a supersonic Hawker fighter and low-level strike aircraft, which left the projected English Electric Lightning (due to fly at more than twice the speed of the Hunter at a ceiling of more than 60,000ft) as the RAF's only supersonic aircraft.[13]

Sandys' plans for strategic defence depended on three missile systems, the intermediate range ballistic missile (IRBM) called Blue Streak that he believed would replace the V-bombers in threatening the Soviet homeland but which needed to be stored in hard silos and took some half-an-hour to fuel; the air-to-ground missile, Blue Steel, due to be carried by the V-bombers to give them extended powers of penetration against improving Soviet defences and the short-range missile system called Bloodhound intended to protect the V-bombers' bases by engaging targets at between 10,000 and 60,000ft at ranges of up to 40 miles. The detailed development of these systems are described in the following chapter.

Sandys' policy was bound to be deeply unpopular with the RAF for it went far further than cancelling a weapon system against a preferred alternative. With the advantages already enjoyed by the American ICBMs and their air-launched missiles, British versions were unlikely to become world leaders, while new iconic military aircraft could. Another major grievance arose from the amount of research and development that had already been invested in the Avro 730, a Mach 2 plus high-flying supersonic bomber due to be armed with a megaton warhead that was to replace the V-Force before it was cancelled in favour of the Blue Streak missile programme. The same anger was felt for Hawker's highly promising thin-wing P.1083 Hunter that had reached a relatively late stage of design before it was also cancelled.

The cancellation of such highly regarded bomber and fighter programmes coupled with the RAF's visceral suspicion of static missiles made it predictable that the service should feel the need for a replacement aeroplane (leading to a specification being drawn up by Vickers and English Electric for a new highly advanced, all-purpose plane) to be called TSR2 – a tactical strike and reconnaissance bomber.

Less foreseeable was the failure of the military aircraft cancellations to release surplus manpower for the anticipated growth in British civil aviation. Things did not turn out as expected because shortly after the publication of the report, production of planes such as the Lightning, the V-bombers, the Hunter and the Javelin was in fact still increasing and this continued until 1964, when military sales had almost regained the 1955 level. Although the numbers of employees on military commitments contracted by 18 per cent between 1957 and 1964 to 267,540, this was still a fifth higher than at the start of the Korean War.

It was also found that the industry's profits fell steeply from 15.7 per cent in 1957 to just 6.3 per cent in 1964 compared with an all UK industrial average of 11 per cent.[14] Some of this resulted from manufacturers taking the opportunity to invest in civil aircraft where sales proved distinctly disappointing (while American orders were rocketing).

Another unforeseen consequence of Sandys was that while the cancellations undoubtedly saved money on research, missiles did not provide full security and it was discovered that the short-range Bloodhound missile still needed manned fighters to help protect the V-bomber airfields. Furthermore, while the cost of guided weapons did not compare with new aircraft programmes, it was not necessarily cheap and was not above cancellation. The cost escalation on Blue Steel, for instance, was 500 per cent.[15] Worse still, when the Blue Streak ballistic missile quickly proved obsolete, it was cancelled at a cost of more than £200 million.

The most damming criticism of the Sandys proposals, however, was that they interrupted the progression of aircraft designs and placed the British aviation industry in a position similar to that of the late 1940s, where it needed a major technological leap requiring massive new investment to match continuing US developments.

Due to the complexity and the depth of opposition to the Sandys proposals, Prime Minister Harold Macmillan decided that a special interdepartmental committee, chaired by Sir Thomas Padmore, the Permanent Secretary to the Treasury, should be appointed. His Aircraft Industry Working Party (AIWP) commenced in the summer of 1957 to review past policy, including Sandys, and concluded that the Sandys recommendations would be most severe for the aircraft industry unless it was rationalised into a few well-resourced firms able to concentrate on export-led civil contracts. Although the British were strong in aero engines, similar successes had not been gained in civilian aircraft construction, where world numbers were expected to double between 1955 and 1961 and again by the end of 1967.[16] As a result, Aubrey Jones, the Minister of Supply, proposed that the Trident airliner currently ordered by BEA should be built by a consortium of firms, which caused de Havilland to join with Fairey and Hunting Aviation for the purpose.

Jones made a further attempt to rationalise the industry over the large construction programme for TSR2. At his urging, several submissions were made by different consortia before Vickers joined up with English Electric to gain the contract. As for its propulsion system, although Vickers preferred an engine designed by Rolls-Royce, the contract for this was eventually awarded to Bristol, where its offer to merge its engine production with that of Armstrong Siddeley and de Havilland gained the day.

With declining military orders, the industry's long-term future appeared to depend on the civil sector, but Jones was well aware of the formidable competition from US manufacturers, buttressed by their huge domestic market, and from countries such as France, who promoted the manufacture of civil aircraft as a deliberate matter of national policy. Although he encouraged manufacturers to undertake development with their own finances, he recognised that 'with the depletion of revenues from defence contracts, few will have the resources to do this and some government contribution is inevitable'.[17]

Following the 1959 General Election, Duncan Sandys succeeded Aubrey Jones to become Britain's first Minister of Aviation. To help counter American domination, Sandys attempted to force the pace of rationalisation by favouring two large groups of companies to whom he promised launch aid for civilian aircraft programmes in return for a levy on sales. Such initiatives were largely responsible for the British aircraft industry regrouping into the Hawker Siddeley Group in 1958 and the British Aircraft Corporation in 1960. Although in July 1960 Sandys ceased to be Minister of Aviation, rationalisation continued with the pooling of industrial resources for the TSR2 project, and the agreement to collaborate with the French on a supersonic aircraft that would become Concorde. Projected new military aircraft developments would include the V/STOL Hawker Siddeley P.1154, where initial financial support came from US-inspired measures, and other collaborative missile, helicopter and aircraft projects with France.[18]

Opinions vary widely about the effects of the Sandys Report. Sir George Edwards, who became Managing Director of BAC and was one of the most notable and influential designers in British aviation post-1945, acknowledged that although at first he was shattered by the Sandys proposals, something he saw 'as essentially pointing the way towards a new technique of waging war in which you didn't need a man (or aircraft) but taking a long view, it was pretty far-seeing as to what eventually happened'.[19] Some years later Edwards went as far as to tell a London audience that he believed the Sandys doctrine had been misinterpreted as it had the great merit of pulling together the confused and sprawling situation following the Korean War to set out a recognisable defence policy. 'Although some of us disagreed with much of its detail (and a good deal of this has been straightened out since) we must recognise that it was a courageous and necessary step.'[20] Edwards' approach was echoed by his biographer Robert Gardner, who concluded that while it destroyed many of Britain's most advanced and promising new aircraft of the period, the carrot of TSR2 successfully forced the industry into mergers, reducing it from some twenty-five airframe companies to two major groups in a process Sir George described as 'a golden welding flux'.

Charles Gardner, BAC's historian, and others were markedly less philosophic. To him the brutal fact remained that in 1957 Sandys killed all the advanced aeroplane projects in the pipeline, together with some of their engines. Gardner could never forgive Sandys, either, for what he saw as demoralising the Royal Air Force and the aircraft industry by setting British military aviation back by a decade. 'Looking back on the period 1946–1958 it still challenges comprehension that such a mess could be made of such a favourable initial situation.'[21]

How favourable the initial situation really was is open to question, but Gardner likened Sandys' bias towards rockets to 'a Dan Dare scenario which might conceivably be valid by the turn of the century, but which bore no relation to the state of the art or the practicalities of life for the 1960s'.[22] Yet, even

he approved of Sandys later mission in 1959 to amalgamate the aviation industry into two airframe groups and two engine groups, each strong enough to
retain the competitive edge in all fields.

Arthur Reed, one-time air correspondent of *The Times*, was even more con-
demnatory than Gardner over Sandys' fixation with rockets. He considered his
belief that the aeroplane was finished:

> the biggest mistake made governmentally that has ever been inflicted on
> the industry because people at once lost faith in the industry and there
> was a complete disorientation of thinking … this unfortunate pause in
> forward planning meant that our American competitors caught up with
> our knowledge on jet propulsion in the military field and were able to
> overtake us because they had no break in the programme. From this we
> still suffer today.[23]

How much Sandys was responsible for the Americans catching up with
Britain's knowledge on military jet propulsion is highly questionable, but a
decade later aviation author Derek Wood wrote in the same vein as Reed,
referring to the Sandys Report as 'wrecking British aircraft development
for a decade and stopping manned military aircraft for five years'.[24] For
Wood the 1957 review could only have been chaired by a heartless and
ruthless chairman.

It is fully understandable that many champions of British aviation should
remain deeply angry and bitter over what they viewed as Sandys' perfidy in
attacking the aeroplane and its constructors and because of what they saw
as his dangerously enthusiastic and uncritical support for missiles (which he
called rockets). They were proved right about aircraft in that, during the succeeding decades, they would continue to play a predominant and flexible role
with air forces throughout the world. Missiles, however, would unquestionably
take the premier role with nuclear deterrence. Without Sandys' cancellations,
such men firmly believed the British aviation industry could have designed
further world-beating military aeroplanes and the apparent high quality of the
prototypes that fell to his defence cuts appear to support them.

On the other hand, Sandys was expressly appointed by Prime Minister
Harold Macmillan to effect savings when economic failure appeared to be a
more immediate risk to the country than major technological setbacks or even
the growing possibility of global war. On 24 September 1956, at the time of
Suez, Macmillan wrote in his diary that 'if this situation goes on too long, it
may well overcome us and we will be driven to devaluation or bankruptcy'.[25]

Harold MacMillan discussing a de Havilland Firestreak missile attached to a Gloster Javelin on 1 April 1959. (Royal Aeronautical Society/ National Aerospace Library)

He was far from alone in believing in the potency of such economic pressures, for in November 1957 Nikita Khrushchev famously overestimated Soviet strength by declaring 'that in the peaceful field of trade we declare a war. The threat to the United States is not in the intercontinental ballistic missile but in the field of peaceful production.'[26]

Macmillan was convinced that in the case of a medium power experiencing major economic crises it was essential to reduce defence expenditure and release resources and manpower for civil production, with the hydrogen bomb representing a cheaper way of confronting the Soviet Union than conventional weapons, which within a few years was likely to be delivered by missiles rather than traditional aircraft. Sandys' proposed economies on defence can therefore be seen as part of wider political efforts to modernise Britain, although putting such radical proposals to the heads of armed forces who had come through a titanic world war and had recently been involved with fighting in Korea was bound to be extremely difficult.

Macmillan proved ruthless over what he saw as necessary changes and it was understandable that the person he chose to bring about such root and branch

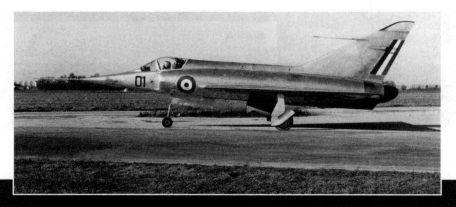

The redoubtable Mirage 1 modified to take a SEPR 66 rocket under its rear fuselage. (Royal Aeronautical Society/National Aerospace Library)

reform should be a hard (and obstinate) hatchet man, although Macmillan maintained that Sandys was far more than that, emphasising that he was 'quite simply good at any job you gave him to do'.[27]

With such directives from his political chief it appears somewhat surprising that aviation commentators should appear nonplussed by Sandys' conclusions, for they were fully aware he was a self-professed and enthusiastic champion of missiles.

Yet while the cards might have appeared to have been dealt against the RAF, support was given to TSR2, while in the late 1950s it was beyond anyone's imagination that Dassault's Mirage should prove such an outright winner or that TSR2 itself should itself be cancelled. It was also tragic that Sandys pursued his reforms at a time when the British aviation industry was diverse and disunited, with its companies requiring regular defence contracts to help finance their civilian projects.

In October 1959, Sandys would show his human side and his genuine regard for the aviation industry when, as Minister of Aviation, he not only pressed for amalgamation but took steps to help the aircraft industry financially to overcome some of the consequences of the heavy reductions in its military aircraft orders. As for accusations that he singled out aviation for reductions, while he undeniably reduced the size of the V-bomber force against the advice of the Air Ministry he also cut the manpower of the Army below the threshold advocated by the Chief of the Imperial General Staff.[28]

In essence, Sandys was given a most difficult assignment that was bound to arouse feelings of anger and betrayal from harassed service chiefs facing major Cold War commitments; a situation made more difficult by the failure of earlier governments to come to grips with the unacceptable cost of British defence policy and the aviation industry's own reluctance to consider amalgamations. Even so, at times Sandys gave the impression he rather enjoyed a fight and no one can deny that at the time of his proposed reforms he was culpable of seriously overrating the capacity of missiles.

As for the results, however dire the predictions about the damage caused by Sandys' recommendations, the value of the air defence industry's output rose slightly from £7.3 billion in 1957 to £7.6 billion in 1960, and by the early 1960s launch aid and other investments had overtaken the cuts introduced by Sandys.[29] Notwithstanding, the value of aircraft exports dropped from £2.4 billion in 1958 to £1.6 billion in 1962, while American exports soared, and it was not until the mid-1960s that output and export revenues returned to those of Sandys' time.[30]

It was also undeniable that at the time of Sandys' sweeping cuts to the aircraft industry's research and development projects, other events were striking hard at British aviation, notably the Comet disasters and the subsequently disappointing orders for British-built civilian airliners. These could be put down to multiple failures to keep up with the Americans and although, with Concorde, a recovery would take place in civilian construction involving European coordination, it would prove a false, if glorious dawn.

By then Sandys' enthusiasm for missiles seemed more justifiable, with an American sea-launched nuclear deterrent that was to serve Britain so well, although its dispatch would be transferred to the Royal Navy and was bound to bring renewed questions about the RAF's raison d'être. This was despite Sandys' championing of all three professional armed forces, which enabled the RAF to continue to play a significant role in later operations, including the Falklands War.

Finally, whatever setbacks were brought about by Sandys to aircraft development, it should be seen against another report in 1965, less than a decade later, when a new financial crisis brought renewed political intervention with even more serious consequences for British aviation. This time it was spearheaded by Denis Healey, Labour's swashbuckling Secretary of State for Defence, bringing more cancellations of British military aircraft and their substitution by US equivalents. Most disappointing of all was its cancellation of the Air Ministry's highly expensive but eagerly anticipated aircraft project, the TSR2. This was followed by the bleak findings of the government's Plowden Report, when after a swift enquiry it concluded that for financial reasons British aviation could never again embark on any major project of its own, that the size of the industry should reflect the actual amount of work it succeeded in obtaining and that the government should not do anything to maintain the industry at an artificially high level.

Whatever the unrivalled cost escalation of new aircraft programmes, to the supporters of British aviation that occupied such a promising position in 1945, the pragmatic safety first – if not defeatist – message of Plowden seemed contrary to the industry's historic high aspirations, including its attendant risks, evident since the early years of the twentieth century.

7

UK MISSILES: IN AMERICA'S WAKE

British participation in missile technology owed much to the government's determination to develop nuclear weapons after the Second World War and Defence Secretary Duncan Sandys' rare enthusiasm for missiles as weapon delivery systems. The movement started relatively early in the war when in 1941 the government-appointed MAUD Committee decided that the construction of an atomic bomb was scientifically possible, following which Winston Churchill gave authorisation for work to proceed under a project code-named Tube Alloys.

Due to more pressing concerns over the country's survival, progress was relatively slow until in 1943 Roosevelt and Churchill agreed to the conduct of a joint US/UK atomic programme through the so-called Manhattan Project. It was as well they did for during the same year Stalin started a sister programme in the USSR that culminated in a successful test on 16 July 1945 of a supercritical mass of fissionable material. Fortunately by then the British and American scientists were ahead with their construction of two atomic bombs, which on 6 and 9 August 1945 were dropped by Superfortress bombers on the Japanese cities of Hiroshima and Nagasaki.

Following this demonstration of their awesome destructive power, the Americans formally ended the Anglo–US nuclear partnership and voted to exclude the UK from their ongoing programme. Attlee's Labour government, however, decided to continue with its own development programme. As scientist William Penny, so-called father of the British Nuclear Programme, expressed it, 'Because the discriminate test for a first-class power is whether it has made an atomic bomb … we have either got to pass the test or suffer a serious loss of prestige both inside the country and internationally.'[1]

US Boeing B-29 Super Fortress. (Farnborough Air Sciences Trust)

For the bomb to be credible, it needed an effective delivery system, which at this time meant purpose-built aeroplanes, and from January 1947 submissions were invited from the British aviation industry for what would become the country's legendary V-bombers, which were expected to become operational during the later 1950s.

In fact, prior to their coming into service, most significant developments took place in the development of nuclear weapons. By 1952 the Americans had tested a thermonuclear weapon, allegedly a thousand times more powerful than an atomic bomb, with the Russians following suit in 1954, before the British exploded their own device in 1957.

During this period Soviet advances in their air defences brought the need for Britain to supplement its delivery systems beyond V-bombers with their free-fall bombs. One possible solution was a supersonic aircraft with a range of at least 5,000 miles capable of cruising at Mach 2 or better, that could fly above Soviet air defences.[2] This requirement might have been met by the Avro 730 advanced strategic bomber, but after its cancellation by Duncan Sandys in 1957 reliance came to be placed on a range of projected missile systems.

These offered different options, with an intermediate-range ballistic missile, (Blue Streak) to deliver the country's nuclear devices on to targets some

2,000 or more miles away, an air-to-ground stand-off missile (Blue Steel) enabling the V-bombers to release their nuclear weapons more than 100 miles away from their intended targets, and a defensive short-range guided-missile system to replace manned fighters in safeguarding the V-bomber bases.

Prior to the construction of Blue Streak, the Americans were already ahead in their development of both IRBMs and air-to-ground stand-off missiles, and to safeguard national security the British government concluded an interim agreement for the installation of American Thor IRBM missiles for a period of some four years until Blue Streak became available. The Thors were allocated to twenty RAF squadrons across eastern England, with each missile embedded in 235,000 cubic yards of concrete.[3] Although officially British owned, their warheads were American and so-called authentication officers from the USF held the second of two keys that had to be freed before launching. While during 1960–63 4,000 RAF personnel staffed these installations, they could never be said to have been under full British control. To achieve this the UK needed its own ICBM, upon which work proceeded during the 1950s despite residual opposition from a UK Treasury wrestling with succeeding economic crises.

The first operational Thor missile in England. (Painting by Richard Green, US National Archives, Licence No. 6344741)

Blue Streak, the British IRBM. (Farnborough Air Sciences Trust)

Blue Streak was somewhat larger than the American Thor missile, being 69.27ft long and 10ft in diameter, compared with the Thor's 64.8ft length and diameter of 8ft. Its range of more than 2,000 miles compared with the Thor's initial 1,500, and with its megaton warhead it was expressly designed to climb above the Earth's atmosphere and re-enter it on a ballistic trajectory to strike strategic targets in the Soviet Union. Construction contracts were awarded to three firms – de Havilland for the vehicle itself, Rolls-Royce for an engine based on the American S3 rocket engine and the British branch of the US Sperry Company for its guidance system. Additional agreement was reached with the US government for the transfer of technology from the US Atlas programme involving the US companies Convair and Rocketdyne.

Harold Robinson from Farnborough's Royal Aircraft Establishment was made responsible for managing the project, although all its departments had some involvement. Work was also conducted from design offices in London and at facilities in Stevenage and Hatfield, with further outdoor development and testing taking place at the remote Cumbrian location of Spadeadam and in South Australia, where, on its Woomera launching range, the missile was expected to be fired during 1960.

Blue Streak's construction involved unrivalled technological challenges for British scientists for it had to survive the most severe conditions on its re-entry and its warhead had to be protected from the heat produced by its own systems. The missile was made up of four sections: a propulsion bay, a tank bay, a guidance bay and a warhead. The propulsion bay, constructed of conventional aluminium alloy, housed two Rolls-Royce RZ2 engines, using liquid oxygen and kerosene, each providing 137,000lb of thrust at sea level. Fuel was fed from its tank bay into the turbo-pumps of each engine through large-diameter fuel pipes by means of power provided by a bank of batteries supplying various voltage outputs, while direction-finding came from the inertia guidance can in the guidance bay which was designed and manufactured by Sperry.[4]

The management of such a complex missile required extensive instrumentation where accurate measurements of the flow, shaft speed, temperature, pressures, liquid levels, vibration and stress levels had to be made both during ground operation and in flight. Its large stores of fuel always posed serious safety risks but to the design team's credit, throughout the missile's operational life no accident nor injury occurred. This was achieved by strict test and control procedures and by the containment of its electrical and electronic ground support equipment in two designated road trailers, which along with their manpower actually cost more than the missile.[5]

Following preliminary tests the missile was assembled and delivered by road trailer to the test site at Spadeadam where, before it was packed up for its long journey to the Australian launch site, static conditions were created for its anticipated 154 seconds of real flight on the other side of the world.

With its liquid oxygen and kerosene fuelling arrangements and inertial guidance system, the missile was not only the first of its kind in the UK but it offered a major opportunity for the country to make significant technological advances. Although its construction team initially required technical information from the US Atlas programme, they soon gained their own expertise in developing reliable mechanical, electrical and electronic systems that involved some of the first computers and transistors used in the UK.

Unsurprisingly, its flight conditions were found to be more challenging than with any other mode of transport, with very severe heating and vibration levels that necessitated some of the electronic equipment being installed in pressurised containers, and for new methods of jointing the stainless-steel piping being used throughout. Among other firsts was the acquisition of knowledge about cryogenic technology, the development of structural ceramics and a novel type of electric cabling (later used on Concorde) together with high-density electrical plugs.

Blue Streak's 100 per cent safety record compared well with the earlier and far shorter US Thor programme that suffered missile losses, although before the British missile's somewhat prolonged completion further technological advances by the Soviets brought disturbing questions about its utility. The strongest doubts about its deterrent value came from the time needed to prepare its liquid fuel for launching and because it could not be long held in a fuelled-up state. It was even felt that due to estimated improvements in Soviet missile accuracy the missile's concrete silos offered convenient 'bullseye targets'. As a result, by the time of its completion there were already a number of powerful calls for its abandonment.

Throughout its development, it had encountered opposition from the Treasury, and RAF historian Humphrey Wynn, for instance, was convinced that the overwhelming problem of the cost of a large complex and entirely new kind of weapon was never to be solved and finally brought an abrupt ending of the programme.[6]

In contrast, Sir James Lighthill (Director of the Royal Aircraft Establishment at Farnborough, 1959–64) believed the calls for cancellation were for the most part due to political calculation, arguing that the RAF sought to preserve its traditional role of operating manned bombers by giving its support to the V-bombers assisted by the air-launched system Blue Steel (and its successor

Sir James Lighthill.
(Farnborough Air Sciences Trust)

the US Skybolt) rather than relying on an intermediate-range ballistic missile (IRBM). He went further, believing that the Royal Navy apparently supported the RAF in the hope that the development of the Skybolt missile would fail (which it did), leaving a submarine-launched, ballistic missile system as the only option.[7]

Professor Solly Zuckerman, eminent chief scientific advisor to the MoD, took up another approach, believing Blue Streak ceased to make sense as a deterrent from the moment that the government decided that it should be buried in silos.

Whatever such formidable opposition, it was the Soviet launching of Sputnik in October 1957 that proved a watershed for British and American nuclear planning and led to fresh assumptions about Soviet SS-3 and SS-4 IRBM capabilities based on known US ones. This led to a reduction in the anticipated warning time for a potential Soviet attack from ten to fifteen minutes to an over-pessimistic six minutes, which could not, in fact, be countered by Blue Streak forces, whose reaction time in 1958 was believed to be a minimum of seven minutes – although the Air Ministry claimed it was actually only four-and-a-half.[8]

As a result, in mid-1959 an interdepartmental study group under Sir Richard Powell, Permanent Secretary of the Ministry of Defence, was assembled to consider the question of Blue Streak's continued viability. This estimated, for instance, that the Soviet SS-3 could carry a 3-megaton warhead and the SS-4 a 1.8-megaton one, whereby it concluded that 98 per cent of the Blue Streak Force could be destroyed by a not inconsiderable 300 to 400 missiles and could only be effective if it was fired first. All such calculations, based on exaggerated Soviet capabilities, served to create what appeared to be an unchallengeable strategic case against Blue Streak and led the Chief of the Air Staff, Sir Thomas Pike, to join the other chiefs in recommending it should be cancelled.

The anticipated decision to cancel came in April 1960 amid charges in the House of Commons that the project should never have been initiated at a cost of some £600 million, or the equivalent of £20 billion in 2012 prices, with absolutely nothing to show at the end of it all.[9] After accepting Blue Streak's vulnerability, Parliament also decided that from 1963 onwards the US Thor missiles based in Britain should be progressively phased out. The decision provoked no uproar for although Blue Streak gave Britain an opportunity to catch up with American technology, its relatively slow development compared with the US and USSR meant that by the time of its cancellation the two superpowers (in military terms, at least) were already moving on towards alternative systems.

Not all were so easily convinced and, with his pride in the RAE's achievements, Professor Lighthill, for one, remained very unhappy about Blue Streak's demise, declaring during a lecture tour of the US that:

> In this technical sphere, the experiment can be claimed to have produced excellent results. Financially estimates rose by a large factor but no more than has been the standard experience with large products all over the world. Politically the project collapsed but technical deficiencies were never adduced as reasons for this, indeed Blue Streak is now seen to have been ahead of its time in several important respects.[10]

While this might have been true, Professor Lighthill could not disprove the British IRBM's diminishing deterrence capability, whether based on over-pessimistic estimates or not.

In any event, by the time of Blue Streak's cancellation work was being conducted to improve the V-bombers' capabilities by modifying their bombs and constructing air-launched missiles for them to carry. In addition to Red Beard – a free-fall parachute-retarded bomb – with its kiloton warhead, there came about the development of Yellow Sun, a ballistic bomb with a megaton warhead.

Most important, however, was Blue Steel, an air-launched missile carrying a nuclear warhead. This was considered the RAF's best means of enabling its bombers to operate without going into areas in which they would be exposed to concentrated guided-weapon attack.[11] Blue Steel had a body length of 35ft and a 13ft wingspan. Its canard configuration featured small delta-shaped foreplanes and a rear-mounted wing with inboard ailerons. Made of stainless-steel, its power came from a hydrogen peroxide-kerosene steam turbine with direction-finding achieved through an inertial navigation system. Designed for launching from both Vulcan and Victor bombers, upon its release it was capable of accelerating from transonic to supersonic speed in pursuit of its target.

In 1956 the Air Ministry chose the Avro Aircraft Company as its constructor rather than putting the specification out for competitive contract, with four other organisations sharing major responsibilities: Armstrong Siddeley for its propulsion motors, Elliott (working under RAE design authority) for the inertial navigation system, de Havilland for the power supply turbines and the appropriate department of the RAE for its armament system.

From a range of studies undertaken at the RAE during 1953–54, it was decided that to ensure the V-bombers could release their missiles clear of the Soviet defences, Blue Steel needed a range of 100–150 miles and as the V-bombers were not originally designed to carry such a weapon it also had to be of an acceptable size and weight. They also concluded that the missile required a pure inertial navigation system, thereby enabling the bomber crews to update travel information in flight to ensure that following its launch the missile could come under the control of an autopilot, making it very difficult to be located.

During 1957, extensive wind-tunnel calculations were supplemented by a series of free-flight trials using one-eighth scale models. These were dominated by the fact that a large part of any trajectory was spent in acceleration and in unsteady flight and that a large proportion of the propellant was consumed in reaching cruising speed and altitude.[12] For the first time such trajectories, along with the aerodynamic heating and risks of collision between missile and its parent aircraft shortly after launch, were computed on an IBM 650 machine.

Despite the missile's complexity, by early 1959 most of the laboratory work was complete and air-launched free flights had taken place. Additional tests followed to establish the extent of the vibration encountered during the missile's supersonic flight, the nature of the conditions inside it during long periods of carriage by an aircraft at high altitude and the successful transfer of hydraulic and temperature controls at its time of release.

Blue Steel air-to-surface missile, installed on a Valiant B1 bomber. (BAE Systems Heritage)

With such a bold design concept and the time constraints, it was considered that 'there were a number of substantial risks to be run'.[13] By modern standards its potent warhead was not only very large and environmentally sensitive but it needed air conditioning (both warming and refrigerating) to safeguard its arming circuits, while before the age of transistors the missile's inertial navigator was comparatively large, with its guidance functions producing considerable waste heat that needed a refrigerating system using arcton gas.

A considerable number of structural and system connections were required between the missile and its parent aircraft for it to separate cleanly during a process that was not altogether straightforward, for in the case of the Vulcan 'the missile's wing tips had to be turned down to clear the plane's engine fairings while the plane dipped its opposite wing'.[14]

As for its systems, although the rocket motor promised great success, its oxidant was both volatile and corrosive. Its pioneering doubled-skinned airframe required the development of novel stretch-press methods of manufacture at a time when there was much less information about high-temperature materials and ways of alleviating thermal stress, and when hardened stainless steel remained the most suitable structural material that could be easily weldable.

Blue Steel's flight trials were shared by the United Kingdom range at Aberporth and the Australian one at Woomera, with both authorities understandably requiring satisfaction about the absolute reliability of the missile's destruct system.

In the event Blue Steel did not pass into squadron service until December 1962, six years after the contract was placed and three years after its intended date. Space historian C.N. Hill (writing afterwards) believed that the Ministry of Supply made a bad choice in selecting Avro for Blue Steel's development and – even more serious – that delays in the programme, the cost overruns and the difficulties in handling the missile combined to reduce even further the reputation of the British Aircraft Industry.[15]

It was a full two years later, in April 1964, before Blue Steel was able to be used with the Vulcan quick-reaction alert aircraft. Such progress did not match American procurement times and the three-year delay in its delivery was bound to shorten its service life. Even so, it served three Vulcan and two Victor squadrons and helped form the British deterrent for more than six years at a cost of just 8 per cent of the total spend on the V-Force.

During this time, another major tactical change to the British deterrent became necessary when it was recognised that the V-bombers were too vulnerable to overfly enemy territory at high altitude and they would have to adopt contour-hugging measures. Fortunately the requirement was met by a relatively inexpensive modification to the missile's flight-rules' computer to accept new release data.[16] The RAF's Victor squadrons were phased out by the end of 1968, while the last flight of Blue Steel with Vulcan followed on 21 December 1969.

In addition to questions about Blue Streak's strategic capability, by 1959 doubts were being raised about the viability of Blue Steel. These centred on its limited range of up to 130 miles when Soviet ground-to-air weapons were thought to have been extended to cover main areas of vulnerability rather than 'point targets only'. In view of this Avro's Weapons Research Division was considering the construction of a Blue Steel Mark II, where rather than rocket power it would be equipped with four ramjets, giving it a much-extended range of 850 miles. A one-sixth scale model of the Mark II had actually been flown in free flight at Aberporth, just before the whole Blue Steel contract was cancelled, a decision made possible by the presence of a longer-range US missile called Hound Dog. This missile was, however, subsequently found to be too bulky to fit on to the V-bombers and

Polaris submarine-launched ballistic missile at the start of its journey. (US National Archives Licence No. 6 375 196)

the British Chiefs of Staff decided to opt for the much-vaunted American Skybolt, which was already at an advanced stage of development and reputedly had a range of 1,500 nautical miles.

In 1960 agreement was reached between Prime Minister Macmillan and President Eisenhower during their meeting at Camp David about supplying Skybolt to the UK. There it was also agreed that US submarines could be based in the Firth of Clyde at Holy Loch. The latter was because the American Navy was currently proceeding with a new system, a solid-fuelled, sea-launched strategic missile called Polaris, with a range of 1,000 to 1,500 nautical miles. Polaris' first successful launch from a submerged submarine – the USS *George Washington* – took place on 20 July 1960, followed three hours later by a second. Thus, the US Navy declared a strategic capability.[17]

By now rumours were circulating about the US Skybolt system being in trouble and in December 1962, when Macmillan went to Nassau in the Bahamas to meet the new US President John F. Kennedy, he learned that it was about to be cancelled. By this time the UK had spent £27 million to accommodate it on the V-bombers and the Blue Steel Mark II contract had already been cancelled. After protracted discussions it was finally agreed that the UK would purchase Polaris missiles, whose warheads would be made in Britain.

However much Polaris might improve Britain's deterrent capability it represented a massive blow for the RAF and its current bomber/air-launched missile system. With Polaris the RAF would lose its deterrent responsibilities. What was more, there seemed no turning back. Admiral Mountbatten anticipated that Polaris would last for a minimum of twenty to thirty years for he could see no prospect of anti-submarine measures being able 'to attack Polaris submarines over the millions of square miles of ocean or under the North Polar Ice Cap'.[18] Britain's purchase was made all the more attractive for not only did the US agree to the country having the longer-range A3 variant of Polaris but for its expenditure to be capped at the retail cost of the missile plus 5 per cent as a fixed contribution to the development programme.[19]

The Sandys White Paper's recommendations to use missiles rather than aircraft in a tactical role involved the use of ground-to-air, short-range guided systems for defending the V-bomber airfields rather than using manned fighters. The first of an intended family of missiles called Bloodhound (the Army's equivalent was Thunderbird) entered service in June 1958 at North Coates in Yorkshire. During 1958–61 a total of 352 Bloodhounds were deployed in four wings: at Lindholme to cover the northerly V-bomber bases, at North Coates for the V-bomber airfields of Coningsby, Scampton and Waddington, at Luffenham for the more southerly bases and at Watton for the East Anglian ones. These were controlled from a tactical control centre[20] with a master radar station that decided whether to rely on Bloodhounds or scramble fighters.

The Bloodhound was designed by Bristol Aircraft with Ferranti providing the radar guidance and related servo control equipment. It relied on a target-illuminating radar (positioned at its launch sites) to lock its semi-active, radar homing device on reflected signals from its targets, where on approaching a lethal range its high-explosive warheads were able to be detonated by a proximity fuse. The missile was equipped with independently pivoted wing fins and a tailplane, and its four solid-propellant rocket motors boosted it to speeds approaching 2,200mph at around 2,000ft, at which stage two Thor ramjets took over.

Thunderbird, the Army's short-range defence missile. (Farnborough Air Sciences Trust)

Bristol Bloodhound, the RAF's air-defence missile system. (Farnborough Air Sciences Trust)

Despite Bloodhound I's successful development, it, too, fell short relatively quickly, proving susceptible to electronic jamming and not providing the level of defence offered by manned interceptors, despite their longer reaction times in getting airborne. Within three years it had succumbed to defence cuts.

In 1964, Bloodhound II, an improved air-transportable version with a maximum range of 80km and ability to strike at targets as low as 300m, entered service in Cyprus and West Germany until it was returned to West Raynham to defend air bases on the eastern side of the United Kingdom. With the reducing numbers of manned interceptors such missiles might still have had a genuine role to play had it not been for easing East–West tensions that led to Bloodhound II's successor, Bloodhound III – costing £6 million – also falling victim to defence cuts.[21]

In sum, during the 1950s and 1960s, the UK missile programme followed the pattern of the country's many other initiatives involving high-technology projects being affected by financial limitations, changing strategic requirements and superior advances by others, particularly the US.

Although the development of the Blue Streak IRBM represented a triumph for British constructors, its Rolls-Royce engine builders and management team from Farnborough, its restricted levels of funding meant that it could never match the speed of construction achieved by the American Douglas Aircraft Company with its Thor system. After being awarded a contract, Douglas succeeded in delivering its rocket within an incredible ten months, launching it three months later in January 1957, when no other weapon in this category was available.

Although Thor's first four launches failed, the fifth succeeded, seemingly restoring the balance of power between the West and Russia.[22] In any case, with Blue Streak positioned within range of Soviet missiles it was sure to suffer from multiple credibility problems. Although its silos were built to withstand a 1-megaton bomb burst 1,000 yards away, there were still major uncertainties: the explosion's noise was likely to damage some of the missile's controls, while debris would most likely obstruct the silo's exit and the intense nuclear radiation disable further instruments. Major difficulties also arose over choosing acceptable locations. It could not be sited downwind of nearby towns, nor where there were vulnerable water tables, nor near geographical faults. In any event, for a small country such as Britain, the damage from a Soviet first nuclear strike promised to be horrendous.

The situation was not that dissimilar with Blue Steel. Following the earlier cancellation of the Avro 730 supersonic bomber its use was necessarily limited to the slower V-bombers, where its comparative short range left them very vulnerable against Soviet ground-to-air weapons.

As a consequence, the IRBM Blue Streak was rapidly ruled out, and although Blue Steel was considered technically capable of being developed to carry multiple independent re-entry vehicles (MIRVS), by this time the US had embarked on its own multiple warhead programme.

Whatever the technological achievements of the British rocketry programme, its greater financial limitations and necessarily lower ambitions than those of the superpowers finally brought it to depend on weapon systems designed and built by its American ally – despite remaining responsible for their warhead development. Nonetheless, on 13 April 1960 Harold Macmillan's incoming Defence Minister Harold Watkinson followed his announcement in the House of Commons about the cancellation of Blue Streak by giving a confident message about continuing British space involvement, declaring that a civilian space programme revolving around the two launchers had government support. However, the announcement of an allocation of just £5 million (with strings attached) raised questions about whether in fact the government was more interested in deflecting the opposition's charges about the alleged waste of public money on Blue Streak than supporting an indigenous space programme.

Such charges seemed credible enough when up to this point the UK government had shown very little enthusiasm for space research, with the country lacking a dedicated body in support of a space programme, like America's NASA (National Aeronautics and Space Administration) or the later French Centre for Space Research (CNES). In contrast, the so-called 'British National Committee for Space Research' was founded to liaise with COSPAR, its sister committee concerned with international aspects of space research activities, rather than acting in an executive role to further the development of a British civilian space programme.

Regardless of this, proposals concerning missiles for civilian purposes had already been made at Farnborough during April 1957, some three years before the launching of Blue Streak – when two research scientists, Desmond King-Hele and Doreen Gilmour, produced a paper about how Blue Streak and (the smaller missile) Black Knight could be continued to form a (reconnaissance) satellite launcher.[23] This paper included detailed calculations to prove that although Black Knight was fifteen times smaller than Blue Streak its motor was capable of burning for 145 seconds to achieve a height of some 135 miles.

Whatever the financial restrictions, following Harold Watkinson's announcement about continuing work to develop a satellite launcher, the Ministry of Aviation circulated all the firms involed outlining a provisional programme

Black Knight launcher system. (Farnborough Air Sciences Trust)

for the construction of a Blue Streak Satellite Launch Vehicle (BSSLV) called BlackPrince using Blue Streak as the first stage and Black Knight as the second.

The plan was for eight firings to be carried out at Woomera: the first two were scheduled to be with unmodified Blue Streak missiles, numbers 3, 4 and 5 were with Blue Streak carrying dummy upper stages, while numbers 6, 7 and 8 firings, due to be carried out by March 1966, were to involve combined Blue Streak and Black Knight launchers with a third stage.[24]

In the event political support for the provisional programme proved far from unanimous. When a committee under the Cabinet Secretary Sir Norman Brook consulted the government's chief scientist, Sir Solly Zuckerman, he proved notably critical, maintaining that Blue Streak's liquid-fuel technology was obsolescent, even though it would be used by derivatives of the Thor and Atlas rockets some forty years later. Moreover, Zuckerman took pains to point out that the anticipated research and development (R&D) expenditure for the British space programme was set at some £15 million per annum out of Britain's total R&D defence budget of £220 million. The significance of this became apparent when he cited a conversation between himself and the US Assistant Secretary for War, who had suggested that the UK joined the US in space work. However, when Zuckerman told him about the level of our intended financial commitment he replied that even if we made over all our defence R&D funds for space it would not be enough for us to become starters in a US/UK collaboration programme in rocketry and satellites.[25] With the high costs associated with space research Zuckerman raised the question about whether Britain could even justify the comparatively small amount of £15 million per annum when it did not have the same need as the US and when British intelligence enjoyed access to much American information.

Whatever Zuckerman's doubts and Farnborough's enthusiasm for launching a number of experimental satellites, the funds allocated were inadequate, particularly as there were no satellites for the proposed launchers. In an effort to save the programme Peter Thorneycroft, the new Minister of Aviation, visited the old commonwealth nations of Canada and Australia to persuade them to share in the costs. Neither proved interested; a Canadian satellite was due to be launched by NASA and Australia would not go beyond supporting the work being done at Woomera.

A country that did show interest was France, even if its greatest concern appeared to be finding out design information for its own ballistic missile project. For the satellite launcher it proposed inserting a French second stage to Blue Streak with a third stage coming from another European source. Following prolonged Anglo–French talks, on 29 March 1962 the European Launcher Development Organisation (ELDO) was formed aimed at constructing a launch vehicle called Europa. Its convention came into force on 29 March 1964, following ratification by seven signatory states: Belgium, France, the UK, Italy, the Netherlands, the Federal Republic of Germany and Australia.

In practice the countries varied widely in their enthusiasm and pledges of support, with commentator C.N. Hill going so far as to consider ELDO 'a model example of how not to carry out a joint European project, and technically Europa had modest aims and even less success'.[26] Britain was responsible for its first stage, France for the second and Germany for the third, with Italy agreeing to build the Satellite Test Vehicle (STV). Using the facilities at Woomera, ELDO carried out eleven launchings of Europa, during which Blue Streak performed faultlessly, in contrast to the second and third stages.

The disappointing progress overall was exacerbated by different political aims, language problems and incompatible technical systems. Britain shared in the political trickery; although a reluctant member, the 1964 Wilson government found it was unable to end its commitment but this did not stop it demanding a reduction in the UK's share of the budget by arguing that it was interested in developing the technology that went with the satellite rather than the launchers.

By 1968 the UK government had virtually washed its hands of the organisation, before on 27 April 1973 the programme was finally abandoned when 'after eleven launches and literally hundreds of millions of pounds, the vehicle was still not ... flight worthy'.[27]

As yet neither Britain nor other members of ELDO had fully appreciated the potential economic advantages of launching satellites and neither the Europa nor the earlier British missile, Black Knight, ever succeeded in putting a payload into orbit. In fairness, Black Knight's twenty-two flights at Woomera were primarily designed to test problems of re-entry and the use of separate re-entry heads. In any case, costs were relatively modest, totalling £6 million in all, and its performance gave the RAE observers valuable experience in designing Black Arrow, their much smaller derivative launcher, upon which they carried out extensive work while Britain was still a member of ELDO.

While Black Arrow was by any measure an inexpensive programme wholly designed for civilian applications, it was constantly under financial threat with permission to go ahead only granted after the cancellation of Black Knight. Although five launch vehicles were built for a three-stage rocket using tried and tested technology 'involving nothing new or exotic', its total payload was restricted to 132lb and its launch cost was about one sixth of a Europa one.

Static tests on Black Arrow's rocket motors were conducted at High Down, on the Isle of Wight, following which the vehicle was stripped down prior to being sent to Woomera for active launching. In the event, Black Arrow was extremely fortunate in being allowed to take its opportunity. The decision to go ahead came during the last days of Sir Alec Douglas-Home's Conservative administration prior to an incoming Labour government that intended to review many scientific projects, including Black Arrow, and whose Minister at the Department of Trade, Frederick Corfield, actually cancelled the programme on 29 July 1971. Despite this, at Woomera the four firings that had already been arranged went ahead. The first two, code-named R0 and R1, were launched without a third stage. R0 was unsuccessful and its vehicle was destroyed by ground command but R1, launched on 4 March 1970, was completely successful. It was therefore intended that R3 should put Prospero, a satellite formed of eight faces covered with 3,000 solar cells, into orbit.

Having arrived at Woomera in July, R3 was finally fired on 28 October 1971 – three months after the cancellation order – during what was described as a

Launch of the Prospero British space satellite. (Farnborough Air Sciences Trust)

cool, fresh Australian spring day with clear skies. Following a smooth lift-off the telemetry stations north of Woomera reported that everything had been successful, although it was only after the global satellite station at Fairbanks reported an operational signal from a satellite on a frequency of 137MHz that the control team knew it was orbiting.[28] Despite the uncertainties, with this the UK became the sixth nation to place a satellite in space.

Prospero would in fact prove to be the only British satellite, for R4 was never fired and it is now on display in the Science Museum at Kensington. Following the decision to cancel, after Prospero's success all further UK attempts at constructing launch vehicles ended. The decision meant it became the only nation to abandon its own orbital launch capability.

The achievements of the British space programme up to the mid-1970s proved disappointing. Even so, the launching of Prospero and the construction of versatile test vehicles such as Black Knight and the Farnborough-inspired, solid-propellant rocket Skylark for upper-atmosphere research went some way to challenge Professor A.D. Baxter's sweeping observation that with the vast projects by the US and the Soviet Union the efforts in Britain and elsewhere were insignificant.[29]

The reasons for the UK's modest space achievements are not hard to find. Aviation writer Stephen Hastings put it squarely down to a disproportionately low level of investment, maintaining that:

British expenditure on space has been pathetic and treated as a luxury … the cost of a puny space programme as a percentage of GNP proportionately less than that of France and many tens of times less than that of the US …we have completely neglected our own national programme.[30]

On the other hand, Douglas Millard, Senior Curator of Information, Communication and Space Technologies at the National Science Museum, has somewhat grandly pointed out that 'the UK conducted activities in almost all of the recognised space sectors in that it designed, built, launched and operated spacecraft with its industries operating at the forefront of European and Space endeavour'.

Yet Millard himself acknowledged that the UK's space programme never came under the aegis of a single government department or ministry with its own dedicated vote or budget, and at the time the country never formed a government space agency.[31] The disadvantage of not having a dedicated agency was demonstrated shortly after the Prospero launch, when after British aircraft manufacturer Saunders-Roe had devised an improved form of Black Arrow with a fourfold increase in its payload, it attracted no official interest.[32]

The nub question remains about whether, as Stephen Hastings suggested, in the UK space was seen as something of a luxury. Although in 1957 Britain was the only nation apart from the US and the Soviet Union with the required scientific and technical experience for space exploration, between 1957 and 1972, the US launched 145 reconnaissance satellites – admittedly to spy on Soviet rocket sites – compared with Prospero's purely experimental and non-commercial tasks. With the US assuming the initiative, the UK never felt the strategic need for space research and the scientists involved, like many of their foreign colleagues, lacked the imagination to consider its commercial utility.

However meritorious, by the time Britain's IRBM, Blue Streak, was complete, the US already had its own versions in service and the air-launched missile Blue Steel had too short a range to be militarily viable for any length of time. Yet whatever the dire effects of financial restrictions, it is probably fair to say that in the thirty years after the Second World War the British space programme lacked an outstanding prophet, unlike France for instance, where from 1927, airman and thinker Robert Esnault-Pelterie had been convinced that once the atmosphere had been conquered there remained nothing more but to strike out into the empty space of the universe.[33]

Britain did not lack for brilliant individuals. There was for instance, physicist Sir Harrie Massey, whose work on atomic and ionic collisions ensured that Britain had a well-established research programme unequalled outside the superpowers; Arthur 'Val' Cleaver, a propeller expert who designed the RZ-2 rocket engine for Blue Streak and the equivalent for Black Arrow, who according to his colleagues could have been the British von Braun; Dr Leslie Shepherd, concerned with fast reactor technology at the Atomic Energy Department, who co-wrote (with Val Cleaver) one of the first detailed papers on the application of nuclear energy to interplanetary flight; and astronomer Bernard Lovell, with his world-renowned 250ft radio telescope.

However successful in a technical sense, they had to watch their country being forced to rely on American missile systems for its strategic defence and a lack of funding preventing its indigenous space programme from sharing in the subsequent scientific and commercial opportunities offered by satellite launches both up to and beyond our period of concern.

8

VC10, TRIDENT AND BAC 1–11: RESTRICTED MARKETS

Whatever the disastrous weaknesses of the early Comets – which were eliminated in later models – British manufacturers continued to demonstrate their capacity for producing world-class aircraft with their designs for the VC10, Trident and BAC 1-11 airliners. Whether they could be sold in the quantities required against strong American competition was, of course, another matter.

The VC10 was not only the largest of the three aircraft but the largest airliner to be put into production in the United Kingdom. Its genesis began with its ill-fated predecessor, the Vickers V1000, designed to carry service personnel and freight anywhere in the world – including locations with short runways – at a speed similar to that of the country's V-bombers. The V1000 was scheduled to be powered by advanced Rolls-Royce Conway Engines and George Edwards, chief designer at Vickers, decided on a parallel civilian version, the VC7, which would be capable of flying on BOAC's Empire routes and making lucrative transatlantic flights.

A government order for the V1000 prototype was placed in January 1953 and for the production aircraft the following year. The specification was for a far more robust aircraft than the Comet 1A with spars machined out of solid material for a fuselage 137ft 11in long with an all-up weight of 260,000lb, compared with the Comet's 93ft length and all-up weight of 115,000lb.[1]

By this time Vickers had produced the Valiant, its first four jet-engined bomber, and both the V1000 and VC7 owed much to that aircraft's design.

The V1000 was scheduled to fly in the early months of 1956 and enter service during 1959–60. Along with the civilian VC7, it would have been the world's first four-engined, bypass jet aircraft designed for long-haul routes and was sure to have occupied an advantageous position with Boeing's 707, which entered service in August 1959, and Douglas's DC-8, which followed two years later.

All such advantages were lost when, in early 1956, despite having reached an advanced stage of production, the V1000 was cancelled by the Ministry of Supply on the grounds of it being one of the most costly items on the Air Staff's budget.

In fact, apart from lukewarm support by the RAF, the government wished to give priority to the slower, turboprop Britannia, production of which guaranteed work for Short at Belfast, where closure was threatened following the cancellation of contracts for the Swift and Comet 2 aircraft. In fact, the Britannia had already been ordered by BOAC, whose chairman, Sir Miles Thomas, was sure it would dominate the market. Although Reginald Maudling – the Minister of Supply – attempted to keep the V1000 project going through its VC7 civil version, Sir Miles rejected it on the convenient, if unproven, assumption that its increased weight would make it incapable of flying non-stop across the Atlantic.

In later years, Sir George Edwards, Chairman of Vickers, would conclude that the Treasury-led cancellation of the V1000 with its superior performance over the initial Boeing 707 'was the greatest blunder of all' for British aviation, while Derek Wood, editor in chief of *Jane's Defence Weekly,* went so far as to believe it marked the point at which British airliner development 'really began to go wrong'.[2]

Despite its decision, the Conservative government of the day appeared to retain a belief in British-built aeroplanes successfully competing in the burgeoning civilian market. Although following the cancellation of the VC7, Harold Watkinson, the Minister of Transport and Civil Aviation, approved BOAC's purchase of fifteen Boeing 707 aircraft (to be powered by Rolls-Royce 17,500lb-thrust Conway engines, which had been destined for the VC7) it was with the proviso that from then on the airline should look for a British-built plane for its eastern and Empire routes.

It was hoped this plane would be the result of a private venture within the aircraft industry rather than depending on taxpayer support. In the event, the only company strong enough to undertake such a project was Vickers, which had made good profits from its turboprop Viscount. In response, the company undertook to produce its VC10 long-range airliner for £1.25 million per air frame (roughly equivalent to £43 million in 2017) on condition that BOAC ordered thirty-five aircraft, later increased to forty-two when a transatlantic version was added. The RAF undertook to place an order for five (later increased to fourteen) for a plane that was expected to perform passenger transport, freight and casualty evacuation duties.

Officials from the Ministry of Aviation subsequently conceded that the total of thirty-five aircraft might have been a bit high for BOAC's needs but Vickers believed it was the minimum number needed to launch the aircraft as a private venture, with the company's break-even figure reckoned to be eighty. Vickers expected the additional sales to come through exports, although it warned that if the specifications from BOAC were too restrictive, they would hamper its appeal to a broader market.

Such risks became only too apparent when in March 1957 BOAC issued an exceptionally severe set of requirements for an aeroplane somewhat smaller than the Boeing 707 to operate on routes to Africa and Australia, where conditions combining high temperatures with high altitudes and relatively short runways were the most exacting in the world.[3] Even so, the plane was required to carry a payload of about 35,000lb for nearly 4,000 miles in still air.[4]

To meet this most demanding specification, Vickers produced a 139-seat, rear-engined, pressurised aeroplane, whose four Rolls-Royce Conway bypass engines gave it a cruising speed of 450 knots, and its low unobstructed wing proved capable of carrying a payload of up to 20,000lb and operating from 2,000-yard runways under both normal and tropical conditions.[5] Its rear engines provided a new standard of passenger comfort through reduced cabin noise and vibration. On the debit side, to achieve such a performance it had to be somewhat heavier and more highly powered than its main competitors – a feature bound to restrict its worldwide attractiveness.

Vickers VC10, an airliner that raised the bar. (Farnborough Air Sciences Trust)

Work began in 1957 and in January 1958 BOAC placed an order for thirty-five VC10s with an option for a further twenty, which, with the sweep back of their wings increased from 31 to 32.5 degrees and their greater wingspan giving increased fuel capacity, were unquestionably well equipped for transatlantic operations. However, the more advanced specifications entailed serious financial penalties for Vickers, who in 1959 warned BOAC that the costs of developing the VC10 had increased and the airline would have to find the money to cover the difference.[6]

In June 1959 the company went further, forecasting serious difficulties unless it received direct government aid as it was apparent that its original cost estimates for each aircraft had been set too low; a more realistic £1.4 million per airframe was put forward but the non-recurring costs for its development had apparently reached astronomical figures despite the most stringent controls.[7] Vickers asked the Treasury for £15 million to cover the increased costs of both BOAC's VC10 and its VC 11 short-to-medium-range transport, intended for BEA. In response the current Minister of Aviation, Duncan Sandys, offered to support Vickers providing BOAC took the longer-range Super VC10s that would prove more attractive to other airlines. Under this arrangement Vickers' own contribution totalled £21 million, with the company estimating the government would get its money back at a 10 per cent rate if eighty-five VC10s and 110 VC11s were sold.[8]

In January 1960 the Cabinet gave its support for the VC10 despite optimism being mixed. Sandys himself admitted it was hardly 'a promising civil project' but he told them it was necessary to tide Vickers over and prevent it going out of business before 'a group of sufficient strength has been created'. The consortia he had in mind were, of course, BAC (British Aircraft Corporation) and Hawker Siddeley Aviation.

Sandys put immense pressure on BOAC to acquiesce and in April 1961, despite the airline's concerns about the VC10's unfavourable operating costs compared with the Boeing 707 and the Douglas DC-8, it agreed to take fifteen standard and thirty Super VC10s, if to a somewhat scaled-down design.

Predictably BOAC's own financial position soon became parlous but Julian Amery, the new Secretary of State for Air who would become Minister of Aviation in July 1962, rejected any cuts to its order for Super VC10s. The result was only too predictable. In 1963, with BOAC's deficit topping £64 million, Amery appointed City of London accountant John Corbett to review its finances. Following a ten-month inquiry, he reported that the VC10 was the largest single burden on BOAC's resources and a new chairman, Sir Giles Guthrie, appointed to put BOAC back on its feet, hinted at cancelling a large part of the order. He was unable to fulfil his threat for as a major condition of BOAC's capital reconstruction the government required it to take seventeen Super VC10s (with the RAF taking an extra three of the standard model).

The VC10 received its certificate of airworthiness on 23 April 1964 (some four years later than that scheduled for the V1000 and VC7) and it commenced a regular service from London to Lagos before taking over services to other parts of Africa and to the Middle and Far East. Although it was tailored to the needs of a single airline, and entered a market where most of the world's leading airlines were already equipped with American Boeing 707s and Douglas DC-8s, it proved a very special aircraft. It was remarkably popular (and safe), attracting 10 per cent higher passenger loads than the 707 during much of its seventeen years' service with BOAC and giving more prolonged service to the RAF on transport and tanker duties than could ever have been anticipated.

In this context the author was fortunate to travel on VC10s for more than ten years, during which time their smooth flight and reliability proved outstanding (except at Washington where the plane tended to suffer from a series of mysterious minor problems that gave its crews an extra twenty-four hours or so in such a popular location).

As Sir George Edwards said, 'The VC10 had to be better than the 707, not just different and we succeeded that requirement in many ways.'

In this he was strongly supported by its chief test pilot, Brian Trubshaw, who believed that:

> The VC10 was a beautiful aircraft to fly and its designers went on to create Concorde. The VC10 provided a level of comfort not seen before. The 707 was indeed a fine machine, but it was not – in design, manufacturing or flight – the engineering and design advance that the VC10 represented. Many of the VC10s' innovations are now seen in today's commercial airliner designs ...[9]

Vickers champion Dr Norman Barfield believed it could fairly be regarded as a generation ahead of its competitors.[10] In forty-eight years' service it had just two fatal accidents, neither of which were due to the aircraft itself. One was with Nigeria Airways' 5N-ABD, which crashed on the approach to Lagos due to crew error, while East African Airways' 5X-UVA overran the runway at Addis Ababa during an aborted take-off.[11]

However, whatever the VC10's excellent qualities, it has to be acknowledged that it was never a commercial success. The especially demanding technical and operational specifications for BOAC's Empire routes meant Vickers provided a better-performing aircraft off the ground than the market actually needed.

Just twelve standard VC10s and seventeen Super VC10s were acquired by an American-leaning BOAC during 1964–69. More serious still, Vickers failed to penetrate the international market and only fifty-four planes were built in all, compared with 1,010 Boeing 707s and 556 Douglas DC-8s, which thus established an impregnable position. Had Vickers entered the market some four years earlier with its VC7 the results would surely have been very different.

Despite this sad outcome for large British jet aircraft, during the 1950s the market for medium-range types still appeared to offer massive opportunities.

However, like Vickers with the VC10, the manufacturers needed sufficient domestic orders from which to launch their international sales campaigns. An opportunity appeared in 1956 when BEA, Britain's second airline, issued a requirement for a 100-seat jet airliner capable of flying at 600mph over a minimum range of 1,000 miles. While BEA had successfully operated the turboprop Vickers Viscount since 1953 and had ordered the larger Vanguard, increasing interest from overseas customers in the rear-engined, jet-powered French Caravelle led its chairman, Lord Douglas, to acknowledge that on such routes extra speed had become an important factor.

De Havilland offered a plane to meet BEA's requirement and in May 1957 BEA granted it a contract for twenty-five DH.121 aircraft at a total cost of

Vickers Vanguard, the turboprop airliner that came late to the market.
(BAE Systems Heritage)

£574 million. These were scheduled to be powered by three Rolls-Royce Medway turbofans mounted at the rear end of the fuselage, each with an output thrust of 14,000lb (thus offering plenty of stretch potential). The DH.121, whose first flight was due in 1961, was scheduled to carry 110 passengers over a maximum range of 1,800 nautical miles at a markedly higher cruising speed than the French Caravelle.

By any standard, the DH.121 was a handsome aircraft and Professor Keith Hayward wrote enthusiastically about 'the plane's, elegant, aerodynamically efficient contours and powerful engines that gave it a superb performance in the cruise, with speeds of up to 600–610mph', de Havilland was confident that the plane – about to be called Trident – would repeat the success of the earlier Vickers Viscount and with such hopes in mind the company's market research department forecast sales of 550 aircraft by 1965.[12]

In spite of having a strong competitor in the shape of Boeing's 727 (to whom de Havilland had naively given full data about the Trident's research and development during an official US visit to Hatfield[13]), there appeared good reasons for such optimism.

Sadly, as with other potential British winners, its prospects were to change for the worse when in March 1959 BEA discovered that air-traffic trends had

De Havilland DH.121 Trident medium-range airliner, offering speed and economy. (Farnborough Air Sciences Trust)

shown a significant dip during 1958–59. Instead of viewing it as a temporary slippage, BEA's board panicked and decided that with fewer passengers available, the Trident had to be cut down in size (to eighty-seven seats) and given a less powerful engine (the Rolls-Royce 163 Spey).

At a stroke, the task of de Havilland's consortium changed from designing an aircraft for international customers to meeting the specific (and mistaken) needs of a single European carrier. Nevertheless, following its earlier misfortunes with Comet, de Havilland was desperate to finalise the contract and it vetoed its sales and market research department from entering into discussion with overseas airlines so that all could be concentrated on the limited BEA specification.[14]

Although BEA paid de Havilland £200,000 for the changes (and the company received additional government support), they not only reduced the aircraft's international attractiveness but added six months to its development schedule.

This proved disastrous; by January 1964, just forty-four Tridents had been sold, thirty-three of them to BEA, compared with the Boeing 727 that was always on the open market. The Boeing was strikingly similar to the original Trident, being designed for 130 passengers to travel at around 600mph over a range of some 1,000 nautical miles whose design – like the Trident's – gave scope for further 'stretch'.

The 727 proved an instant success, with a total of 131 orders from seven different airlines received by November 1962. In all, more than 2,000 727s would be sold, compared with the smaller Trident's 115, whose break-even sales were set at 100.

Despite such grave disadvantages, de Havilland should surely have adopted a more aggressive development programme. The first Trident flight occurred on 9 January 1962 but the first revenue-carrying service was not until 11 March 1964. This compared with the Boeing 727's first flight on 9 February 1963 and its first revenue-carrying one on 1 February 1964, one year later.

In de Havilland's defence, there were understandable reasons for some of the differences; the weather was generally better in Washington State, the home of Boeing, and the amalgamation of the British aircraft industry saddled the Hawker Siddeley Group (including de Havilland) with an unexpectedly heavy workload. Additional commitments also arose during the development of the aeroplane, including its Autoland facility, an automatic landing system. Whatever such justifications, the process took well over a year longer than that of the Boeing 727.

Notwithstanding this, like the VC10, when regular Trident services started on 1 April 1964 they proved very popular. By 1966, nearly all BEA flights from London were by Trident and these continued until 2 April 1983, when the plane was withdrawn due to the enforcement of more stringent noise regulations.

Nothing, however, could compensate for BEA's decision – like BOAC's with the VC10 – to specify an aeroplane for its special and limited requirements when in its original form the DH.121 was not only well-suited for international needs but ready to take advantage of its unquestionable technological advantages. Professor Keith Hayward was in no doubt BEA's actions 'lost the British aircraft industry an opportunity to forestall Boeing's successful entry into the medium–haul jet market with the three-engined 727, which would subsequently dominate the sector for a generation'.[15]

The decision was doubly unfortunate because at the time the Ministry of Supply was not happy with BEA's changes and recognised that 'the aircraft was evidently tailored to meet the needs of BEA where it was unusual in having no stages longer than 1,400 miles [2,250km] and a preponderance of stages under 1,100 miles [1,770km]'.[16]

By the time de Havilland (now within the Hawker Siddeley consortium) realised they should produce a larger, more powerful, variant of the Trident – more or less back to what BEA had originally requested – the main chance was lost for the Boeing 727 had already made big inroads into the international market.[17]

Whatever the disappointments with large- and medium-sized airliners, the short-range market still beckoned, where the Vickers Viscount had already proved so successful and where many British firms were involved, including Hunting Aviation, which was setting about designing a jet-powered replacement with its H.107. At the time of the British Aircraft Corporation's acquisition of Hunting in 1960, this aircraft had grown into an 80ft, five-abreast airliner with two Bristol Siddeley BS.75 engines of around 7,000lb thrust, giving it a 500mph cruise speed and a range of 600 miles.[18]

In March 1961, it was decided to install the more powerful Rolls-Royce Spey engine with 10,330lb thrust that had already been used in the Trident and the plane became the BAC 1-11. The aircraft was scheduled to carry sixty-five passengers – sixteen first and forty-nine tourist class or eighty-nine single class – and qualified for £9.75 million launch aid from the British government.

Plans were made to produce an initial run of twenty for a plane whose average journey was estimated at just forty-five minutes, and whose maiden flight was due in the spring of 1963 prior to it being delivered by the autumn of the same year to Freddie Laker's independent British United Airways.

Such was the confidence in the new aeroplane that Sir George Edwards, now Executive Director of BAC, predicted it could take 40 per cent of a 1,000-aircraft market, potentially equalling the success of the Viscount.[19] His confidence

A BAC 1-11 short/medium-range turbofan airliner of Laker Airways.
(Farnborough Air Sciences Trust)

was supported by BAC's excellent marketing campaign – whose team visited eighty-nine airlines, where they emphasised the 1-11's ability to cater for a broad spectrum of customers. Particular attention was paid to the American market, where in April 1963 the wider-bodied, ninety-seater DC-9, powered by two rear-mounted Pratt and Whitney engines – providing significantly more thrust than the 1-11's Speys – was launched and quickly picked up pre-orders.

With American interest in mind, BAC also did the right thing by announcing the availability of two other versions, its series 300 and 400, with their more powerful Spey 511-14 engines giving the same cruising speed of 548mph over a doubled range of 1,400 miles.

By the time the first BAC 1-11 was rolled out at Hurn airport on 28 July 1963 it had obtained sixty orders from eight airlines, including American ones, and hopes were understandably high.

However, following a successful maiden flight, although development work was proceeding normally, on 22 October 1963 during tests to assess stability and handling characteristics, the plane entered a deep stall and crashed, killing all seven of its test crew. Much was learned from the incident about the new phenomena of deep stall, which led to the fitting of powered elevators, modifying the wings' leading edges and adding a stick pusher to the controls to draw the crew's attention to the likelihood of a stall.[20] However, the modifications inevitably extended the plane's flight-test development programme, and its Certificate of Airworthiness (CoA) was not issued until 5 April 1965.

In the meanwhile, there had been two forced landings, one due to limitations with the plane's elevators and the other because of pilot errors. The apparent succession of mishaps brought adverse publicity, which led to Alitalia and Iberia cancelling their orders, although the remainder of the flight programme actually proceeded uneventfully and the plane flew a total 1,900 hours and carried out more than 2,000 landings prior to gaining its full certificate of airworthiness.

Between 1967 and 1971, 120 1-11s were built and, following the plane's initial problems, the vast majority were for BEA. However, in spite of the firm's early declaration of intent, it was not until the late 1960s that the 500 series, a more powerful stretched version for ninety-nine passengers, was produced and delivered to BEA. The airline began using them on fare-paying routes on 17 November 1968 and its successor British Airways continued to do so until 1993.[21]

Although the majority of the BAC 1-11s were constructed during the late 1960s and early 1970s, the type continued to be built until 30 May 1984. Of the 236 subsequently manufactured in Britain (222 at Hurn and thirteen at Weybridge) only thirty-five were completed during its last twelve years. By the early 1980s, the plane was due to receive a new powerplant in the shape of the more powerful and quieter Rolls-Royce Tay 650 engine, capable of producing 15,100lb of thrust, which was expected to increase take-off performance by 32 per cent. Unfortunately, after two aircraft were converted it was found that the tailplane shook when applying full reverse thrust and only a limited certification could be granted.

Another serious reverse occurred in 1979 when hopes for large overseas orders from Romania foundered due to the rapid deterioration in that country's economic and international standing. Only nine aircraft in all were produced under such arrangements. Even so, the BAC 1-11 proved a reliable, popular aircraft over some seventeen years until in 1984 more stringent noise restrictions led to its engines – which were notoriously 'thirsty' – being considered unacceptably noisy as well.

During the early 1960s major British expectations for civil aviation rested on the three airliners described. While all three were intended for use by British airlines, there were high hopes for them breaking into the international markets, including the prime American one. In the event, while they undoubtedly succeeded in engineering terms and were remarkably popular with all who flew in them, the sales of the VC10 and Trident proved deeply disappointing, while the BAC 1-11 took only half its anticipated share of the overseas market and little of the American one.

The reasons were clear enough. The VC10, following the setbacks with the Comet and the phenomenal success of Boeing's 707, came late to an already established marketplace bearing the irreversible disadvantage of being designed

with a short take-off capability, when the rapid development of modern airports rendered such a requirement unnecessary. To make things worse, BOAC
did not purchase enough planes to make the VC10 economically viable and
the RAF's orders for an aircraft that suited its needs so admirably were too low
to help reduce production costs. In contrast no fewer than 820 707s (in their
KC-135 designations) were purchased to serve the needs of the US Air Force.

Whatever the VC10's undoubted virtues as an aircraft, its sales total of fifty-
four was never large enough to make a desired impact on the world scene, nor
to dent Boeing's sales of more than 1,000 707s and Douglas's 556 DC-8s.

The Trident was no less handicapped by its association with a British airline. In its initial stages, it compared directly with Boeing's 727 but BEA's
demand for a smaller, less-powerful aeroplane put it at a grave disadvantage to
its American competitor that could only be overcome by a major new development programme for a market where the opportunities were diminishing.
Most of the Tridents sold overseas were variants that came closer to the planes'
original specification than for BEA's downsized version and these could never
compare with the sales of Boeing 727s, which approached 2,000.

In the case of the BAC 1-11, with the dynamic Sir George Edwards as the
firm's Executive Director it was to be expected that lessons would have been
learned from the adverse experiences of the VC10 and Trident and that the
1-11 would be marketed vigorously for its reputed worldwide utility.

Tragically it, too, missed the boat with its prolonged development time causing it
to lose out to the DC-9, particularly as its extended version did not follow quickly
enough. As a result, by 1972 its sales had faltered and the more powerful engines so
sorely required were never widely installed. Even so, 236 were manufactured, 200 of
them by 1972, so that prior to the appearance of the Rolls-Royce RB211 engine
it was the country's biggest dollar earner. However admirable its sales figures, they
could never compare with those of the rival Boeing 737, which were measured in
thousands and whose production continued for more than forty-five years.

Although the main reasons for the disparate sales of civilian airliners
between Britain and the US during the 1960s could rightly be attributed to
the restricted and specific demands made by Britain's national airlines, government vacillation and the restricted size of the UK's home market, it has to be
acknowledged that industrial practices within the British aviation industry also
played an additional and significant role.

British producers, for instance, failed to move from design to production as
quickly as the Americans. Although the VC10's first flight was on 29 June 1962,
it did not come into service until 29 April 1964, while the Boeing 707 entered
service within a year of its initial flight. In the case of the Trident, the gap between
its first flight and its first revenue-earning one was more than two years compared

with half that time for the Boeing 727. The period between the BAC 1-11's first flight and its first official one was one year and eight months, compared with the Douglas DC-9's just eight months, and during that time a succession of accidents significantly affected customer confidence in the British airliner.

British manufacturers were much slower at producing stretched versions of their aircraft, partly due to a shortage of capital. While the standard VC10 made its maiden flight on 29 June 1962, it was almost two years before the much-needed Super VC10 did so (on 7 May 1964). In contrast, Boeing routinely prepared individual variants for customers, which it indicated with a number following the 707. Its 707-300C for instance, indicated a quick-change model from passenger to freight configuration.[22]

While Trident needed a stretched model to compete head to head with Boeing's 727, it was three and a half years before the series 3B was rolled out at Hatfield.[23]

Although the BAC 1-11's entry into service was a great success, an enlarged version was not on offer for six years. In contrast, within two months of the Boeing's 737's start date, it had a stretched version, while the DC-9 came to be stretched again and again.[24]

BAC should also have offered Pratt and Whitney engines as an alternative powerplant and if the company had come near to meeting the development routines practised by Boeing and Douglas, it is likely the 1-11 would have enjoyed several times its actual sales.

Unsurprisingly, such comparisons caused concern and by 1969 a working party convened by the Royal Aeronautical Society came to the conclusion that the US repeatedly put twice as much effort into aeroplane R&D and twenty-five times as much effort into aeroplane proof-of-concept activity.[25]

Aeronautical author Stephen Skinner went far further, believing there was a 'lack of focused direction on the part of British Aviation and the Government where civil aviation is concerned'.[26]

Dr Norman Barfield echoed such criticism with his conviction that the VC10's fortunes were 'grossly frustrated by the extreme vacillations of the management, the politics of the airline itself and national political factors far beyond Vickers' ability to influence'.[27]

Whatever the reasons, the relative lack of commercial success with the VC10, Trident and BAC 1-11 meant they would be the last major civilian aeroplanes produced by British aero-firms during the thirty years after the Second World War. Henceforth, escalating costs and greater technical complexity would compel them to enter assisted and collaborative projects, most notably with the Anglo–French supersonic Concorde.

PART 3

INDECISION AND CANCELLATION

9

THE HARRIER: UNDERVALUED TREASURE

In his book *Harrier*, aviation writer Francis Mason leaves his readers in no doubt about the wide-ranging and formidable opposition to this remarkable V/STOL aircraft because of its smallness, subsonic speed and very unorthodoxy. He expresses his delight that it survived against all odds to become a shining example of British genius, ingenuity and perseverance – in the face of what he saw as undisguised hostility, lack of political and professional backbone and, possibly most of all, ignorance where intelligence should abound.[1]

Hawker Harrier jump jet. (Farnborough Air Sciences Trust)

Although Mason was a special pleader, during the early post-war years against a confusing backdrop of periodic economic crises and fast-changing defence needs any projected British military aircraft had to win over the current service chiefs. Without their support it could never obtain the Treasury's backing for development before attempting to make a mark in the fiercely competitive overseas market, where the US was the largest prize of all.

As Mason perceived, in the case of the Harrier things were even more difficult because it was being developed following the 1957 Sandys White Paper on Defence where the emphasis on the growing dependence on unmanned guided missiles had, in fact, halted work on new combat aircraft except for the English Electric Lightning. This was notwithstanding the fact that V-bombers on a high state of readiness represented a better deterrent against the Soviets than Britain's Blue Streak IRBM in its concrete silo that, according to the mad logic of the time, positively invited showers of incoming missiles. Even so, formed up on their runways the V-bombers themselves were far from immune from Soviet tactical nuclear weapons, either rocket- or aircraft-borne, nor were second- and third-generation jet fighters, which needed up to 2,500m of asphalt for take-off.

Such vulnerability seemed sure to attract interest in Britain and the US in aircraft that didn't need runways for, although the principle of vertical take-off was as old as aviation, it had almost wholly been concentrated in the helicopter rather than a high-performance military aircraft. The root problem was how to bring such a vehicle into a robust and practical form.

Its potential had already been recognised by German designers when, among their other advanced aeronautical work during the Second World War, they had built the Focke-Achgelis Fa 269 shipborne fighter using thrust vectoring, which had been intended to operate from platforms on merchant vessels. Its single radial engine drove a pair of propellers that could be rotated downwards to give vertical thrust and rearwards for horizontal movement, but due to its serious power limitations and more pressing priorities elsewhere it was abandoned.

After the war the advent of jet power delivered through second and third generations of gas turbine engines appeared to offer new hope and during the early 1950s jet pioneer Dr A.A. Griffith, working with Rolls-Royce at Derby, had considered a complicated VTOL system depending upon 'a battery of vertically mounted, specialised, high thrust-to-weight ratio lift engines used only for the take-off and landing phases of flight, quite separate from the horizontally installed cruise flight propulsion system'.[2] Lift technology had been demonstrated in 1953 when Rolls-Royce produced its so-called 'Flying Bedstead' using two Nene turbojets to achieve stable hovering flight.

At around the same time, French engineer Michel Wibault considered moving a vital stage further, namely to the earlier German vectored system of diverting the gases from a turbojet downward for take-off and landing and rearwards for horizontal flight.[3]

After failing to interest either the French or American governments in his new concept, Wibault approached Colonel Willis Chapman of the United States Air Force (USAF), who headed an American-sponsored organisation called the Mutual Weapons Development Team (MWDT) dedicated to encouraging promising military projects of interest to NATO that might otherwise die for lack of funds. Following Wilbault's visit, Chapman went to see Dr Stanley Hooker, who had left Rolls-Royce to become Bristol Aircraft's technical director, to gain his views on Wibault's proposals. Hooker was initially not very enthusiastic due to the unrivalled amount of thrust needed and the relative inefficiency of contemporary centrifugal blowers to provide it. However, he passed the project on to Gordon Lewis, a senior engineer in his team, who recommended employing the more powerful Bristol Orpheus engine rather than that proposed by Wibault. Even more importantly, Lewis suggested making crucial changes to the propulsion system by replacing Wibault's centrifuges with a single axial compressor with one pair of rotating nozzles and a simple rear deflecting jet pipe.[4] As a result, in January 1957, shortly before Wibault's death, a patent in the joint names of Wibault and Lewis was taken out on these lines but leaving the rear nozzle configuration open to adaptation. At Bristol the subsequent design progressed rapidly and a brochure for an engine numbered BE53 was passed by Hooker to Colonel Chapman early in 1957.

The programme still needed a powerful champion to give it impulsion and it found it in Hawker's famed senior designer, Sydney Camm, who was at the time wrestling with requirements for the TSR2's advanced design needs while keeping his eye on British and US attempts towards V/STOL flight.

Camm was sceptical of Rolls-Royce's lift jet ideas and sent one of his typical letters to Stanley Hooker at Bristol, opening with the words, 'Dear Hooker, what are you doing about vertical take-off engines?'

Hooker replied by enclosing details of the Wibault–Lewis engine (a preliminary of the famed Pegasus), which Camm passed to his Kingston design office for their reactions. At Kingston, whilst there were strong doubts about whether the 11,000lb thrust needed to raise a V/STOL plane was attainable, one of Camm's senior project designers, Ralph Hooper, suggested that if only all the 'bolt thrust' from the engine's split tailpipes could be vectored downwards, it might be achieved.

In June 1957, Hooper went on to sketch a basic airframe around such an engine, originally for a three-seater aircraft. This proved the foundation for the Harrier, which was allotted project number P.1127. Hooper developed the design, to arrive at a 'viable single-seat high performance aircraft in which the hot gas exhaust from the engine was also passed through rotatable nozzles so that four such nozzles could direct the turbojet's entire thrust vertically downwards for take-off and then by progressively rotating them afterwards, accelerate the aircraft into horizontal wing-borne flight'.[5]

Following Hooper's work, Hooker received another telephone call from Camm in which he asked him, 'Why haven't you been to see me? – I have designed an aeroplane around your Pegasus engine and it is about time you took an interest in it.'

Hooker immediately went to Kingston, where he met Camm and two members of his senior staff, John Fozard and Roy Chaplin, and was shown a drawing of the P.1127.[6]

Most importantly, Camm was impressed enough by the progress so far that he decided to use his company's resources to build private venture prototypes based on Hooper's latest design. This enthusiasm was in marked contrast to the negative response from the Ministry of Supply, which told Hawker that although some tunnel testing facilities might in due course be made available, there was little chance of obtaining a research contract for the P.1127 as there appeared to be no civil potential.[7]

Camm encouraged Hooker to approach Colonel Chapman for financial help towards the engine development and the American-funded MWD programme agreed to provide 75 per cent of the initial development costs, with

Bristol's chairman Geoffrey Vernon Smith guaranteeing the remaining 25 per cent. Hooker told Colonel Chapman that six engines were needed, 'four for bench testing and two for flight testing', and after visiting Camm at Kingston, Chapman agreed to Hawkers' having them.[8] Contact was also made with NASA and model testing took place both in the US and at Kingston.

The first Pegasus engine ran on the bench in September 1959 and during the second half of the year – with Camm's continuing support for the Harrier as a private venture – metal was cut on the first of the three prototypes for an aircraft that, for practical reasons, Camm believed should have its sophistication restricted as far as possible.

By 27 October there was evidence that the government was in fact considering support for a preliminary contract of £75,000 to cover further design and development work for a tactical ground support aircraft to replace the Hawker Hunter.[9] However, things were still less than certain, for when Duncan Sandys visited Hawker at Kingston he proved far from receptive about the P.1127, although the new CAS Air Chief Marshal Sir Thomas Pike came to take a personal interest in the aircraft for which, of course, Sydney Camm's backing remained vital.

Camm was fully aware about the value of his role for during the aircraft's development Hooker had to report to him at 10 a.m. every Monday. On one occasion Camm greeted him with the words, 'Have you got a sufficient sense of grief and shame?' to which Hooker replied, 'What do you mean?'

'Well,' Camm continued gleefully, 'You come here every Monday, spending the country's money on this hair-brained scheme of vertical take-off. Have you no sense of shame about it?'[10]

In June 1960, the Ministry of Aviation finally signed a contract to undertake the full development and manufacture of two P.1127 prototypes for research into V/STOL flight. The first flight engine was delivered to Hawker in September 1960, but although its top thrust had been increased to 11,200lb, this was barely enough to lift the P.1127 off the ground after everything possible was removed and the fuel was limited to three minutes' flight. Camm remained unabashedly optimistic: 'The damned thing will fly beautifully. What we wish to do is the hovering test straight away.'

On 21 October 1960, Hawker's chief test pilot, Bill Bedford, prepared for the plane's first vertical lift, although the circumstances were far from propitious because a few days earlier he had broken his ankle in a car accident. He was compelled to demonstrate his continuing dexterity by flying a glider, a helicopter and several other aircraft before the RAF Central Medical Board cleared him to fly – and then only in tethered mode. Even so, in his hands, the plane rose a few inches off the surface of a special grid while still restrained by its cables.

There followed five weeks of further tests before, on 19 November, the tethers were discarded and 'like a bird freed from its cage' the plane rose by means of a Pegasus engine rated at 10,400lb thrust. Tests continued during the winter of 1960/61 and a second prototype joined in the process. By 8 September 1961, both had progressed to making conventional flights.

Some idea of the challenges to the test pilots at that time can be gathered from Bill Bedford's comments on the first lifts:

> Slowly we were becoming less ignorant about control of V/STOL aircraft. We realised that in essence the P.1127 was rather like a house brick supported by a jet fountain, but possessing no natural stability nor damping and that controlling it satisfactorily with these jet reaction controls was going to extend our ingenuity to the limit.

On 14 December, they suffered a crash when a fibreglass nozzle was blown off XP836, although Bill Bedford ejected and was unhurt. Following the installation of steel nozzles, the flight programme continued, using Pegasus engines that had been upgraded to 13,500lb thrust.

During 1962 the P.1127 successfully performed vertical and short take-offs and landings together with high-speed runs past enthralled crowds at the Farnborough Air Show, while on 8 February of the following year Bill Bedford flew prototype XP831 on to the deck of HMS *Ark Royal*, despite having never before landed a combat aircraft on an aircraft carrier.

Flying at the Paris Air Show of 1963 an embarrassing incident occurred when the aircraft flopped down, causing extensive damage to the airframe, if no injury to Bill Bedford. The cause was put down to a tiny piece of grit jamming a valve in the system that regulated nozzle angles, with the chances of it ever being repeated estimated at many thousands to one.[11]

The advances at Hawker took place amid strong scepticism from some of the Air Staff towards the V/STOL concept, including surprise at the limitations of the P.1127's powerplant (whose performance, however, was steadily advancing) and doubts about the plane's operational role despite it giving much increased operational flexibility. Insupportable horror was expressed, for instance, about the price of the aircraft, which amounted to £560,000 each, when even refurbished Hunters were costing around £300,000.[12]

In spite of the doubters, the prototypes went from strength to strength and Larry Levy, an American with the MWDP in Paris, came to the conclusion that what NATO most needed was for the plane to show how V/STOL could actually be used under battlefield conditions.

To this end, he succeeded in persuading the American, British and Federal German governments to fund a tripartite squadron, for which each accepted one-third of the development cost of nine improved examples of the P.1127, to be called Kestrel, for extensive testing.

The so-called Tripartite Agreement was signed on 16 January 1963 and the manufacture of the Kestrels was started by the middle of the year. On 5 March 1964 a concentrated flying programme under operational conditions commenced with pilots from the RAF, the Luftwaffe, the USF, the US Army and the Royal Navy, with the latter two flying on to the USS *Independence* and *Raleigh* aircraft carriers. This continued for some eleven months, during which 938 sorties were conducted involving twenty-four missions per aircraft and 600 hours of flight, before the squadron was disbanded.

After the Germans declined to buy their aircraft, the Americans took six Kestrels back to the United States. Despite their pilots' enthusiastic reactions towards a plane that far exceeded their own V/STOL prototypes, the USF still indicated a preference for aeroplanes that used airfields and however adaptable the Kestrels, their short fifty-hour engine life was considered a grave disadvantage.

In Britain, V/STOL flight operations continued to progress and by 1965 the Pegasus engine's thrust had been increased to 19,000lb and its engine life extended sixfold to 300 hours. With such advances, the aeroplane acquired a radius and endurance as good as any Hunter, while it was now capable of carrying greater payloads.

In 1964 while Denis Healey's cancellation of other advanced aeroplane systems, including the intended supersonic V/STOL P.1154, meant that the British aircraft industry could no longer supply such military aircraft to the NATO air forces nor support the full range of aircraft needed for Britain's own forces, it led to increased support for the subsonic Kestrel in enhanced form with the Pegasus 6 engine.

The newly formed Ministry of Technology issued a contract for six pre-production models of a plane where 90 per cent of its original components had been changed and where it was able to vector its engine through 98.5 degrees, with all four nozzles moving in unison by means of a single lever in the cockpit.

This now became the P.1127 (RAF), with the name Kestrel giving way to Harrier. An initial production order was made for Hawker to produce sixty aircraft, the first of which was due to make its maiden flight on 31 August 1966. Despite this, in both the RAF and beyond, the Harrier still had its British detractors.

Two F-4 Phantom II aircraft during Exercise Gallant Eagle '82. (US National Archives Licence No. 636 7185)

In the case of the RAF, continuing enthusiasm for large supersonic fighters and bombers made it difficult for many officers to appreciate the role of a new subsonic aircraft, however versatile it might prove. For them, it seemed a step backwards technologically.

As for senior politicians, Labour Chancellor Denis Healey, in his quest for standardisation and economic rationalisation, favoured its cancellation and replacement by the excellent American McDonnell F-4 Phantom which, however, entirely lacked V/STOL capabilities.

Whatever the critics, they had to acknowledge that the Harrier met the need for a combat aircraft that could be dispersed from orthodox airfields to escape potential air strikes. However, by the mid-1960s, instant nuclear retaliation against potential Soviet strikes on airfields was giving way to the doctrine of flexible response, whereby NATO's conventional forces would be built up and nuclear weapons only used when one's conventional forces failed. In this context, the use of V/STOL aircraft would be primarily tactical.

On 2 February 1965, Harold Wilson talked about a limited development programme for an aircraft 'that will, in fact, be the first in the field, with vertical take-off for close support of our land forces'.[13] Specifically, such close support meant reconnaissance and low-level attacks on the enemy's second echelon armoured units, using cluster weapons and 68mm SNEB rockets.

The RAF's continuing reservations were revealed in its modest order for sixty aircraft to provide one squadron in Britain and another in West Germany, although in the British Amy of the Rhine (BAOR) when used during large-scale NATO exercises, its ability to take off and land independently of airfields quickly became appreciated.

Yet had it not been for a quite unexpected but deadly war in the Falkland Islands, some 8,000 miles from the UK, the essential Harrier story, as far as land operations went, might have been limited to a supporting role with British NATO forces in both BAOR and the UK.

Due to the aircraft's unique performance in the Falklands and with the US Marine Corps in their major out-of-theatre operations, the Harrier story goes far beyond our book's thirty-year period. Even so, in the first instance the British armed forces were hardly its strongest champions for, whatever the RAF's lingering doubts, the Royal Navy's interest came later still.

Although the first of a series of landings by the P.1127 prototype XP831 on HMS *Ark Royal* had taken place as early as February 1963, it was not until 1970 that the Navy's interest escalated, during which year the RAF's No. 1 (Fighter) Squadron had again taken its Harriers to practice landings on HMS *Ark Royal* while it was off the Scottish coast. The main cause for the Navy's increased attention was the decision to replace its large aircraft carriers with small through-deck cruisers that were originally intended for helicopters only, but when equipped with Harriers were seen to be capable of performing much wider roles.

The first of the through-deck ships, HMS *Invincible*, was launched in May 1977. She was due to begin her sea trials on 26 March 1978, by which time the Navy had gained Treasury approval for the development of a naval version and had ordered twenty-four Sea Harriers, six each of which were intended to be carried by the Invincible-class ships, along with ten Sea King helicopters.[14] The Sea Harrier's essential changes from the RAF Harrier, by then the GR.3, included a Ferranti Blue Fox radar, raised cockpit for better pilot view and the conversion of the Pegasus Mk.104 engine cases to aluminium to avoid sea corrosion. The Sea Harrier's primary role was to act as an interceptor of enemy ship-based fighter aircraft, with secondary responsibilities for reconnaissance and strike attack against ships and shore targets.

By 29 January 1982, twenty-nine Sea Harriers had been delivered to the Navy and just over two months later, on 2 April 1982, the Argentine armed forces – which included 200 potent aircraft – carried out a military invasion of the Falkland Islands. Between 3 and 5 April, when the Naval task force set sail from Portsmouth to the Falklands, its two fleet carriers HMS *Hermes* and *Invincible* were loaded with twenty Sea Kings and twenty Sea Harriers of 800,

Sea Harrier FRS.1. (Farnborough Air Sciences Trust)

801 and 899 squadrons, together with their personnel and a force of Royal Marine Commandos.[15] Fourteen further Sea Harriers and six GR.3s of the RAF were taken aboard the merchant ship *Atlantic Conveyor*, for passage to the South Atlantic where they would be expected to join the Task Force.

At this stage, twenty-four Sea Harriers and six RAF Harriers comprised the total number of fixed-wing aircraft supporting the Task Force and, due to the late build-up of its air arm, several of the Navy pilots were newly arrived while the twin mountings for the planes' excellent US Sidewinder missiles were yet to be installed.

The Falklands operation has been described extensively elsewhere and we are restricting our account to the statistics relating to the air campaign. During the early phase of operations prior to the British land forces being put ashore, the Harriers mounted 'softening up' raids, which inflicted considerable losses on the Argentine Air Force, although in the process the Task Force lost 15 per cent of its own aeroplanes.

From such a small force, these losses were most serious but they were made good by two notable initiatives: four RAF Harriers were flown out from England via Ascension Island over a protracted journey that required multiple inflight refuelling, with a further fourteen Harriers (eight Sea Harriers and six GR.3s) joining the carriers after fortunately being flown off the large merchant ship *Atlantic Conveyor* before it was struck and sunk by an Exocet missile.

On 21 May 1982, the Harriers supported the assault forces as they went ashore by providing a screen against Argentinian air attacks and giving ground support. Although they were only able to muster about eight aircraft simultaneously, the Sea Harrier squadrons destroyed at least seven attackers, while the RAF Harriers, flying up to four sorties a day, destroyed others. On that day the Argentinians reported a total of twenty-three aircraft lost while the British casualties were one Harrier and five helicopters.

With their sparse numbers and the fact they were positioned on carriers some distance away from the point of the battle, the Sea Harriers could never prevent a number of raiders getting through and, for instance, bombing the frigate *Ardent* and the destroyer *Antrim*, where the *Ardent* was lost. Yet such was their success that on the following day, the Argentinian Air Force failed to follow up its initial attacks and the assault forces consolidated their positions without interruption.

Final victory came with the Argentinian surrender on 14 June after a campaign where the achievements of the Harrier units were considered to have far exceeded their small numbers. Despite being very significantly outnumbered and unable to prevent serious losses to the Navy and other ships, while on their missions they dominated the skies. In the course of the campaign twenty-eight Sea Harriers and ten RAF Harriers flew more than 2,000 combat sorties, destroyed at least twenty-eight enemy aircraft in air combat and achieved an overall serviceability rate of more than 90 per cent.[16] Although six Sea Harriers, four RAF Harriers and twenty-six helicopters were lost to ground fire and other causes, no Harriers were lost in air combat. In such engagements with planes that were not only more numerous, more heavily armed and frequently much faster, the Harrier's capacity for accelerating and decelerating, increasing its rate of turn and flying at abnormally slow speed, proved outstanding.

How far pilots in the Falklands operation actually took advantage of the Harrier's capabilities for such tactics, remains uncertain, but with their Sidewinder infrared homing missiles, they undoubtedly took a heavy toll on their Argentinian opponents.

The fitting, if not excessive, reward for an aircraft that had previously overcome so much pessimism and then so distinguished itself in a unique military operation, was an announcement by the British government of an order for just fourteen Sea Harriers to replace their lost machines and marginally increase the strength of their established squadrons.

No account of this brilliantly designed British aircraft can, however, ignore the signal part played by the US both in its development and subsequent use in combat operations. This commenced with the early support for the Pegasus engine from Colonel Chapman and his Mutual Weapons Development Team and continued with the Tripartite Agreement of 1964 where, after US participation in a concentrated flying programme with the Kestrel, it continued to evaluate the six aircraft it took back to the US.

Although the type was rejected by the USF, following further extensive trials, the US Marine Corps would come to display a growing enthusiasm. This resulted in a visit by two US Marine Corps pilots, Colonel Tom Miller and Lieutenant Colonel Bud Baker, to the Harrier chalet at the 1968 Farnborough Air Show to request clearance to fly the Harrier. After being given every opportunity, they returned to the US with glowing reports of its performance and, following a further US evaluation, approval was given by Congress to purchase twelve Harriers during the 1970 fiscal year as part of a declared intention to buy 114 planes by the mid-1970s.

Characteristically, US business interests were not neglected, for the purchase was conditional on Hawker Siddeley entering into a fifteen-year agreement with McDonnell Douglas 'assigning to the American Company exclusive rights for the sale and manufacture of the Harrier and its derivatives in the US and agreeing to the mutual exchange of data and drawings on vectored thrust V/STOL configurations stemming from the Harrier during the same period'.[17]

In fact, during the first five years of the procurement programme more than 100 Harriers were constructed in England by Hawker Siddeley because it was far cheaper to build them there. Further collaboration between the two countries came about with the production of a more advanced form of the basic AV-8A, as it was designated in the US, used by the Marines. McDonnell Douglas developed a new, supercritical wing constructed largely of carbon fibre composite that, combined with the Rolls-Royce Pegasus II (MK.5) engine's improved thrust of 21,750lb, doubled the AV-8A's payload radius.[18] In due course the US Marine Corps signalled its requirement for 340 such Harriers, known as AV-8Bs. The RAF also ordered sixty aircraft based on the American AV-8s and these entered service in 1989 as the Harrier GR.5.

The RAF retired the Harrier prematurely in 2010 due to defence cuts and only in 2018 did the service regain an aircraft capable of vertical flight with the delivery of the supersonic Lockheed Martin F-35B Lightning, some 138 of which were due to be purchased by the UK at the time of writing and 2,457 by the US. In the Lightning's STOVL (short take-off and vertical landing) form, the Harrier concept continues – if no longer in the hands of British manufacturers.

The Harrier story illustrates so many of the predominant themes in post-war British aviation. Despite the many early obstacles and lukewarm support at home, the plane proved an outstanding triumph for British aeronautical design, for out of seventeen separate V/STOL projects undertaken by different nations, including America, by 1987 only the Harrier and the Russian Yak-38 'Forger' survived. Although much inferior, the Forger was kept flying for political reasons.

John Fozard, the chief engineer on Hawker's Harrier project, believed its success came about because the plane was:

> supremely simple in principle and hence safe and flexible in operation. Its engineering has reflected and indeed nourished this basic virtue. Thus the vectored thrust concept and its execution are fully deserving of the word elegant, well-proportioned, refined, having a fine sense of beauty or propriety.[19]

Vital contributions to its emergence were also due to the perspicuity, personal pride and skills of outstanding individuals such as Stanley Hooker, Gordon Lewis and Ralph Hooper and, once his doubts were resolved, to Sydney Camm. The designer emphasised as he had always done with his earlier planes the need for simplicity of operation, and, as with the Hurricane, pledged his company's financial support towards the aeroplane. Once committed, in his inimitable manner he forced the project forward. Such men, working in an adverse political environment at a time when the RAF still needed convincing about the plane's utility, made what Fozard claims was the most important contribution 'to the operation of tactical jet airpower, since the introduction of the jet engine itself' – a capability that still remains to be exploited by civil aviation.[20]

The V/STOL Harrier created by British inventiveness, practically and faith was undoubtedly aided by US-inspired financial help. Even so, in the country of its birth it took an unexpected and distant war for its unique offensive qualities to be fully appreciated by the RAF and Royal Navy, where it much benefited from the last-minute installation of the simple to operate but deadly US Sidewinder missile.

The Americans needed far less persuasion. From a relatively early stage the US Marine Corps appreciated its unique manoeuvrability, which it summed up as 'vectoring in forward flight', along with the advantages it gave to supporting out-of-theatre operations, where its load-carrying ability proved outstanding. As US Marine General Joe Anderson acknowledged, it brought the USMC into the world of flexible basing and the 'concept of vertical [flight] development'.[21]

The type really came into its own with the US forces in 1991 during Desert Storm's forty-two days of combat, during which eighty-six AV-8Bs flew 3,380 sorties, totalling 4,112 flight hours, delivering more than 6 million pounds of ordnance and maintaining a mission-capable rate in excess of 90 per cent.[22] The US Marine Corps was so appreciative of its performance that it extended the life of the AV-8B Harrier to 2030.

With the scheduled replacement of the AV-8B Harrier with the Lockheed Martin F-35B Lightning, V/STOL capability continues to feature in the West's aerial armoury, something that would have delighted inveterate US inventor Thomas Edison, who had decided earlier that:

> The airplane won't amount to a damn, until they get a machine that will act like a humming bird – go straight up, go forward, go backward, come straight down and alight like a humming bird. It isn't easy … Somebody is going to do it.[23]

However exciting and ultimately triumphant the Harrier story might be for British design capabilities, like so many other advanced aviation developments, responsibility for and production of the latest V/STOL aircraft is now in American hands.

A measure of the continuing sense of anger and loss among some of those involved is apparent from a review of Tony Buttler's 2017 book *Hawker P.1127, Kestrel and Harrier*, published in the RAeS Magazine *Aerospace* for September 2017. The review was by former senior Harrier pilot Graham Williams, who wrote: 'Sitting here today, I can scarcely believe that after all that effort and superb engineering, we sold away the whole fleet of the latest Harriers for a pittance. Stanley Hooker, John Dale, Ralph Hooper, John Fozard et al. would be appalled.'

10

TSR2: STIFLED AT BIRTH

Of all the aviation projects that were cancelled following the Second World War the one that still evokes the strongest reaction is that of British Aircraft Corporation's TSR2, the tactical strike and reconnaissance aircraft that was said to mark as great a technological leap forward as the V-bombers had in 1947 and concerning which there were such immensely high expectations. These were all the greater because the Sandys Defence White Paper of April 1957 had proposed that the RAF's traditional means of aerial defence – through manned fighter aircraft – should be succeeded by ballistic missiles.

Support for an advanced tactical strike and reconnaissance aircraft had been apparent prior to the Sandys Report, based on the understanding that although the coming of nuclear weapons had massively increased the powers of destruction, their horrific nature made global war far less likely and the possibility of limited wars occurring beneath the nuclear umbrella had undoubtedly increased. Whatever the capabilities of ballistic missiles, they could not be used to attack unknown targets nor to carry out reconnaissance missions, and by any standard they were a most uneconomical method of delivering traditional high explosives. In spite of Duncan Sandys' enthusiasm for missiles, the RAF Air Staff believed that tactical strike and reconnaissance missions had to be carried out by an advanced form of manned aircraft.

The result was the Air Staff's General Operational Requirement 339, which laid down the most demanding and varied roles for an all-weather aircraft destined to replace both the Valiant and Canberra bombers; 'a plane capable of low and medium altitude offensive tactical operations with either nuclear or conventional weapons, with a photographic reconnaissance capability and the ability of taking off from a short (1,000 yards) unconcreted runway.'[1]

However comprehensive, by 1959 the requirements were made even more demanding when the plane's speed was upped from Mach 1.7 to Mach 2 and its range increased to 2,500 nautical miles. Two years later, following the abandonment of Britain's Intermediate-Range Ballistic Missile, Blue Streak, it was decided that TSR2 should assume a strategic nuclear role by carrying two tactical nuclear bombs, thereby enabling the British government to cancel the development of Blue Water, the tactical nuclear weapon intended for use in BAOR.

The need for TSR2 to deliver the British nuclear deterrent was then reinforced by the American decision to cancel its air-launched Skybolt missile, which brought an inevitable delay before Britain received the US Polaris sea-launched missile.

With so many requirements, TSR2 not only incorporated some of the aircraft systems that had been cancelled but it was destined to replace the Canberra, which was expected to reach the end of its life by 1967 or very soon afterwards. As a result, on 15 December 1958 HM Treasury agreed to £150,000 – soon to be increased to £600,000 – for a design contract to meet the specification for GOR.339.

At this point the government decided on an additional unrelated function for TSR2. Although in 1957 nine separate firms made submissions for its construction, it was announced that preferential contracts would be given to groups of firms, thereby encouraging much-needed rationalisation. Sir George Edwards, as the future managing director of the British Aircraft Corporation (the largest of such groupings), had no doubts about the political implications of the TSR2 contract as an instrument to help bring about the major rationalisation of the British aircraft industry. As he observed, 'This meant that it was inextricably bound up with both national and international politics and put us in a situation that was like nothing else that any of us had ever had to tackle before.'[2]

The outcome of the enforced rationalisation was far from predictable. One result of the shotgun marriage between Vickers-Armstrong and English Electric, whose consortium would build the TSR2, was the need for fundamental changes to their management structures.

The chief engineer of the TSR2 project, Sir Freddy Page, observed critically that the award of the contract to Vickers, with the work shared on a fifty-fifty basis with English Electric, only served to prevent the formation of a properly balanced project team and led to delays and increased cost.[3] The consortium, for instance, needed greater resources, including the doubling of the main computer installation. In addition, the programme's tight timescale and seemingly ever more demanding contractual specifications placed heavy additional pressures on the aircraft's construction staff. Its improved performance requirements that included reducing the plane's low-level penetration height from some 1,000 to 1,500ft to an extremely demanding 200ft brought inevitable penalties. In 1957, its total weight had been set down by English Electric at less than 70,000lb but by the 1960s this had been raised to 100,000lb.

The enforced amalgamations brought other problems. Left to itself, Vickers would have undoubtedly chosen Rolls-Royce engines for its power plant, but government officials opted for the Bristol Siddeley Olympus 22R turbojet, with Vickers not becoming aware of the extra costs involved until it was too late. The plane's increased weight and need to fly at higher temperatures brought the need for a major redesign. Uncertainties over external support also affected the duration of the building programme: while it seemed reasonable to hope that from June 1960, once the amalgamation had been accomplished, progress would have been relatively swift, government enthusiasm for providing financial support was already waning.

This caused the infant British Aircraft Corporation (BAC) to make do with a series of smaller design contracts or finance the project from its own resources. Progress was also seriously hampered by the hierarchy of committees appointed by the Ministry of Aviation, which included officials lacking in the required technical expertise who proved unduly slow to give their approvals.

The supersonic TSR2, expected to be all things to all men. (Farnborough Air Sciences Trust)

Yet whatever the financial penalties and other impediments, with such an advanced plane cost increases were inevitable. In 1960, the Ministry of Aviation recognised this: while it decided on a submission for the TSR2's development programme at an estimated £62 million, it made it subject to a possible extra amount of £25 million.[4] However brilliant its design, TSR2 was undoubtedly over-specified, a situation that was bound to bring major cost overruns and make it financially unviable unless a major export order could help reduce the costs of its individual airframes.

In reality, the chances of this happening were never high, for the aircraft seemed too complex for most countries and the United States was about to produce its own rival in the form of the swing-wing F-111.

In such circumstances it must have come as a pleasant surprise when Australia emerged as a serious would-be purchaser. It had, hitherto, bought British and with its Canberra bombers nearing the end of their lives, an all-weather strike and reconnaissance aircraft appeared the ideal solution for Australia's far-ranging defence concerns, including Indonesia and Southeast Asia.

An order for TSR2 appeared to offer advantages for both countries and the Australian Chief of the Defence Staff, Air Chief Marshal Scherger, was sent to London to meet his opposite number, Lord Mountbatten, to discuss his country's plans for purchase.

During their conversations Mountbatten unforgivably suggested to his no doubt surprised guest that TSR2 was likely to be abandoned and that the RAF would probably opt for the Royal Navy's Buccaneer instead. This was bad enough but when a subsequent Australian evaluation team visited Britain to consider the possible timings of delivery dates[5] it discovered the British government had still not made a definite offer to supply the plane.

Following such mixed signals and because of Australia's growing belief in establishing closer ties with America, the country decided on the F-111, which the Americans were marketing energetically. Despite last-minute attempts by Britain to reverse the decision, the opportunity to sell TSR2 to Australia had been lost. In fact the advantages provided by the F-111 proved below expectations, with Australia receiving it some six years later than planned at a cost almost three times above the original estimate.

Whatever the circumstances, Australia's withdrawal meant the entire burden of TSR2's development and purchase fell upon the British taxpayer. With Britain's continuing balance-of-payments difficulties and unexpected fatigue problems arising with the V-bombers, it was vital that the TSR2's construction programme should not exceed its latest cost projection and keep to schedule.

Blackburn Buccaneer – no replacement for TSR2. (Farnborough Air Sciences Trust)

F-111 during testing of B-83 nuclear bomb dummies. (US National Archives Licence No. 636 2287)

In the event, this proved unattainable. Although the components for its airframe were being assembled during November 1961, shortages of particular material (particularly titanium for bolts) were already delaying progress, and a lack of communication between the Ministry of Aviation and BAC meant that news of delays at the subcontractors did not reach BAC for weeks or months after the problems surfaced.[6] As a result, by March 1962, production of the first airframe had slowed, with progress on some of its jigs up to five months behind schedule and most of the equipment needed to make it up almost nine months behind schedule (delays that came to be replicated with the second and third aircraft). In extenuation, in 1963 the British weather played a malign part, with the coldest winter since 1795.

In such circumstances there seemed no prospect of the first prototype being delivered early that year. By May 1965, however, the situation had improved and by August the construction of the first aeroplane was well advanced, although its first flight date had been put back to January 1964, with the plane's initial release for RAF service now scheduled for October 1966. When January 1964 came and went without a flight, BAC's managing director, George Edwards, assumed personal control. His major changes included putting Freddy Page in control of the plane's construction and instituting a system of value engineering designed to bring about cost reductions. In spite of an unexpected problem with the selected aluminium–lithium alloy, which was found to fracture badly when large stresses were applied to it, the first aircraft – XR219 – was complete by the beginning of March 1964, although it was immediately dismantled for transportation to Boscombe Down where there were superior runway facilities. Unfortunately its reassembly took longer than expected and the plane's taxiing tests were repeatedly deferred due to problems with engine development. By this time, although the second aircraft was complete the programme's misfortunes continued when it was damaged when it fell off its lorry on arrival at Boscombe Down.

After a summer of negative publicity things improved markedly with TSR2's first flight taking place on 27 September 1964, and during the following month, with improved arrangements being agreed for transferring the final assembly of other airframes from Weybridge to Samlesbury near Preston.

Even so, as author Damien Burke concluded, these came too late to redeem a most serious situation where:

Delays, poor management (at all levels from subcontractors through to BAC and onward to the Ministry of Aviation and beyond), development problems and an underestimation of the complexity of the overall weapons system had all conspired to raise the development costs to previously unheard of levels.[7]

Despite BAC's desperate efforts to get XR219 ready for its second flight, this did not take place until 31 December 1964, by which time three significant developments had already occurred that would affect the fate of TSR2: the RAF realised it could not afford it in the numbers already agreed; the Americans' own variable-wing sweep aircraft was close to making its first flight and a new cost-cutting British government had been elected.

It was crucial for TSR2 to reveal its unique capabilities, and in fact startling flight progress would be achieved with XR219.

In all, twenty-five flights took place between 27 September 1964 and 2 April 1965; by 6 February 1965 major problems with its undercarriage were largely solved and supersonic handling trials took place on the 22nd of that month. The evidence of the plane's first six flights enabled chief test pilot Roland Beamont to write triumphantly:

> The flying qualities in this configuration are as good or better than predicted in every case and it is without doubt the easiest high performance aircraft to land that I have flown. All six landings to date have been, we are told from the visual point of view, perfect ...[8]

By the end of the flight sequences all three of its test pilots were describing the handling of the plane as easy and pleasant.

At the beginning of April 1965 BAC had high hopes for the second aircraft – XR220 – to fly later in the month or at worst during early May (despite the mishap when it was being taken to Boscombe Down) and for the third – XR221 – to fly around June. Of the initial twenty aircraft, seventeen were well advanced.

All such activity was brought to an end when, on 6 April 1965, Harold Wilson's Chancellor of the Exchequer, James Callaghan, announced in his budget speech that the TSR2 programme had been cancelled and orders had been sent out to stop all test programmes and destroy all the construction rigs.

More than half a century later the cancellation of TSR2 can be viewed in a more considered fashion, including the part played by Denis Healey, arguably the most influential of the major figures involved.

One can, for instance, dismiss the early widely held conviction that the cancellation came like a bolt from the blue. From as early as 1962 the Treasury had been voicing grave concerns, and on 15 November 1963 Sir Alec Douglas-Home, the Conservative Prime Minister, had written to the Ministries of Aviation and Defence, saying, 'I am rather troubled about this project. It seems to be turning out to be considerably more expensive than we thought ...

Ought we to have … a new look at the whole venture and satisfy ourselves that it is still an integral element in our defence programme?'[9]

By the first half of 1964 the Air Ministry had begun to ask serious questions about 'whether in fact the RAF programme could bear the cost of TSR2 and about its effectiveness in terms of performance with regard to its conventional strike capability at night or in bad weather'.[10] In view of its ballooning costs, the Air Ministry even went as far as to ask the Ministry of Aviation for a fixed price contract.

In any event, it was no secret that if Labour won the general election of October 1964 it would review defence expenditure with a view to bringing down the total budget of £2,400 million to £2,000 million at 1964 prices. With so much defence spending allocated to personnel for their necessary pay, accommodation, pensions and training, equipment was bound to face especial scrutiny, with the RAF's proposed new aeroplanes, the P.1154 replacement for the Hunter, the HS.681 jet transport and TSR2 – where the chances of containing its costs, let alone reducing them, were minimal – certain to be at the top of Labour's hit list.

By the end of 1964 there were growing rumours that TSR2 was due for cancellation, although the possibility of large-scale redundancy in the aviation industry was far from palatable for a Labour government depending on large support from the trades unions.

In 1997 an in-depth study was carried out by Sean Straw and John W. Young about the deep differences of opinion in the Cabinet at this time, which featured in contemporary issues of *The Times*.[11] Although Labour's majority was only four, Harold Wilson talked confidently of both modernising British industry and maintaining the country's global presence, but while TSR2 undoubtedly bolstered Britain's technical superiority and promised to help the country maintain a world role, it was quickly seen as a possible victim of Labour's declared economy drive on defence. This was fuelled by the understanding that although Britain spent a large proportion of its R & D budget on advanced military aircraft projects, they only produced a paltry 2.5 per cent of British exports.

Even so in September 1964, prior to the election, *The Times* was still writing about the government's full confidence in TSR2 and of Denis Healey being widely mistaken in his estimation of its ballooning costs. Although it acknowledged that Sir Alec Douglas-Home was fully conscious of the cost overruns and had said 'that whether in the cold mathematics of cost and effectiveness it will be a justifiable project is another matter' the newspaper emphasised that its development had reached a stage where it was unlikely to be abandoned even if a Labour Party should come to power in October.[12]

The TSR2 demonstrates its performance in flight. (Royal Aeronautical Society/National Aerospace Library)

Whatever Douglas-Home's confidence in TSR2 continuing, when Healey became Defence Secretary in the new Labour administration he quickly showed his future intent by requesting a breakdown of aircraft requirements and their costs. Along with other key ministers and the military Chiefs of Staff he attended a weekend conference at Chequers to determine future defence strategy, where the Ministry of Aviation under Roy Jenkins brought the cost estimates of the three major aeroplane programmes HS.681, P.1154 and TSR2 to be considered against possible American replacements. At this stage, despite its high costs, the gathering still appeared to believe that TSR2 would be successfully completed, although it was agreed to make further enquiries about the costs and capabilities of its American rival, the F–111.

As a consequence, on 6 December 1964, Healey and other ministers flew to Washington for discussions with the US Defence Secretary Robert McNamara, where Healey and McNamara subsequently had separate talks about a possible preferential deal for the purchase of the F–111. After Healey flew home he secretly sent a group of Ministry officials under Air Marshal Sir Christopher Hartley to discuss the technical details and costs of F–111 with the Americans. They told the delegation that they expected the F–111's first flight to be quite soon, although their plane was unquestionably behind the

Denis Healey. (National Portrait Gallery)

TSR2's development, which *The Times* reported was flying again and proving easy to land.[13] The paper observed that Healey had set up a study of air power for all three British armed services.

By the opening of 1965 opinion at the Air Ministry also appeared to have moved in favour of replacing TSR2 with the F-111, although the American plane was considered less capable. On 15 January the debate about the TSR2's future both broadened and intensified when senior figures from the aircraft industry and the unions met Harold Wilson at Chequers. The Prime Minister seemingly gave little away, being most concerned about how to mitigate the effects of cancellation if it had to come. During the discussions, Frank Cousins speaking as both a trade union leader and Minister of Technology, voiced his concerns over cuts in military aircraft and their effects on employment, workers' morale and the export trade.

Prior to the Chequers get-together *The Times* still voiced its belief that the fate of the country's three main military aircraft remained in the balance, but on the succeeding day it must have suspected that opinion might have been moving towards cancellation for it sternly warned about cuts to the aircraft industry for 'the reduction to a shadow of its former self of an industry in which Britain is one of the world's leaders in order to find room for further welfare plans or simply to bolster home production would be unforgivable'.[14][15]

During the next few days, although *The Times*' articles reported the continuing debate over TSR2 and the other aircraft programmes, it assured its readers that no decisions would be taken on its future for a week or two.[16]

Also on 15 January, TSR2 and the other aircraft projects came up for discussion by ministers in the Defence and Overseas Policy Committee (OPD). There Healey made his pitch, arguing strongly for all three aircraft to be replaced by American ones on the grounds of achieving savings of £600 million to £800 million over ten years. He stressed that the impact of the purchases on the country's balance of payments would be reduced because Robert McNamara required no substantial payments for three years and had agreed to use Rolls-Royce engines in the planes as well as undertaking offset purchases of British military goods. As for the effect on the British aircraft industry, Healey somewhat naively argued that even with the cancellation of all three aircraft it would still be larger than France's.

In contrast, Harold Wilson was much more concerned about the effects of cancelling TSR2, which he believed was the most vital project for the aircraft industry and maintained that there were good industrial and social reasons for considering the situation further. He asked Healey and Jenkins to come to a consensus about the extent of the savings from buying the F-111 and decide how the aviation industry could cope with the possible cancellations.

At a second meeting of the OPD a week later no agreement had been reached about the cancellations, although concerns were voiced about their likely effects on employment within the aircraft industry and on the continuing need to export civil airliners. In a further complication, on 23 January, *The Times* and other newspapers reported enthusiastically on the success of TSR2's low-speed flight tests and made no reference to possible cancellations.

Even so, the mood of the next OPD meeting that took place six days later was decidedly different. This recommended the cancellation of both the P.1154 and HS.681 and the purchase of American Phantoms and Hercules in their place, with Healey pressing for the additional replacement of TSR2 by the F-111. The cost of TSR2, which was put at some 30 per cent higher than the F-111, gave powerful support to his arguments, while on 28 January the aircraft's champions had suffered a setback when under heavy static-load testing its wing suffered an early failure.

During the meeting Jenkins floated the unlikely possibility of cost savings for TSR2's R&D through co-operation with Europe rather than America. In its favour he cited the Concorde project, which had been confirmed with France the previous month. In the event this provided no immediate help for TSR2, with the cost of the Concorde's undertaking bound to increase financial pressures on the Treasury.

On 1 February 1965 the Cabinet approved the recommendations of the OPD towards the cancellation of the P.1154 and HS.681, and Wilson told his ministers that TSR2 presented a most difficult problem due to its mushrooming costs and with the American F-111 still at the early development stage. He acknowledged, however, that a decision was required within two months; according to Healey, Wilson let slip to him at the time that he intended to smuggle the cancellation into the Chancellor's Budget speech in April.[17] Those present were also made aware of attempts to cut TSR2's expenditure by getting the manufacturers to give fixed cost levels and persuade the Ministry of Aviation to accept fewer roles for the aircraft – although there was a feeling that these initiatives had probably come two or three years too late.

Whatever hostile arguments were being marshalled against TSR2, Jenkins continued to reassure the manufacturers that the project was not yet dead, while BAC continued to publicise the plane's exciting capabilities through its fast-developing flying tests. These were so successful that on 23 February, *The Times* joined other newspapers in reporting that the plane handled like a fighter both at supersonic speeds and in turbulence.

On 29 March a further OPD meeting was again dominated by the future of the TSR2. If it were to be cancelled, the possibility was raised about another British aircraft – such as the Buccaneer – replacing it rather than the American F-111. Its findings were reported to the full Cabinet on 1 April, where two long meetings followed.

By now Healey was determined to get his way. At the initial morning session a majority of ministers favoured cancelling TSR2 without taking an option on the F-111 – despite Healey producing an array of statistics arguing that the American option would save £28 million over thirteen years.[18] Healey refused to take the decision, insisting on a second Cabinet meeting the same day, by which time he believed a number of members would be likely to want things brought to a speedy conclusion.

In the interval he contacted Robert McNamara about keeping open the favourable conditions of purchasing the F-111, even if the commitment to buy was delayed. McNamara agreed and undertook to keep the price of an improved F-111 at the original level. In spite of what appeared a most generous American offer, as midnight approached there were still ten ministers arguing against Healey's solution as opposed to the twelve for it. It was not until 12.30 a.m. that the balance of opinion finally came round to Healey's proposition, namely cancellation followed by an option on the F-111, with only six ministers still standing out against it.

The result was that, on 6 April – as Wilson had planned – the announcement about the cancellation was made during James Callaghan's budget speech. The expected news was heard with widespread resignation, but when Healey attempted to make an additional statement it caused uproar because, by tradition, budget debates only allowed financial decisions to be discussed. Healey maintained that his subject was financial and he informed the House about the £357 million option on the American F-111A and about carrying out part of TSR2's commitments with Buccaneers or Phantoms.

On the following day he confirmed that the Americans had offered the F-111A at less than half the price of TSR2. The day after, in an article entitled, 'The End of TSR2', *The Times* presciently reminded its readers that the most serious aspect of the decision concerned the future of the British aircraft industry.[19]

The government made sure there was no going back on the decision. Although the RAF and Ministry of Aviation proposed further flights to test the equipment of the TSR2's prototypes, Callaghan not only ordered the jigs destroyed but the prototypes to be cannibalised, although in fact two specimens still exist, XR220 at the RAF Museum at Cosford and XR222 at the Imperial War Museum at Duxford.[20]

More than half a century later the high emotions associated with the cancellation of TSR2 have subsided and we can come to more considered conclusions about a subject that caused so much furore and bitterness at the time.

In the first place, despite the powerful folklore, there was never any question of TSR2's cancellation coming out of the blue. By 1964 its massive cost overruns and repeated delays had led to it becoming the centre of heated political controversy among Britain's two main political parties, who wrangled over it during the October 1964 General Election.[21] The Conservatives generally believed in continuing with it despite the escalating costs, while Labour was more open to the possibility of Healey's solution of scrapping it in favour of purchasing the rival US F-111, with the aim of saving the British taxpayer many millions of pounds.

However, when the new Labour government took up office it came to a fuller realisation about the seriousness of killing off such a highly advanced, multirole aircraft and the deleterious effects on those involved with the aviation industry. In the government's early weeks the arguments continued during a flurry of pre-budget and ministerial meetings where, contrary to the assertions of Stephen Hastings, to many of those taking part TSR2 was far more than 'a Tory thing upon which a wicked government was spending large sums of money which they preferred to see put into socialist things'.[22]

MPs generally believed the building of advanced aircraft in Britain was worth continuing with to preserve national security.

That they eventually changed their minds, as they did, was due in the main to the redoubtable Denis Healey, whose powerful and persuasive arguments eventually prevailed in favour of the F-111. In his memoirs he alluded to 'my decision to cancel the TSR2', and his actions after becoming Defence Secretary were consistent with his earlier attacks on the aeroplane, where he scaldingly put down its champions with the taunt, 'We are not here to support over-grown mentally retarded schoolboys.'[23]

Fellow minister Barbara Castle had no doubt about his aims and methods at the time, alluding to him as 'a brilliant and ruthless operator ... not too scrupulous about drowning opposition with a flood of expertise, whose validity we were not equipped to refute'.[24] His approach was certainly in marked contrast to that of Premier Harold Wilson, who could always be relied upon to leave all options open.[25]

Healey was never reluctant to court controversy and he remains an enigmatic figure to the present day. An undoubted intellectual heavyweight with a double first in classics from Oxford with a lifelong love of classical music and poetry, he was never disposed to court favour with the rank and file of his party. Once the cultured hedonist, the war had a profound effect making him determined to seize the opportunities that life gave him. As a major in the Royal Engineers he had apparently come under prolonged and sustained fire both as a beach master during the Anglo-US landings at Anzio and in later operations, and the memories of lost friends stayed with him for life. Such experiences helped him immeasurably when, as Secretary of State for Defence, he needed to establish relationships with the three service heads and their staffs.

Healey apparently amazed his wife, Edna, with his continuing determination and awesome reserves of energy when as a right-centrist he battled for the soul of the Labour Party during long and bitter battles against left-winger Anthony Wedgwood Benn. During the exchanges he came to be reckoned as the greatest 'duffer up' of all who, with his analytic powers and command of language, could strip an opponent bare, while in his party he was known to remain aloof with those he believed lacked his mental powers and vision.[25] Jim Callaghan, for instance, saw him as a lone wolf who seemed to prefer a carapace to cover his essential beliefs.[26]

When such an individual set himself on a path of action his opponents' targets were undoubtedly vulnerable. On becoming Secretary of State for Defence he considered cuts were essential and to him the most logical solution was to cancel the complicated and expensive pursuit of advanced aircraft, notably TSR2, and opt for American substitutes that were undoubtedly cheaper. Intent on winning the argument, one would expect him to be less aware about the effects it was likely to have on the British aircraft industry, still suffering from the effects of the measures imposed by Duncan Sandys in 1957. In any case, by the 1960s Sandys' plans to save defence costs by replacing manpower with weaponry were beginning to unravel, with costs increasing faster than the rate of inflation.

What defence had TSR2 against such a formidable enemy? As a multirole aircraft system it was expected to save the costs of individual systems, while offering full operational capability. In reality, the penalty of its multifarious capabilities was the need to breach the known barriers of technology, something not only complicated but beyond the maximum financial costs for the RAF budget at the time.

Even so, if it had come into production quickly enough, such an outstanding aircraft might still have confounded its critics. This was made impossible by the Conservative government's decision to use its construction as a way to force through mergers and takeovers to streamline the aviation industry. The union, for instance, of airframe manufacturers Vickers-Armstrong and English Electric, with their quite different traditions, required them to combine their separate preliminary designs and share in TSR2's construction work, with the rear fuselage assembled at English Electric's Warton plant in Lancashire and the front assembled by Vickers-Armstrong at Weybridge, Surrey. After being joined together at Weybridge, the first airframes had to be transported by road to Boscombe Down in Wiltshire.[27]

A wide number of other contractors were needed to develop the aircraft's multiple navigation, autopilot and weapons aiming systems: Elliott Automation for automatic flight control, Ferranti for its navigation/attack system, EMI for the sideways-looking radar, Cossor for the identification friend or foe system, and Plessey and Marconi for radio and general avionics. The integration of so many different systems inevitably took longer than anticipated, although most delays occurred with the engines.[28]

All this meant there was no chance of producing it on time, whereas the advanced American F-111 did not appear to have the same initial problems and offered a cheaper alternative; as we now know, it too suffered from long delays before coming into service.

In retrospect there was, in fact, an alternative choice of construction: if English Electric had been the senior partner in the consortium with Vickers-Armstrong it was likely to have proceeded with its P.17A aircraft, possessing terrain-following radar and V/STOL capability if lesser range and speed than

TSR2. Powered by a standard Bristol Siddeley Olympus engine, it could have been flying as a prototype by 1963, well before either the TSR2 or F-111. It wasn't progressed and neither was a submission by English Electric and Short for a relatively simple aircraft with a separate VTOL lifting platform.[29] As a result, Healey's relentless campaign prevailed.

With the cancellation of TSR2 and British aviation's two other major military aircraft projects in favour of American alternatives, Britain's production of major military aircraft ended (except for the relatively unconsidered Harrier) and the path was opened for collaborative programmes that, however successful, would depend on foreign partners. Ironically, in spite of the great advantages to Healey of his agreement with Robert McNamara over the purchase of the F-111, this too fell victim to the ending of the country's east of Suez defence liabilities.

Because he had persuaded the RAF to cancel the TSR2 by guaranteeing the F-111 in its place, Healey was apparently on the point of resigning, although in the end he decided against it, remarking later that, 'I would have found it impossible to justify to the Party or the Public by resigning over the cancellation of the F-111.'[30]

In his autobiography, Healey wrote with more than a flash of defiance and pride that, 'I imagine historians will best remember my six years at the Ministry of Defence for the liquidation of Britain's military role outside Europe, an anachronism which was essentially a legacy from our nineteenth century empire.'[31]

Among aviation enthusiasts he might best be remembered for virtually ending Britain's independent aircraft industry and destroying what might have been its best plane ever. Yet while Healey was the formidable figure bent on demolition, it was the decision to end Britain's east of Suez military liabilities and the parlous state of the country's finances that made the cancellation of TSR2 near inevitable.

As for his remark about it being an anachronism, the turn of history's dice during the later twentieth century brought renewed requirements for advanced multirole aircraft in new conventional conflicts. What Healey ensured was that, with the exception of the brilliant Harrier, the British aircraft industry would never again play a sole role in supplying them.

BRITISH HELICOPTERS: SETTLING FOR LICENSING AND JOINT VENTURES

In 1971 Sergei Sikorsky gave an address to the RAeS on behalf of his famous father Igor on 'Sixty Years of Flying' that emphasised the unique characteristics of the helicopter as 'the only vehicle yet devised by man' that gives you unlimited freedom of transportation without the need for airfield runways.[1] Writing thirty years later with the knowledge of the impact made by V/STOL aircraft, British defence commentator Matthew Uttley was still able to point out the helicopter's continuing progress, which had turned it into a major form of aviation technology and which 'facilitated important evolutions in battlefield and naval operations, making it a key element in modern warfare'.[2] He might equally have mentioned its impressive number of civilian applications.

As a concept the rotorcraft captured the imagination of the earliest air pioneers, featuring during the 1480s in Leonardo da Vinci's well-known sketch of a screw-like machine that he believed when turned swiftly enough would spiral into the air. Three hundred years later the idea would surface in Britain through the more empirical experiments of the so-called British father of flight, George Cayley, who in 1809 flew a small toy helicopter powered by elastic band before progressing in 1843 to his convertiplane model. It featured side by side contra-rotating rotor arrangements, where for its propulsion Cayley experimented with an unsatisfactory gunpowder motor.

As with orthodox fixed-wing aircraft, the full realisation of rotary vehicles hinged upon a viable power source. Although in 1888 Italian inventor Enrico Forlanini used steam power for an unmanned helicopter to take off vertically and hover for some twenty seconds, it was not until after the First World War

– with the advent of internal combustion engines – that such craft would fly with any reliability.

The first successful flight by a rotorcraft took place on 9 January 1923 at Getafe aerodrome, near Madrid, under the direction of Spanish nobleman and air pioneer Juan de la Cierva, who by the age of 18 had already constructed kites and gliders. Assisted by other young enthusiasts, he had drawn up plans for a three-engine aeroplane that – partly due to pilot error – crashed and was destroyed. Cierva rightly decided that the basic cause of the crash was the aeroplane's inability to fly both slowly and safely, which led him to construct an autogiro that did not need a large fixed wing to rise off the ground.[3]

Cierva's hybrid aircraft was pulled through the air by a propeller like a conventional fixed-wing aircraft, although it was sustained in flight by an overhead rotor whose blades turned through the action of the air flowing through them (by autorotation or windmilling). Distinct from a helicopter rotor, which is power-driven and gains its propulsion by being tilted forward, the key development of the Cierva Autogiro was the direct take-off.[4]

Following the failure of his first three experimental models, Cierva gave his rotor blades more flexibility by installing joints at their bases to make them automatically self-adjusting to the stresses of flight, upon which he flew successfully.

Cierva Autogiro. (Farnborough Air Sciences Trust)

Britain became involved with the new technology when in 1925 Cierva brought his C.6 to Farnborough, where it was demonstrated to the Air Ministry. He was invited to continue his work in this country and in 1926 founded the Cierva Autogiro Company. Upon receiving financial support from the Scottish industrialist James G. Weir, and with Avro supplying the chassis, the first British autogiro was built. Work proceeded on refining the aircraft, with manufacturing licences sold to France, Germany and the United States.

In 1928 Cierva demonstrated his autogiro's reliability over a journey of some 4,800km within the UK. He then flew his C.8 across the English Channel to Paris and on to Spain, where he toured the country giving flying demonstrations. Later in the same year Cierva, went to the United States, where he was greeted by a fleet of four American-built machines. By 1930 the autogiro was riding the crest of a wave and by 1932 pioneer British airman Alan Cobham incorporated one into his fleet of aircraft giving public air shows across Britain.

With the Cierva Company based in the UK the British aircraft industry acquired a sound knowledge of rotor technology and British manufacturers built gyroplanes under licence, two of which were acquired by the Air Ministry in its hunt for a better air observation platform (AOP) capability.

Cierva had high ambitions for his craft, which included installing autogiro parking spaces in city centres, but all these ended in 1936 when he was killed in a crash involving a conventional aircraft at Croydon airport. In any event, by now, other pioneers had taken advantage of the aerodynamic advances achieved by Cierva and work was commencing on helicopters with powered rotors that could genuinely hover. In February 1938 the first (single-seat) helicopter, the German Focke-Wulf Fw 61, flew in the hands of the famed female test pilot Hanna Reitsch inside Berlin's huge Deutschlandhalle.[5] Among those watching were Charles Lindbergh and Igor Sikorsky, who in September 1939 flew his own VS-300 helicopter.

Whatever the German and US initiatives, British technical capabilities with rotorcraft were state of the art, with the British Weir W.6 arguably the most advanced helicopter prototype under construction, while the Austrian Raoul Hafner – who came to England in 1932 – ranked with Cierva and Sikorsky as a helicopter visionary. In 1935 Hafner demonstrated an advanced system of cyclic pitch control with his AR III gyroplane. In view of such developments it seemed very likely that Britain would remain at the leading edge of future helicopter development.

Such expectations were halted when in July 1940, following Dunkirk, the British government decided to suspend indefinitely all indigenous helicopter work (including the Weir W.6), divert its workforce elsewhere and rely on helicopter technology being developed by the US. The Americans were alerted to Britain's likely needs and British design and development knowledge was put at their disposal. With the threats to the UK at this time it seemed a justifiable decision despite the relatively limited financial and manpower commitments needed to continue work on rotorcraft. In the event it turned out to be as unfortunate for the indigenous British helicopter industry, as the one suspending civilian aircraft construction would prove for the industry as a whole. The subsequent decision by the Ministry of Aircraft Production (MAP) to give priority to other aviation projects was made considerably easier because of the general view within the RAF at this time that 'there was no demonstrable specific need for aircraft of the helicopter type'.[6]

In consequence, US firms gained a significant lead in helicopter design, development and manufacturing capacity.[7] While in Britain the RAF limited its wartime use of Cierva autogiros to help calibrate a high-level radar station, it also authorised the construction of Rotachutes that would be developed by Raoul Hafner, who had by now acquired British nationality. These were the lightest, man-carrying rotorcraft ever flown, but although twenty were built they never became operational.

In contrast, the Royal Navy emerged as pacesetters in the use of rotorcraft – especially helicopters – for anti-submarine operations in the Atlantic and for its extensive search and rescue (SAR) work, sending some of its pilots for training in the US on the new Sikorsky YR-4 helicopter. This was under-standable for in America at this time, pioneers such as Frank N. Piasecki, Arthur M. Young (Bell Aircraft), Stanley Hiller Jnr (Hiller Aircraft) and Igor Sikorsky were all developing working helicopters, although the Sikorsky company was the first to place them in volume production before the end of war.

As early as 14 September 1939, Sikorsky's first tethered flight in his VS-300 helicopter had revealed its exciting possibilities, and on 13 May 1940 invited guests looked on in amazement as Igor flew 'backwards, sideways, up and down, and even turned on a spot'.[8] By 10 January 1941 his prototype remained aloft for twenty-five minutes (still considerably short of the French Brequet Giroplane some six years before), but on 6 May 1941, Sikorsky seized the lead in worldwide development with a flight of one hour thirty-two minutes.[9]

He followed his VS-300 with the much-improved Sikorsky YR-4 (to which the British Royal Navy was attracted), which he delivered to the US Army on 3 July 1943. Sikorsky's smaller YR-4B was subsequently taken up by the US Navy following a request from the Royal Navy for 150 to help in its campaign against U-boats. The British order triggered an increase in resources

Saunders-Roe Skeeter. (Farnborough Air Sciences Trust)

to assist Sikorsky develop and produce his helicopters, but US forces were given priority and the Royal Navy eventually received forty-five YR-4Bs late in 1944, which it named the Gadfly, when the U-boat menace was declining.

With the end of the war in sight, British interest in rotorcraft activities revived with companies such as Auster, Bristol, Cierva, Fairey, Hunting, Percival, Saunders-Roe, Servotec, Handley Page and Westland all seeking to get involved.

In spite of the impressive progress in America, earlier British dominance in Cierva-produced autogyros appeared to offer its reformed industry good chances of success. This seemed apparent when by 1948 the Cierva Company had made flight tests with two prototypes: the W.14 Skeeter two-seater; and the Air Horse, the world's largest helicopter, with an all-up weight of 17,500lb.[10] However, in 1951 Saunders-Roe took over the Cierva interests at Eastleigh, including the Skeeter, development of which will be explained later. In the case of the Air Horse, after completing its initial flight-testing it crashed during a further training flight with the loss of three lives. Its development was discontinued after the withdrawal of financial support from the Ministry of Supply, which believed that a slower pace towards a larger payload was advisable.[11]

During the early post-war years British helicopter companies not only had to work with an overcautious and parsimonious Ministry of Supply but also with the RAF, which maintained its wartime priorities for strategic rather than tactical airpower, and had shown lukewarm interest. This contrasted with the USAF, which as part of the US Army came rapidly to appreciate the range of tactical opportunities offered by rotary-wing aircraft.

As a consequence, large capital resources were made available for US helicopter production through development funds, amounting to $265,000 for the Sikorsky XR-4 helicopter, with authority for Sikorsky's officials to ask for up to 3 million for the special buildings and machinery needed to construct its R-5.[12]

Apart from receiving levels of funding unmatchable in war-torn Britain, the American helicopter industry was able to move forward to consider the merits of consolidating its design expertise – something not seriously considered in Britain until the mid-1950s.[13] Moreover, while the British looked towards the US for open co-operation, by 1943 the American administration had taken steps to protect the commercial interests of the emerging US helicopter industry by stemming any claims the British might have to such American wartime developments.[14] To make matters worse, British politicians proved far less supportive of their infant helicopter industry than American ones. They received serious warnings from J. Weir, pre-war chairman of G. & J. Weir Ltd, that the UK was being left behind by the active interest of American firms in post-war markets, together with strong messages that the UK was losing ground from Wing Commander Reggie Brie, one time flying manager of the Cierva Autogiro Co. Ltd, who went to the US towards the end of the war to help purchase helicopters for the Royal Navy. In spite of the warnings, the politicians displayed little urgency.

In fact, civil servants in the Ministry of Aircraft Production proved unbelievably laid back about the likelihood of the Americans establishing a comprehensive lead in helicopter design, persisting in the belief 'that any threat to post-war British Commercial helicopter activities was marginal and did not require an immediate programme of development'.[15]

Whatever advantages the US might gain, it was the task of the new Ministry of Supply (which had replaced the Ministry of Aircraft Production) to help establish structures through which UK helicopter procurement could be carried out. The Air Ministry asked it to place three distinct types of helicopters on its research and development programme for 1946–47: a two-seat air observation post (AOP), an eight-to-ten-seater for transport and general service and a flying crane with a 10-ton lift capability.[16] The request was made in the full expectation of a buy British purchasing policy leading to the production and sale of helicopters, making the UK self-sufficient in helicopter design and able to bid for potential future export markets.[17]

In line with such expectations, the Brabazon Committee received preliminary specifications for helicopters to join its classes for future aircraft, although the chances of British helicopters succeeding both in Britain and overseas would, of course, depend on the abilities of the firms involved in their construction.

By 1947 four British firms were actively engaged in helicopter development; the Bristol Aeroplane Company, Fairey Aviation, Cierva Autogiro Co. and Westland Aircraft. In British fashion, they took quite different approaches: Bristol decided to develop helicopters in house that generally conformed to the configuration established by Sikorsky; Fairey's helicopter division opted for compound helicopters to take advantage of both helicopter and autogiro designs, while Cierva viewed its participation in helicopter development as a continuation of its pre-war business, including work on Weir's W.6 helicopter.

Westland sought a different solution when, on 21 January 1947, it came to an agreement with Sikorsky for the licensed production of its four-seater S-51 helicopter, which could be manufactured and marketed anywhere but the US and Canada, thus giving the company the opportunity to produce such vehicles well in advance of the other indigenous makers.

As a result, during the three years 1947 to 1950 only Westland-licensed helicopters obtained production orders. By late 1948, when Bristol's Type 171 Sycamore was still far from complete and the Fairey Gyrodyne project remained at the development stage, Westland was able to meet the Royal Navy's requirement for heavier lift helicopters by securing orders for twelve license-built Sikorsky S-51s.

Orders followed from the Air Ministry because, whatever its previous reservations, during March 1949 the communist-inspired insurrection in Malaya brought an urgent need for helicopters to carry out casualty evacuation. With indigenous helicopters still unavailable, Westland was the only option as the other firms not only faced development time lags but suffered from adverse and convoluted financial arrangements within the War Office, where requests for funds for helicopters had to be conveyed through the Air Ministry. Due to the Air Council's view that helicopter R&D was of marginal importance compared with fixed-wing development, it proved reluctant to authorise expenditure from its procurement budget. As a result, between financial years 1946–47 and 1950–51 helicopter funding from the Ministry of Supply proved negligible 'with its total R&D Budget, remaining below 1 per cent of the total expenditure in each year'.[18]

Westland Dragonfly. (Farnborough Air Sciences Trust)

In contrast, Westland benefited from its rights to buy helicopters from Sikorsky, a firm that had already received significant financial allocations from the US authorities for technical innovations.

With such limited financial support the indigenous helicopter firms even had to consider whether certain technical developments would increase the chances of orders or not, while their inability to land early large-scale production orders meant that the largest British aero-engine manufacturers proved unwilling to enter the helicopter field, forcing British helicopter designers to rely on engine technology originally designed for fixed-wing aircraft.

Whatever the particular difficulties of the three other firms, Westland understandably did everything to strengthen its hand. It began by 'anglicising' Sikorsky's technical drawings so that every part became different from the original – including its engines – thus enabling the firm to provide so-called British-built helicopters. It also raised the capital to produce a batch of thirty Sikorsky S-51s as a private venture, thereby avoiding any objections from the Treasury over balance of payments issues. In any case with no other all-British alternative yet available, the Treasury faced the choice of buying Westland or spending its scarce dollars on buying US production helicopters off the shelf.

Westland progressed from obtaining production orders for 159 S-51s – whose anglicised version the Royal Navy called Dragonfly – via a general-purpose

Bristol Sycamore. (Farnborough Air Sciences Trust)

helicopter similar in weight to the Dragonfly that it named the Widgeon – to Sikorsky's larger eight-seat S-55, which the company named the Whirlwind, and which appeared to meet the specifications of the second type of helicopter required by the Air Ministry. In the process the firm gained know-how to further develop its own R&D ability: between 1953 and 1966 for instance, it built a total of 364 Whirlwinds, some seventy of which were for export customers.

Understandably, the other British manufacturers responded with major new initiatives of their own. In 1950 Hunting Percival, for instance, formed a helicopter division committed to producing jet-driven models that brought a serious technological challenge to Westland, for its first turbine-powered Whirlwinds were expected to come later.[19] Whatever such initiatives, with the indigenous manufacturers having to build their helicopters from scratch, a number of serious problems were virtually bound to arise.

This became evident with Bristol's Sycamore, a four-seat single-rotor helicopter designed by Raoul Hafner, who joined the company in 1944. Although its prototype first flew on 24 July 1947, the rotor disintegrated during a second attempt and it required a strengthened version. Although it received its first certificate of airworthiness on 25 April 1949, its move to production was relatively slow and it did not enter RAF service, in its standard HR.14 form, until April 1953. It proved an eventual success as 183

Westland Wessex. (Farnborough Air Sciences Trust)

Sycamores were produced in all, with the RAF becoming Bristol's largest customer. Due to the delays, its export orders were limited to just fifty for the Federal German Government, seven for the Royal Australian Navy and three for Belgium.

During the 1950s the RAF used the Sycamore in both Malaya and Cyprus along with Westland's Dragonfly, which had come into service during 1950. In Malaya the latter's performance proved much affected by the high temperature and humidity: when carrying out casualty evacuation it could only take one stretcher patient and then fly for just thirty minutes at 60mph.[20] Even so, on 1 June 1950 the Dragonfly was the first to be used on scheduled service for British European Airways, flying between Cardiff and Liverpool and then via Wrexham, but the service proved only moderately successful and it was terminated on 31 March 1951.

By 1953 Westland had strengthened its position through its contract for Sikorsky's S-55 (Whirlwind) and this, including its turbo-engined form, would gain 30 per cent of the total UK helicopter output between 1945 and 1960, with the primary demand coming from the Royal Navy.[21] The Navy used it for search and rescue and anti-submarine duties, although during its twenty-one-year life it saw service with the RAF in Malaya and Cyprus, while also serving with the Queen's Flight between 1958 and 1967.

Despite the Whirlwind's undoubted success, the Ministry of Supply attempted to support the indigenous manufacturers as well. Apart from Bristol's Types 171 and 173 (designed by Hafner) and Saunders-Roe's Skeeter light helicopter, it also sponsored the development of Bristol's torqueless rotor designs to help it catch up with the Americans. The policy enjoyed varied success. Although Hafner's Type 173, designed to meet the Air Ministry's requirement for a helicopter suitable for personnel and casualty evacuation, flew on 3 January 1952 and was the first tandem motor helicopter using two sets of Sycamore powerplants in a thirteen–sixteen-passenger layout, it was cancelled in 1956.

Bristol also spent a considerable time developing analogous models: the Type 191 for a Royal Naval ship-based general-purpose helicopter, the Type 192 for the RAF and Type 193 to Canadian specifications. Of these, the Type 193 was soon cancelled due to a Canadian economy drive and the Royal Navy cancelled the Type 191 in favour of Westland's version of Sikorsky's S-58, which, after being called the Wessex, became its main anti-submarine helicopter. The Wessex Mk1, fitted with twin Rolls-Royce Gnome gas turbines, entered service in 1961 and was immediately successful. It entered RAF service in January 1964, where it was used for troop carrying, search and rescue and for VIP transport with the Queen's Flight. Some 400 Wessex helicopters were produced and they would, in fact, remain in service until 2001.

Bristol Belvedere heavy-lift helicopter. (Farnborough Air Sciences Trust)

This left Bristol's Type 192 – again designed by Hafner – which first flew on 5 July 1958. Equipped with two 1,465hp gas turbine engines, it was the RAF's first twin-rotor heavy lift helicopter, capable of carrying eighteen fully equipped troops up to a capacity of 6,000lb, twenty-six of which were ordered. Named the Belvedere, it was used in all the RAF theatres of operation before being withdrawn from service in 1969. Its performance proved sound rather than spectacular, but after its withdrawal it was more than ten years before it was replaced in 1980 by Boeing's Chinook, an aircraft that had first flown in 1962 but offered a vastly improved performance.

Another indigenous project that reached production was Saunders-Roe's Skeeter light helicopter, on which design work had begun as early as 1947. This was originally constructed by Cierva but after being taken over by Saunders-Roe it used its own resources to complete the second and third prototypes. Following lengthy development and the installation of the de Havilland Gypsy Major 200 engine, sixty-four were ordered for the British Army and it was, in fact, the first helicopter to enter service with the newly formed Army Air Corps, for which seventy-seven were ordered. Deliveries commenced in the late 1950s, with six additional Skeeters ordered by the West German Army and four more for the West German Navy, making it the only Saunders/Saro helicopter to achieve a quantity overseas order.[22] It was withdrawn from German service in 1961 and its service with the Army Air Corps was limited to the United Kingdom and West Germany due to its poor hot-climate performance. The Skeeter replaced the fixed-wing Auster aircraft formerly used by the Army Air Corps and it was itself replaced by Saunders-Roe's improved Scout helicopter, which as the Westland Scout (following Westland's takeover of Saro) was delivered to the Army Air Corps during 1967 and 1968.[23]

The other notable Ministry-sponsored helicopter was Fairey's Type Y – known as the Fairey Rotodyne – which initially appeared to offer high hopes for the company's future. This was a large transport helicopter built in the late 1950s, which, although notably noisy, incorporated advanced features in design. Powered by two 300hp Napier Eland turboprops, its rotor was turned by pressure jets at the blade tips supplied with air from compressors driven by the engines. At sufficient height the Rotodyne was intended to convert into an autogiro with the rotor auto-rotating, the wings providing much of the lift and the turboprops driving propellers for forward propulsion.[24]

In early 1959 it succeeded in setting a world speed record over a 100km closed circuit of 190.9mph, but although BEA had declared an intention to buy thirty, it subsequently cancelled its order, following which Rolls-Royce (to which Napier had been amalgamated in 1961) withdrew support for its

Fairey Rotodyne. (Farnborough Air Sciences Trust)

Eland engine.[25] Official funding ended in February 1962, with the novel Rotodyne broken up towards the end of the year.

During the 1950s, the restricted nature of funding from the Ministry of Supply for the indigenous British firms, together with their more limited production opportunities, made it difficult for them to match American helicopter technology, let alone surpass it. American constructors also benefited from sharp increases in demand for their helicopters during the Korean War, where invaluable lessons were learned about their capabilities under extreme conditions and necessary modifications made. When on 27 July 1953 hostilities ended, the US Army owned no fewer than 1,000 helicopters, a total that by 1955 had risen to 1,200.[26] Their importance had become apparent because 'more than any other factor the helicopter reduced the death rates from battlefield injuries in Korea to the lowest point in the history of warfare, a rate less than half that suffered by wounded American troops in the Second World War'.[27] In the process light helicopters built by the Bell and Hiller companies evacuated more than 20,000 wounded, including British troops.

As for Sikorsky, although its S–52 (H–18) was not widely successful in Korea, the company's larger and more mobile S–55s (H–19s) with their impressive lift capacity, distinguished themselves in the war's final stages.

The growing importance of helicopters in Korea led Westland to request funding for the manufacture and in-house development of Sikorsky's S–52, S–56 and S-58. Although at a meeting held on 18 October 1953 the Ministry of Supply did not endorse the proposals, by early 1954 it would find itself facing the choice between getting into or getting out of the helicopter development field, and when in 1955 further reductions were made to its R&D estimates it had to withdraw its support from major indigenous helicopter programmes.[28] This meant phasing out funding for both Hunting Percival and Saunders-Roe, once its Skeeter project had been completed, with Bristol's Type 173 and its variants reclassified as civilian projects and funds already allocated to Westland's S-56 Westminster for financial year 1958–59 also being cancelled.

Although the Westminster programme did not prove immune to the financial crises affecting the British helicopter industry as a whole, the company's arrangements for the speedy acquisition of much-needed helicopters from Sikorsky and its shrewd decision to assemble them, using British components, not only enabled it to survive but to acquire a genuine design and development capability. By such means it came out as by far the best of the country's helicopter constructors and by 1960, after a series of takeovers, it had become Britain's sole helicopter design and manufacturing firm.[29]

Westland Sea King. (Farnborough Air Sciences Trust)

Like so many other aircraft projects following the Second World War, the indigenous British helicopter industry lost out to superior and better-funded American competition. Westland proved the exception by acknowledging US superiority through its licensing of Sikorsky's advanced helicopters and then anglicising and modifying them to build up its own expertise to a high level.

A notable instance of this came with the licensing of Sikorsky's large helicopter, the S-61 (to be called Sea King), which was some 72ft long with a 62ft, five-bladed main rotor. Westland's licence enabled it to use the machine's basic airframe and rotor head and make modifications to permit the use of an alternative British engine, the Rolls-Royce Gnome H1400 turboshaft.[30] The first production contract was announced on 27 June 1966 and the twin-engined Sea King was taken on by both the Royal Navy and the RAF and exported to West Germany, India, Norway, Egypt, Pakistan, Belgium and Australia. During 1968–90 Westland would build a total of 321 Sea Kings.

The company followed this with its second-generation, medium-sized, utility helicopter designed to meet a joint service requirement issued in June 1966 in which the British government wanted the company to collaborate with the French to build a range of helicopters to cover the needs of both the British and French forces.[31] The proposed helicopter would be called the Lynx where, contrary to the Sea King, its many new design features, including some that resulted from Saunders-Roe's research, put it apart from Sikorsky products.

On 17 May 1965 a memorandum of understanding was signed by the British and French governments by which three types of helicopters would be constructed. Apart from the Westland-led medium-sized Lynx, which in its two proposed versions was also considered for an armed reconnaissance role with the French Army and an anti-submarine warfare role with the French Navy, the French firm Aerospatiale was scheduled to design and build the Gazelle, a light observation helicopter, along with a larger transport helicopter, the Puma.[32] The agreement gave Westland a new design and production role and a guaranteed market. Through it the company was able to produce 70 per cent of the Lynxes, with the remainder being built by Aerospatiale. In the case of the French-designed Puma and Gazelle helicopters, Westland built forty-eight of the former for the RAF and 262 Gazelles, primarily for use by the British Army.

The Westland Lynx proved an outstanding helicopter, which attracted export orders from sixteen other nations, and it would distinguish itself during the 1982 Falklands War.

Westland Lynx. (Farnborough Air Sciences Trust)

Even so, in spite of Westland's undoubled achievements through its licensing of American technology and its later collaborative arrangements with France, it has to be acknowledged that during 1945–75 the indigenous British helicopter industry did not fully justify the high hopes raised by its re-establishment immediately after the war. The Royal Air Force and the British Army both carry some responsibility, with their early irresolution about the battlefield utility of helicopters, an attitude all the more unfortunate when the US armed forces came rapidly to appreciate their worth in Korea and especially in Vietnam, thus contributing hugely to the American helicopter industry becoming a world leader.

In this regard, distinguished soldier and defence analyst General Anthony Farrar-Hockley confirmed the RAF's emphasis on strategic airpower and its doubts about the helicopter's validity in a 'hot' war against Russian defences, and he also believed it was not until 1957, following the formation of the Army Air Corps, that the Army came to fully appreciate the wide uses of helicopters. He believed this resulted in a situation where, 'British helicopters and their service clients had the disadvantage that they were latecomers to the industry.'[33] He also considered that the Army expected too much of its helicopters, not only the fragile Skeeter but the Scout as well. More contentiously, Farrar-Hockley believed that the service's early ambivalent support contributed to the Lynx being late in delivery, underdeveloped and underpowered when deliveries began.[34]

Farrar-Hockley was by no means alone in his criticisms; air observer Raymond Prouty bemoaned the British helicopter industry's failure to produce an attack helicopter such as the Bell AH-1 (Huey) Cobra or the Hughes OH-6 Scout that the Americans used in Vietnam. He also pointed out Aerospatiale's remarkable later successes with helicopters, bringing orders from around the world.[35]

Because of the UK's fast-increasing requirements for civil helicopters with the North Sea oil industry and for roles such as rescue and evacuation one might reasonably have expected more initiatives in this field, too.

Whatever the reasons, including valid financial ones, it has to be acknowledged that despite the country's participation in the 1930s, during the early post-war years there appeared to be a lack of imagination, if not dereliction, towards helicopters in Britain. The first report of the Interdepartmental Helicopter Committee after the war, for instance, limited civil helicopters to 'the carriage of passengers' freight and mails between provincial towns and cities and for speedy and convenient connections between international airport and sea ports and the provinces', when by 1956 the American Bell company had seen its helicopters used in fifty-five countries for tasks such as fogging to kill insect pests, spraying to control weeds and parasites, dusting to increase crop yields, the inspection of power and pipe lines, for construction in rugged terrain, surveying for oil and minerals and providing patrol and executive transport, apart from their many military tasks. [36][37]

In 1966 Raoul Hafner talked bitterly about helicopters being seen by many in Britain in the late 1940s as a kind of Heath Robinson device of no particular significance, an observation repeated twenty years later by journalists Richard Gardner and Reginald Longstaff, who wrote that 'although it was for many years considered a relatively low priority, less in defence budget terms, the Falklands proved again that a military helicopter is probably the most important aircraft type in the services armoury'. [38][39]

For whatever reasons, following the Second World War the British establishment appeared to have a blind spot about the dramatic possibilities of helicopter technology in which it had participated earlier. Fortunately, the Westland company took the opportunity to gain the benefit of American advances and then collaborate with France to provide the British armed services with many of the helicopters they needed – if at the cost of superseding many of the exciting developments by the other indigenous firms that (prior to amalgamation) had struggled to create a distinctive and world-leading British helicopter industry.

PART 4

FLIGHTS FROM REALITY

12

CONCORDE: QUEEN WITHOUT AN EMPIRE

In the mid-1960s supporters of the British aircraft industry might well have wondered what sort of a future remained when cancellation of the two advanced military aeroplanes – the HS.681 freighter and the Hawker P.1127 supersonic vertical take-off fighter – was followed in April 1965 by that of the RAF's so-called flagship aircraft, the TSR2. A further blow came at the end of the year with the report of the government-appointed Plowden Committee with its bleak recommendations about not only reducing the scale but ending the national independence of new aircraft construction. In the circumstances it was fully understandable that queries should be raised about the individuals who made up the committee and their qualifications. Its potential critics could hardly have been reassured that its chairman was Lord Plowden, chairman of Tube Investments, rather than from an organisation with aviation connections, who on hearing that TSR2 was to be cancelled asked Prime Minister Harold Wilson to relieve him of his appointment and had to be persuaded to carry on.

Apart from the Conservative MP Aubrey Jones, who was not only a friend of Harold Wilson but a one-time Minister of Supply who previously had exercised authority over the aviation industry and who would produce a minority report against government ownership of it (while remaining in favour of up to 50 per cent government support for major civil projects), its members came from disparate non-aviation backgrounds, including banking, the trades unions, the oil industry and the Royal Navy.

Unsurprisingly, Plowden rejected the advice of the Royal Aeronautical Society to bring in a panel of its 'independent assessors' to help his committee come to its decisions, although he also declined the opportunity to travel around the country to see what actually took place in the aircraft factories.

This did not prevent his committee coming to fundamental and, to many, unwelcome conclusions about an independent British aircraft industry, one of which was that Britain should never again consider undertaking major new aviation projects on its own. This stemmed from its recommendation that Britain should take the initiative in arranging a conference of European aviation ministers with the object of formulating a common, long-term policy for aircraft manufacture and procurement in Europe.[1]

Plowden even went so far as to propose that 'no new British staff requirement for an aircraft or guided weapon system should be endorsed by the Ministry of Defence, until the views of our allies and the prospects of launching a co-operative project with them have been thoroughly explored', at the same time suggesting to the United States that it should remove all forms of discrimination against defence projects produced abroad.[2]

The committee favoured a reining in of what it saw as previous unrealistic and expensive ambitions, which it seemed to believe were more likely to be achieved through a measure of public shareholding in both BAC and Hawker Siddeley. It suggested that more stress should be put on research that could contribute to the more modest aircraft and weapons that the industry was likely to embark on in future, and on civil aircraft.[3]

Its final recommendation was that the government should set its research establishments a firm target for reducing their aeronautical activity. 'A reduction of 20 per cent in the present annual budget for intramural aerospace research and development, effected over about five years, is suggested.'[4]

Many in the aviation industry were horrified by such recommendations and on 17 February 1966 the Royal Aeronautical Society (whose earlier offer to help had been rejected) held a one-day conference on Plowden's findings, where feelings of both anger and betrayal were evident.

The conference chairman, Sir George Gardner, opened with the hope that it was not too late to re-establish a British initiative 'which will greatly ease many of the difficulties relating to finance and markets so depressingly commented upon in the Plowden Report'.[5][6] Contrary to Plowden, he declared he was clear beyond doubt that the government fully accepted the case for the UK having a substantial aircraft industry, both military and civil.[7]

He was followed by three other keynote figures, who while equally critical of Plowden, acknowledged that there had certainly been grave weaknesses in British aviation policy since the end of the war.

The first was Peter Masefield, who had acted as Secretary to the War Cabinet Committee on Planning for Post-war Civil Air Transport and who concluded that the Plowden Report 'just didn't get down to saying what should be done to get British aviation back on its feet in the world as we found it today'. He believed that what had been lacking since the war (with the exception of the Brabazon Committee) had been really adequate professional planning, and he corroborated the president's wish for a British Aerospace Master Plan.[8]

Masefield was followed by Henry Gardner, technical director of the British Aircraft Corporation, who voiced his disappointment with the attitude of the Plowden Committee and went on to propose the formation of teams to define the roles of the present and future aircraft industry.

The third, Professor Keith-Lucas, an aircraft designer who had worked on the design of the Short Stirling bomber and Short S.A.4 Sperrin jet bomber, highlighted the weakness of a system where responsibility for aviation was split between the Ministry of Aviation, the Treasury and the Ministry of Defence. He believed the present cult of amateurism inappropriate and recommended that the political parties and the civil service appoint professionals – trained in science and engineering – to high government office, where their latest experience and understanding could be used to best advantage.[9]

Peter Masefield conducting Winston Churchill and his wife on to an Airspeed Ambassador. (BAE Systems Heritage)

Unsurprisingly, during the discussion that followed virtually no blame was laid on the aircraft industry but on government policy and the Plowden Committee for its lack of expertise and despairing attitude. Individual delegates were more specific in their criticisms, with J.M.L. Reeve viewing the committee as yet another unsuccessful expensive bureaucratic exercise, where 'the government's antagonistic action for the past two years coupled with the apathy of the British nation have brought one of the most advanced technological industries in the world to its knees', and G.S. Henson forcibly pointing out its lack of analysis on the sort of increase in productivity one should get. [10] [11]

Summing up, the chairman rightly said the meeting had demonstrated members' anxiety for the problems that faced them. However, instead of announcing approaches to the government, he contented himself by saying that the RAeS would be summarising the points made and their conclusions for future use by the society. [12]

Most surprising of all, in spite of the conference's stated need for master plans and improved controls over research and funding, little or no concern had been expressed about a distinctly futuristic and potentially very expensive construction programme agreed with France for the supersonic airliner Concorde. While R. Evans alluded to it during the society's discussion period, this was in passing and he merely referred uncritically to Britain taking on a senior role with continental collaboration. [13]

The practice of separating Concorde, with its huge financial significance, from contemporary aviation was also evident with Plowden, which had confined its references to a single paragraph of its report. [14] It was brief and matter of fact, if not faintly dismissive, observing that the money needed and the risks entailed in developing this advanced project were so great that (unlike in the past) the manufacturers had not been willing to contribute to the development costs. It noted that the total British contribution towards developing and proving the aircraft was currently estimated at £140 million and arrangements had been made for a levy on sales of the production aircraft and spares. [15]

What the Plowden Report did not acknowledge was that the reasons for the supersonic aircraft project were exceptional: Harold Wilson had already attempted to cancel what promised to be an exceedingly expensive venture, but with no cancellation clause in Britain's agreement with France and the country requiring President de Gaulle's approval for its application to join the Common Market, the Prime Minister was forced into a continuing commitment.

Although the £140 million estimate was in fact set way too low, these were still unprecedented figures and whether or not they could be mitigated by a somewhat unrealistic levy on the finished aircraft and its spares, no mention was made by Plowden about the inevitable cost rises for a collaborative project that promised to prove by far the most expensive in British aviation history and was bound to impinge heavily on any later aircraft projections.

The Concorde programme had been launched a decade before, on 1 October 1956, at a meeting attended by a group of industrialists, Ministry of Supply and aviation officials, airline representatives and RAE scientists, to discuss the future direction of British civil aviation. It came about because of the Comet tragedy and the Americans taking the lead in jet airliner sales. It was decided to create a Supersonic Transport Aircraft Committee (STAC) to direct Britain's move into supersonic flight which, if successful, it was believed would help to regain the initiative from the Americans.

The committee decided that the nature of the work already carried out at the RAE indicated that such a plane could be constructed with a suitable engine currently being developed for the projected TSR2 bomber. There was never any doubt about the plane being expensive. With the vast technological challenges involved, it was expected to cost at least twice that of the VC10, the dearest British airliner so far, although at this stage the extent of the problems that would arise from its engine noise and sonic boom were far from fully anticipated.

It was a project where the advanced technical requirements and costs would always be major considerations. Whatever Plowden's proposals for international co-operation over future programmes, in the case of Concorde the limited UK domestic market had already made collaboration imperative. As for likely partners, although the United States had been the obvious one there were concerns that it would be sure to dominate such a project. This in fact never happened because the Americans were intent on constructing a Mach 3+ aircraft of their own rather than the Mach 2 Concorde, which the British did not expect to suffer the kinetic heating problems of the faster aircraft.[16]

This left the French, Britain's main European rival who were intent on building a similar, if shorter-ranged version of the British specification. Preliminary talks were held during 1961–62 and by November 1962 a treaty was concluded between the two countries committing them to produce two types of supersonic transport (SST): a Mach 1.8 aircraft and a Mach 2 aircraft, which would be built for BOAC (later BA) and Air France.

In 1964 the slower aeroplane was discarded and the total development costs for a Mach 2 aircraft were estimated to have risen to £250 million, a figure calculated on sales of 150 aircraft.[17]

As was to be expected, the treaty divided costs and development equally between the two countries. The British Aircraft Corporation and Sud Aviation

Concorde flying over Farnborough's black sheds. (Farnborough Air Sciences Trust)

undertook the airframe development while Bristol Siddeley Engines and the French company Snecma were scheduled to build the civilian version of the TSR2 Olympus engine.

The technical development of the Concorde has rightly been called a unique achievement in the face of unprecedented technical and organisational difficulties.[18] In the first place, the plane's basic shape was novel, based on newly discovered aerodynamic principles, which came about from an understanding of the underlying mechanisms of supersonic flight and from the painstaking and occasionally brilliant research of scientists at the RAE at Farnborough and Bedford.[19] Sir Arnold Hall, then RAE Director, began the process by appointing a small committee under one of his deputies – Welshman Morien Morgan – to get some coherence into what Morgan called 'a staggeringly bold aerodynamic adventure'.[20] Its first meeting took place on 25 February 1954, two years before the setting up of the Supersonic Transport Aircraft Committee (STAC), where it was decided that no thin and straight-winged supersonic aeroplane could economically carry passengers across the Atlantic and therefore a new conformation had to be found.

Dietrich Küchemann,
Farnborough's brilliant
aerodynamicist.
(Farnborough Air
Sciences Trust)

The outcome was a slender delta wing design with sharp leading edges in which Farnborough's fluid dynamicist Dr Dietrich Kuchemann was much involved in its development. The design was revolutionary in that instead of aiming for an airflow that would pass smoothly over the wing with separation delayed for as long as possible, the Farnborough scientists decided to provoke early separation to give a proportion of its lifting force in low-speed flight to reconcile the plane's cruise efficiency at Mach 2 with an ability to rise from and descend on to the ground under full control.

The alternative way of achieving this was to adopt variable-geometry wings to enable their outer sections to pivot in flight to match the speed of the aeroplane, a method attempted unsuccessfully with the United States Supersonic Transport programme (SST).

In the case of the slender delta wing, an immense amount of further theoretical work and wind-tunnel testing was needed before deciding on the best dimensions, including the possibility of a fully integrated, all-wing design, without a distinct fuselage. The final shape of Concorde with its thin, heavily angled wings, discrete fuselage, vertical fin and rudder and underslung engine nacelles was reached after hundreds of models had been built and tested in the research laboratories in Britain at the RAE and at ONERA in France.

The 1962 agreement signed by Britain and France to build a supersonic transport aircraft was based on the understanding that costs should be shared together with the proceeds of the sales. Two committees were formed, one to direct the construction of its airframe, the other for its engines. It was agreed that the senior management post should alternate between Britain and France at two-yearly intervals. However, where any collaborative programme with France was concerned, it was to be expected that the first incumbent should be French. He turned out to be General Andre Puget of Sud Aviation, who, in fact, quickly formed a close relationship with the senior British representative, Sir George Edwards of the British Aircraft Corporation. In the case of engine construction, the first chairman was British. The production timetable was for the prototype's first flight to take place during the second half of 1966, with the first flight of the production aircraft by the end of 1968. The plane's certificate of airworthiness was expected to be granted by the end of 1969, with the flight certificate for the engines also scheduled for that time.

In the event it proved far easier to decide on a 50/50 work programme than to implement it. In the case of the fuselage, it was finally agreed that the French should be responsible for the front section of the wing, the centre of the aircraft, the elevons and the landing gear. British responsibility would be for the front part of the aircraft, the engine nacelles, the rear section of the fuselage and the fin and rudder.

To achieve the sought after 50/50 split it was decided that 60 per cent of the work on the airframe would go to Sud Aviation and 40 per cent to BAC, while development work on the engine would be divided into two-thirds for Bristol Siddeley and a third for the French engine company Snecma. Sixty per cent of the engine production work was scheduled to go to Bristol Siddeley with 40 per cent to Snecma.

However careful the allocation of responsibilities, the development of a proposed Mach 2 airliner to carry some hundred passengers over transatlantic distances was not only exceedingly complex but, with two nations participating, bound to be expensive.

The dominating feature in the aircraft's construction was its low payload ratio for passengers and freight, just 6 per cent of the overall weight compared with the Boeing 707's 20 per cent. Any increase in weight was bound to threaten its already limited payload and each national team was required to draw up accurate weight estimates for the components contained in the aircraft sections. This was time-consuming and the two-nation involvement meant double-checking at every point for a craft that aerodynamicist James

Hamilton believed was the most tested aeroplane of all time.[21] This was fully understandable, with the British unlikely to forget the example of the Comet with its disastrous metal fatigue and the far greater requirements this time.

With the Concorde, there was never any intention of taking risks and George Edwards' acknowledgement that '5,500 flying hours were logged before [Concorde's] certificate of airworthiness while the Boeing 747 did about 1,500 hours'[22] was fully understandable, if inevitably costly.

Edwards also pointed out that delays tended to occur because, with no direct western competitor, there was no undue pressure on completion dates and because the final Concorde needed to be superior to its initial specifications.

In spite of this he found the working practices pretty extraordinary; every time he picked an English or French leader for a particular project he had to have a French and English deputy. There was also the existence of two national assembly lines, one in Britain at Filton, the other in France at Toulouse, a practice that any competent manager would have rejected for cost reasons.

The process did not stop with duplication of personnel and production lines, much of the equipment for the aircraft's many ancillary systems came from separate British and French suppliers. This meant that national pride was at stake and in such circumstances a crisis arose when the British decided to change the measuring procedures for the engine intakes from the French analogue system to a British digital one – fortunately with notable success. Another occurred when the brakes were changed to UK computer-controlled ones, bringing weight savings of 1,200lb.

For such reasons, with Concorde things often proved more complex than anticipated, although the overriding principle in its construction was that after creating a new shape to reach supersonic speed, other systems should be relatively conventional and rely on proven technology. This was fair enough in principle but Concorde's performance needed to go beyond previous known limits. Whereas a comparable military aircraft would be required to go supersonic for a few minutes at a time, Concorde had to fly at such speed for hours. Unsurprisingly, the production aircraft also proved heavier than the first prototype, thereby placing additional demands on the powerplant where the combination of the plane's wing air intakes, engines and final nozzles needed to work smoothly under all conditions – from standing still to flying at some 1,350mph at 60,000ft after a period of transonic acceleration.[23]

The British air intakes and the French final nozzles were the two most important components of Concorde's engines and the synchronisation of the temperatures, pressures and airspeeds in the intakes, engines and nozzles during widely different flight conditions proved a most demanding process. It was, however, essential because Concorde was only marginally a transatlantic aeroplane with very little room for error with its fuel consumption. In the process its engines were to become the most efficient thermodynamic machines in the world, even when working at very high temperatures, with the intakes operating at 120–130°C and temperatures through the compressors rising to about 550°C.

In spite of the universally high performances required and the duplication and increased friction arising from bi-country participation, George Gedge – the director of the Concorde programme at Filton – emphasised the advances in production practices achieved during its construction. He talked of closer interpretations between the design and production staff and the successes in assembling the plane's close-packed equipment and systems within its limited structure (in contrast to the roomy proportions of wide-bodied jets). As a result, improved methods of production were adopted, including the sculpture machinery that automatically machined intricate shapes out of a solid piece of metal.[24] This reduced the complexity of assembly and increased the accuracy of manufacture, which helped him come to the conclusion that Concorde was 'a beautiful aeroplane to build'.[25]

The rare dedication of Gedge and his team replicated by their French opposite numbers prepared the way for Concorde's successful first flight and its amazing trouble-free service over the next twenty-five years. This ended on 25 July 2000, when during take-off runway debris burst a tyre that in turn ruptured a fuel tank, causing a French Concorde to catch fire and crash with the loss of 113 lives (100 passengers, nine crew and four people on the ground). Following modifications to the fuel tanks and other safety measures service was resumed but after Air France decided the cost of keeping the type flying had become prohibitive, British Airways had no option but to follow suit, with the plane's last official flight in Britain taking place on 24 October 2005.

In retrospect, Concorde's immense technical successes were always accompanied by massive and unanswerable questions about its financial viability. A basic one was its limited passenger capacity: although capable of flying more than twice as fast as the subsonic Boeing 747 wide-bodied airliner, Concorde's maximum of 100 passengers, together with its veracious appetite for fuel (which proved particularly serious during the rocketing oil prices of the early '70s), compared adversely with the 747's fivefold capacity and relatively thrifty engines.

Above all there were Concorde's development costs and its environmental problems. Wheatever the expected increases through bi-national arrangements, the costs proved astronomic. In spite of skilful marketing that enabled it to attract premium fares, it would always cater for a limited market and the combination of unequalled expenses for British and French taxpayers, together with the lack of aircraft sales beyond Britain and France, prevented any chance of it becoming an economic success.

Escalating expenditure with supersonic flight was, however, not restricted to Britain and France. The Americans experienced ballooning costs with their version of an SST transport plane before suffering ultimate failure. Although their country had become accustomed to being a world leader in premier technical and commercial undertakings, on 24 March 1971 the US Senate turned down a proposal for additional taxpayers' funds for Boeing's projected Mach 3 SST, which if successful would have enabled that country to have an aircraft with unrivalled speed and passenger capacity.

The US SST experience began with a request from the Federal Aviation Administration (FAA) to its aviation industry to design a larger rival to Concorde. Boeing emerged as the selected constructor with a complex swing-wing design for a supersonic giant capable of carrying up to 300 passengers at a speed of Mach 2.7 or beyond. This was to be built primarily of titanium to withstand a skin temperature of more than 500°F (260°C) and dynamic pressures of 1,300lb per square foot on wing surfaces.[26] The company encountered immense difficulties in constructing a swing-wing system, including problems with weight, that were intensified because the plane's payload (like Concorde's) was only half that of a Boeing 707. This forced the company to revert to a fixed delta-wing conformation with a tail and canard foreplane but, despite its best efforts, it failed to meet the FAA's construction deadline of 30 June 1967.[27]

Although Boeing was granted a year's extension, things became more serious still when its struggles to reach supersonic speed amid escalating costs were compounded by determined environmental campaigners, who challenged the plane's potential noise levels and the effects of its sonic boom. William Shurcliff, leader of the Citizen's League Against the Sonic Boom, famously estimated that with the 150 supersonic airliners scheduled to be built, 75 million square miles of boom carpet would be created across the US with an estimated damage bill of $3 million a day.[28] Ironically, the American cancellation of their SST programme when its expenditure had risen to the Anglo-French aircraft's costs of production proved of no benefit to Concorde, because the Malthusian pronouncements of William Shurcliff and other environmentalists about the limited and damaging nature of SST flight adversely affected American attitudes to it.

Although on 21 January 1976 Concorde commenced passenger services to Bahrain and Dakar before crossing the Atlantic to Dulles Airport at Washington on 24 May 1976, permission was not given to land at John F. Kennedy Airport in New York until 31 July 1978. To obtain it required a bruising campaign conducted against US environmentalists that culminated with a successful legal action.[29]

By then they had dealt Concorde a deadly blow by helping to influence airlines such as Eastern, American, Continental and TWA, as well as Japan Air Lines, to ask for their deposits (on sale options) to be returned.[30] Most serious of all, on 31 January 1973 Pan American followed suit and cancelled its order for eight Concordes. With Pan American's rejection Concorde's chances of being bought by International airlines ended and BA and Air France were obliged to go it alone with their fourteen aircraft. Concorde had to carry a ton of fuel for each passenger and although the airlines attempted to expand their supersonic routes there were not enough passengers to pay the high fares required.

Whether the SST airliner was restricted to a specialised niche market or not, the extent of technical knowledge acquired by the Anglo-French constructors in building a safe and reliable aeroplane under such demanding conditions can hardly be exaggerated.

Concorde, an unmistakable profile. (Farnborough Air Sciences Trust)

Sir Morien Morgan, Concorde's strong advocate. (Farnborough Air Sciences Trust)

Concorde was initially upstaged by the Russian Tupolev Tu-144, which flew on 31 December 1968. However, the Tupolev's advantages over Concorde ended there. Following a redesign of its prototype, it crashed on 3 June 1973 while carrying out a flight demonstration at the Paris Air Show, killing its crew and eight civilians in the Paris suburb of Goussainville. Following this the West received only limited information about the plane, before in 1978, its scheduled flights within Russia were stopped. As a result, BAC Chairman George Edwards concluded that it wasn't refined enough to carry passengers across the Atlantic in supersonic flight.[31] This contrasted with the near faultless performances of Concorde's daily take-off from Heathrow for the US, where it accelerated so effortlessly through the sound barrier to Mach 2 that its passengers needed a special indicator to help them mark it.

With Concorde Britain banked on increasing the speed of civilian airliners to supersonic levels to restore the country's technical lead and prestige over the Americans, which it had possessed during the Comet's early days. Like so many other significant developments in British aviation, credit for the emergence of Concorde was due to outstanding individuals. Most notable was the ebullient Welsh aerodynamicist Morien Morgan based at the RAE, who after being appointed chairman of the government's Supersonic Transport Aircraft Committee, sent a powerful endorsement of the plane to Air Chief Marshal Sir Claude Pelly, Controller at the Ministry of Supply.

Morgan wrote:

It seems clear that the earlier supersonic transports will represent the start of a whole new generation of very fast, long-range machines … a decision not to start detailed work fairly soon on the transatlantic aircraft would be in effect a decision to opt altogether out of the long range supersonic transport field since we would never again regain a competitive position … as a leading aeronautical power.[32]

His communication included a favourable but not unrealistic cost estimate of £75 million to £95 million for Britain's share in the collaborative construction programme with France.

As chairman of STAC, Morgan was most influential in the decision to design and build Concorde, which Sir Arnold Hall, his director at the RAE, fully acknowledged. While, without Morgan, Concorde might well have not gone ahead, with his strong advocacy technological objectives were very likely to take precedence over economic limitations to such a degree that even after an agreement had been signed with France for the aeroplane, there was no proper realisation about the extent of the fast escalating costs of the bi-national programme.[33]

Like the American SST, there came a moment with Concorde when cancellation was considered the best option. In 1964 the new Labour administration of Harold Wilson learned that the Concorde estimates had risen to an unparalleled £835 million. However, Wilson's subsequent attempt to escape from the UK's contract with France met with a blank refusal from President de Gaulle and with the high hopes resting on the plane and Britain's continuing dependence on France's assistance for entry to the Common Market, it was decided to carry on. The second opportunity followed Labour's electoral defeat in 1970, but the British aircraft industry packaged the aircraft's rising costs in the most favourable way and soft-pedalled the disadvantages of its undue engine noise and sonic boom to a generally supportive government.

While Concorde went ahead its costs were to attract strong later criticism. In hindsight, leading air commentator R.E.G. Davies believed that Concorde's undue costs brought dire results, including stopping the UK from gaining a respectable share of the mainline world commercial airliner market. Davies passionately argued that if £1 had been allocated to the Trident for every £100 thrown at Concorde, de Havilland could have snatched about a third of the Boeing 727's market.[34] To Davies, British misuse of funds at a time of national financial stringency became more evident still when, in addition to its share in funding Concorde, France found the means to give financial support to the Airbus A300, while Britain's politicians were seemingly forced to opt out of the programme.

Whatever the merits of Davies' arguments, the decision to go forward with Concorde rested on what can now be recognised as a fallacy, namely that supersonic airliners would shape the immediate future of commercial air transport and that national governments could afford to build them. During the autumn of 1969, in the aviation publication *Flight*, Davies continued his criticisms of the Concorde programme in a series of articles about the effects of the British constructors' work patterns on the escalating costs, which had already doubled since the 1966 estimate of £500 million despite only a third of the increase being attributable to design changes.[35] The publication maintained that incentive contracts were not introduced until the programme was in its sixth year and, that from the time of the ludicrously low estimates of the aircraft's development to its ballooning cost levels, no phased approval of its construction programme took place, unlike the process carried out in the US by its watchdog committees.

Even so, it is fair to say that at no time were the British public made fully aware of the plane's financial horror story, which Davies described so vividly. The figure-juggling continued when, in 1986, ten years after its inaugural flights, journalist James Woolsey could write approvingly about the British Airways Concorde division making a £12 million profit for fiscal year ending 31 March 1984, despite the plane using the same amount of fuel as the Boeing 747 carrying its 500 passengers on the North Atlantic run and being four times as expensive to maintain.

In fact, the profit was achieved by charging premium fares for business travellers and through undertaking charter flights round the UK that contributed 10 per cent of Concorde's revenue.[36] While these figures were creditable over earlier returns they were still illusory because BA paid just £65 million for its first five Concordes and received the last two free of cost.

Although nothing can take away the unforgettable sight of Concorde spearing into the sky as the world's only supersonic passenger aircraft preparing to cross the Atlantic in record time and with exceptional safety, its seats would always be the province of the few. Its funding also proved to be a major factor in the UK government's decision to leave the A300 project and R.E.G. Davies for one was convinced that it also played a dominant part in neglecting the further development of the VC10 and Trident airliners.

Aviation author Robin Higham came to other critical conclusions, namely that Concorde was a smokescreen for two other important happenings: the decline and fall of the major British airframe industry from lack of private and government foresight and the determined recovery of French technical supremacy from the ashes of the Second World War.

On reflection, the extraordinary design skills of Dietrich Küchemann and the silver-tongued advocacy of Morien Morgan at the RAE helped lead British aviation into what turned out to be a most glorious but ultimately disastrous diversion (with France) against common sense and logic. Despite the spectacular and impeccable flying qualities of the supersonic Concorde, due to legitimate environmental objections it would always be fated to fly for the most part over the sea. With the 1960s heralding the era of escalating air travel, Britain's relatively scarce resources should have been better spent – as the Americans and a consortium of European nations did – on developing cheaper roomier aircraft, travelling at a subsonic 600mph. Although Britain subsequently rejoined the European Airbus consortium, it was to be on far more adverse terms than those originally offered.

13

BRITISH AERO ENGINES: CREATIVE ENGINEERING, FAULTY SUMS

While at the end of the Second World War the Brabazon Committee had the task of recommending the most suitable types of aeroplanes it believed would play a successful role in civil aviation worldwide, British aero engines had already established a dominant position. During the war the Merlin piston engine compared favourably with those of the UK's competitors, and by its end Britain had a primary position in gas-turbine technology.

De Havilland was one of the first British companies to enter the latter field when in 1941 its designer, Frank Halford, decided on the essential features of a turbojet engine using Whittle's single-sided centrifugal compressor and straight-through flow. By 8 December 1941 the Air Ministry issued a specification for a single-seat jet fighter – the twin-boom Vampire – to be powered by Halford's H-1 Goblin turbojet producing a thrust of 2,700lb. Although the Vampire was too late for the Second World War its public debut came during the victory celebrations of 8 June 1946.[1]

In spite of Halford's achievements and those of the Bristol Aeroplane Company, which in 1948 produced a turboprop system capable of being fitted to the Hermes V airliner, by far the greater contributions to the new technology came from Rolls-Royce, which after helping pioneering inventor Frank Whittle bring his jet engines into production, went on to develop its own.

In world terms, former Royal Air Force aeronautical apprentice Whittle came very early to jet technology when, after becoming a commissioned officer in 1932 aged 23, he registered a specification for patenting a jet engine relying on a centrifugal compressor.

Although he encountered powerful opposition from Dr A.A. Griffith, head of the Engine Section at the Royal Aircraft Establishment, who initially considered the turbine as a way of driving a propeller rather than a form of direct

Early jet pioneer Flying Officer (later Air Commodore) Frank Whittle. (Royal Aeronautical Society/ National Aerospace Library)

jet propulsion, the RAF offered Whittle the chance to study as a serving officer for the Mechanical Sciences Tripos at Cambridge. He repaid the service's faith by gaining a first-class honours degree, despite having to telescope the first two years of the course into twelve months.

During the course of his studies, Whittle was offered a measure of financial backing from his one-time colleagues at Cranwell to help fund the construction of his revolutionary engine. This enabled him to found the company Power Jets, but its progress proved agonisingly slow with restricted levels of funding leading to major equipment shortages and his engine's first run not taking place until April 1937.

Without additional support further delays and frustrations seemed only too likely. The breakthrough came following Whittle's meeting with brilliant young engineer and mathematician Stanley Hooker, whom Rolls-Royce's works manager Ernest Hives had recruited in 1938. It said much for Hives that, despite massive ongoing involvement with the Merlin engine, he sensed that new types would soon be forthcoming and men of ability and imagination would be needed to help the company achieve the revolutionary developments that were just around the corner. Hive's choice of Hooker brought immediate results when his analytical work on the Merlin supercharger contributed to raising its engine's thrust from 1,000hp to 2,000hp, thus helping to win the Battle of Britain.[2] In 1939 Hives recruited Whittle's bête noire – Griffith – without achieving the same rapid success.

During the summer of 1940, Hooker visited Whittle's Power Jets, which was based in a derelict factory at Lutterworth and, after grasping the logic of his straightforward approach, left believing the jet engine was unquestionably the way forward.

After describing how Whittle's jet engine was already producing similar levels of power to an advanced Merlin, Hooker persuaded Hives to go to Lutterworth. Upon learning about Whittle's difficulties over obtaining new parts, Hives generously offered to make them at Rolls-Royce. Shortly before Hives' departure, Whittle began emphasising his engine's basic simplicity, only to be met with the classic retort, 'Don't worry, we'll soon design the bloody simplicity out of it.'

In spite of Hive's offer, work on Whittle's engine continued to be agonisingly slow, largely because the Rover Company, which were responsible for its production arrangements, had given it a low priority. This led to a serious deterioration of relations between Whittle and both Rover and its main subcontractor British Thomson Houston (BTH), especially when Rover's brilliant young engineer Adrian Lombard began making some assembly decisions of his own.

As a result, by 1942 Whittle asked Rolls-Royce to take over his engine production. Although Rolls-Royce was at the time working at full capacity on other wartime projects, Hives solved things in a most notable fashion. He proposed a meeting between himself and S. B. Wilkes, his opposite number at Rover, which took place at the Swan and Royal Hotel in Clitheroe. There, over a 5s wartime dinner, he raised the subject of Whittle's Power Jets company. In a sixty-second conversation he made the following proposal, 'I'll tell you what I will do. You give us this jet job, and I will give you our (Meteor) tank engine factory at Nottingham,' to which Wilkes rapidly agreed.[3]

Although Whittle's engine had by now been included among the nation's potential war winners, it was not until Rolls-Royce assumed control that production bounded ahead. Hooker was put in charge of operations and Rolls-Royce received a major bonus when Adrian Lombard, soon to become 'one of the world's greatest gas turbine engineers' joined them.[4]

Despite rapid progress, in 1943 it became apparent that even with its faults ironed out, Whittle's W.2B/B.23 (now known as the Welland) with its 1,700lb thrust would never make a very exciting aeroplane out of its parent aircraft,

Dynamic works manager Ernest Hives. (Rolls-Royce)

although by mid-summer the Welland-powered Meteor was being used against German V1s.[5] Hives authorised the development of a modified engine called the Derwent with 2,000lb thrust and at Rolls-Royce, Adrian Lombard, assisted by Harry Pearson and Freddie Morley, started designing the B.41, or Nene, the first true Rolls-Royce jet engine which by 27 October 1944 was running at 4,000lb thrust. The Nene showed great development potential and during November, in a letter to Wilfrid Freeman, Hives wrote, 'The turbine engines have arrived. Our recent success with the B.41 emphasises that on the engine side the efficiency and performance has been well demonstrated.'[6]

At Rolls-Royce the piston aero engine virtually became obsolete overnight and a year after the war, nearly all the engine work at Derby was with the gas turbine.

Hives lamented the blindness of officialdom towards the jet engine: 'The urgency all appears to be concentrated on the Brabazon type of civil machines … One gets the impression that the Air Ministry don't believe in Turbines.'

Hives' enthusiasm for the new form of propulsion appeared fully justified when on 7 November 1945 a scaled-down Nene engine, called the Derwent V, with 3,500lb thrust, enabled an RAF Meteor IV to take the world's speed record at 606mph.

With such progress, by the end of the war, Britain was in the position of having the world's outstanding piston engine in the Merlin together with the fastest jet engine that promised to make piston engines reductant. As gratifying as such superiority must have been, in a situation where military capacity was dominated by the world's two superpowers (where in the civil field America's domestic aviation market was unrivalled in size), retaining the UK's primacy promised to be much more difficult.

Realistically this appeared impossible without major government support and a crusading aviation authority. Bill Gunston believed that in 1945 the British government had 'little interest in aeronautical progress' and made scant effort to take advantage of progress in this field.[7]

Such conclusions appeared justified when, as a singular naive act of good-will, the British government authorised the shipment of twenty-five Nenes to Moscow. These were rapidly put into full-scale production by the Soviet Union as its RD-45 engine, with parallel initiatives in China, where the Nene became the WP-5. With the cat deliberately let out of the bag, Rolls-Royce had little option but to license production of the Nene to its great American rival Pratt and Whitney before concluding further agreements with Australia, Argentina, the Benelux countries, France and Sweden.

The government's release of such information gave Rolls-Royce additional reasons to press forward with further improvements to the Nene and to develop the larger RB.44 Tay, whose use in Britain was, however, restricted to a specialised conversion of the Viscount. With such limited domestic demand Rolls-Royce licensed the Tay to overseas companies including America's Pratt and Whitney and Hispano-Suiza in France.

In 1946 another British engine development came about in the form of the Dart, a relatively simple propeller turbine designed by a Rolls-Royce team at Derby under Lionel Haworth aimed at producing 1,000hp (although it would achieve subsequent increases in power) for installation in the outstanding Vickers Viscount. By this time Lord Brabazon was advocating turboprops for civilian airliners with pure jet propulsion for military aircraft. The Dart was a centrifugal engine using a two-stage compressor to drive a propeller, which soon demonstrated greater reliability than piston engines. Although not rated that highly by Hives, who favoured the pure jet, it remained in service until the 1980s, with 7,100 engines produced in all.

The depth of British aero-engine technology at this time can be appreciated by the formidable opposition facing the Dart from Armstrong Siddeley's 1,000hp Mamba, together with the eleven-stage axial-flow compressor system produced by Roy Fedden's Cotswold company and Napier's 1,600hp Naiad turbine.[8] However, while the current British system of open competition was fair it was undoubtedly wasteful, with the unsuccessful firms investing much time and capital to no avail.

During 1949 Stanley Hooker entered the field of turboprops with his Clyde 3,000hp engine, which despite world-beating potential, suffered from a restricted home market and was never treated that seriously by Ernest Hives. This was followed in the mid-1950s by Rolls-Royce's powerful 5,700hp Tyne, a second-generation turboprop designed for the private venture Vickers Vanguard, for which orders were limited to a disappointing forty-three aircraft, before the engine gained moderate commercial success by way of military transports, maritime reconnaissance aircraft and overseas sales. Although it also proved most fuel efficient, it was to lose out to passengers' fast-growing preference for the pure jet.

By this time, along with the growing conviction that there were too many British aircraft constructors, there was a similar belief about too many engine builders and that the big four – Rolls-Royce, Bristol, Armstrong Siddeley and de Havilland – needed a larger share of the market.

At Rolls-Royce Hives was convinced the pinnacle for jet engines was the axial-jet system (rather than Whittle's simpler through thrust) that had been advocated since the 1930s by A.A. Griffith, with its two shafts, one carrying the high-pressure turbine blades and the other a series of slower-speed fans at the front of the engine to cool the inner jet.[9]

This design evolved into the AJ.65 Avon, whose early development caused so many problems for Stanley Hooker that they led him to quit Rolls-Royce for Bristol. The crisis came about because while Hooker and his team, based at Barnoldswick some 120 miles from Rolls-Royce's main factory at Derby, were wrestling with seemingly intractable problems for a year or more, Hives' skilled craftsmen at Derby were running very short of work on piston engines. Hives' patience finally snapped and early one Monday morning he travelled to Barnoldswick and burst into Hooker's office shouting, 'This jet job is too important to leave in this garage. I am moving it to Derby.' Following a monumental and tragic bust-up, Hooker left the firm he loved. Even so, by 1951, after a marked increase in its turbine efficiency, the Avon was ready to go into production in the Canberra bomber. In 1952 it would power the Vickers Valiant heavy bomber and in 1954 the Hawker Hunter (following the correction of major surge problems). In 1962 this remarkable engine was installed in the supersonic Lightning and in later marques of the Comet and French Caravelle airliners. In total 10,433 Avon engines were built.

Whatever its outstanding achievements, by the late 1950s, the British aero-engine industry was suffering from adverse political developments. The Sandys White Paper of 1957, for instance, swept away Rolls-Royce's RB.128, the more powerful engine scheduled to follow the Avon and the Conway. The latter pioneering bypass or turbofan engine, designed by Adrian Lombard, was much affected by other cancellations. Far lighter than Bristol's BE.10 Olympus, it was destined for both the V1000 strategic transport and its VC7 airliner version, but their cancellation restricted its use to later marques of the Valiant.

With its weight advantages, Rolls-Royce considered the Conway a genuine alternative to Bristol's Olympus engine. It was aimed at the American market and its production was accelerated to make it an optional engine for both the Boeing 707 (whose immense success Ernest Hives believed marked the end of British aviation) and the Douglas DC-8. However, delays meant it lost out to a modified Pratt and Whitney engine with more than twice its bypass ratio and it was installed in just sixty-nine out of a total of 1,519 aircraft of both types.[10][11] Its earlier version was also disadvantaged in the American market because it was designed for installation within the wing rather than in pods below it, and although the Conway was successfully uprated for the British VC10 and Super VC10, only 907 engines were built in all.

At home, the Conway had to compete with Bristol's Olympus, a superbly designed unit whose qualities were being optimised by Rolls-Royce's one-time 'star', Stanley Hooker. After moving to Bristol in 1949 he supervised the development of the most powerful axial turbojet built in Britain, which by 1953 was comfortably exceeding the anticipated power thrust required for the Vulcan bomber. It was accepted for installation in TSR2, where one of the requirements was to fly at a maximum Mach 2.2 for a full forty-five minutes, but its final destination was in Concorde, where it was required to cruise at Mach 2.2 (or 1,450mph) over the major part of its journey. This was quickly achieved by an engine that Hooker believed had no rival in airline service, whose 8,000lb thrust with reheat could run up to 40,000lb and whose total horsepower was equivalent to that of 160 Spitfires.[12] Even so, the refusal of countries to allow Concorde to fly supersonically over land served to ruin its economic prospects, including those of its excellent engines.

In the early 1950s the calibre of British propulsion units ranging from Bristol's Olympus to Rolls-Royce's full range of engines was at the highest level.

By 1953, with the reduced prospects for its engine sales in the home country, Rolls-Royce attempted to safeguard its world position by establishing a permanent position in the prime American market. Although after Pratt and Whitney had declined a similar arrangement, the company succeeded in

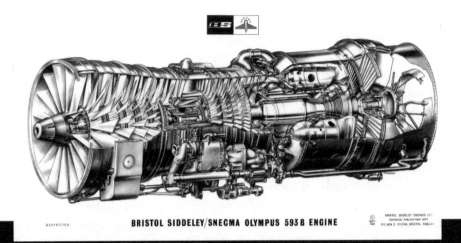

BRISTOL SIDDELEY/SNECMA OLYMPUS 593B ENGINE

Cutaway illustration of the Bristol/Rolls-Royce Olympus. (Rolls-Royce)

concluding a ten-year licensing agreement with the American Westinghouse Company. By 1959 it had come to nothing.

In such circumstances it was compelled to compete for orders in the British market, where in 1957 a major new opportunity appeared with de Havilland's 121 tri-jet the Trident, intended for operation on BEA's European routes. For this Rolls-Royce designed its RB.141 Medway, capable of eventually producing 20,000lb or even 30,000lb thrust, with excellent prospects of both British and worldwide sales. Tragically, in the face of an economic downturn BEA abruptly changed its requirement to a scaled-down engine of some 10,000lb thrust, for which Rolls-Royce offered its RB.163, subsequently known as the Spey, which it hoped would also be used for powering Boeing's new 727 airliner. Although Boeing provisionally accepted Rolls-Royce's upgraded Spey (with more than 12,000lb thrust), in an adverse and unpredictable turn of events the President of Eastern Airlines, Eddie Rickenbacker, rejected it, reputedly saying, 'I won't have a Limey aircraft at any price.' Legend has it that he held a deep grudge because although during the First World War he had been in the UK as a fighter pilot, his German-sounding name had led to his arrest and temporary incarceration in a Liverpool jail.

As a result, Pratt and Whitney designed what was effectively a larger Medway engine. This came to be installed in no fewer than 1,832 of its 727s. A great opportunity to penetrate the American market was lost and, although a very good engine, the Spey was installed in just twenty-one BEA Tridents, although it did power the Fokker F28, BAC 1-11, the Royal Navy's Buccaneer naval strike aircraft and the Nimrod patrol aircraft, while an updated version was eventually taken on by the USF for its A-7 Corsair.

Whatever such modest successes, the ultimate prize of being installed in the Boeing 727 was lost and with it the possibility of Rolls-Royce gaining even larger anticipated sales with the Boeing 737. The seriousness of such setbacks can be better appreciated when, from the late 1950s onwards, the US civil airline market achieved world domination: between 1956 and 1979, for instance, out of a total of 8,558 aircraft, 6,621 (77 per cent) were built in the US.

Nothing like the same opportunities were offered by the UK's relatively small internal market, where its airlines competed with well-developed road and rail facilities. What could be done was to encourage the British airlines to expand by developing additional overseas links and push forward with the long-felt need to rationalise the UK aviation industry by reducing the aircraft constructors into two main airframe groups (which would eventually become Hawker Siddeley and the British Aircraft Corporation). The process continued when in 1960 helicopter producers were reduced to a single company – Westland – and brought to its logical conclusion when all aero-engine manufacturing was brought under the leadership of Rolls-Royce following its merger with Bristol Siddeley in the mid-1960s.

The purpose of rationalisation was to enable British aviation to take part in more expensive projects worldwide, and be better able to compete against the US aviation industry. If anything, the competition intensified and on 5 September 1960 the *Financial Times* warned that with the emergence of the Common Market the increasing number of link-ups between American aircraft manufacturers and their continental counterparts posed new dangers for Britain.[13] In fairness, the paper also acknowledged that, 'There seems to be no reason why the British manufacturers should not do the same.'

In reality, some five years later, when Rolls-Royce was shortly to merge with Bristol Siddeley, it had not yet succeeded in linking up with further American companies and early negotiations about building an engine for the Airbus A300 for a European consortium of Britain, France and Germany had yet to be finalised.

In the meantime it had been experiencing a number of alarming difficulties with its American market. On 20 September 1965 Phil Gilbert, the company's legal adviser in the United States, wrote an internal memorandum pointing out how the company's reputation was suffering from a great shortage of spare parts for its engines (which provided a good source of profits) and how it needed to increase its commitment. At the same time he also recommended that Rolls-Royce should strongly market its new two-shaft turbofan engine – the RB.178 Super Conway – by quoting low prices adjusted to American rates of inflation and quoting in dollars rather than sterling.

Whatever Gilbert's qualms, strong indications of his company's continuing technical ambitions had been evident two years earlier, when its key designer, Adrian Lombard, favoured a forward move from the two-shaft Super Conway to a revolutionary three-shaft engine of a more robust design. His intention was to compete with the American firms Pratt and Whitney and General Electric in powering longer-range, wide-bodied aircraft intended for both passengers and freight. With the new Boeing 747 'Jumbo Jet' about to use the Pratt and Whitney JT-9D engine the thinking was that for Rolls-Royce to maintain its position as one of the world's three major aero-engine manufacturers and seize the opportunity to power the two proposed American tri-jets – the DC-10 and the L-1011 TriStar – it was essential to build a highly advanced engine in the 50,000lb range.

Lombard's projected RB211 would be much the largest engine programme ever undertaken by the company and Rolls-Royce decided to seek assurance from Lazards, its financial advisers, before going ahead. The cost of bringing it into production was estimated at some £170 million, compared with its Spey's £20 million, but encouraged by past triumphs Rolls-Royce decided to go forward with what would be the most advanced engine in the world essentially to compete against American aero-engine makers.

Such a venture could never be without risk, for when entering new engineering territory, initial difficulties were only to be expected. They had occurred previously with both the Dart (turboprop) and the Spey (turbofan) engines but the company had come through successfully on each occasion. With the Dart, Rolls-Royce eventually produced the first turboprop engine to go into regular airline service to accompany the Viscount, Britain's bestselling aircraft since the war. And while the company had lost £4.5 million with its Medway, the investment of a further £20 million on the replacement Spey succeeded in bringing orders from the Ministry of Defence for both Phantom and Buccaneer aircraft.

In 1970, when Rolls-Royce was already experiencing grave difficulties with the RB211 programme, its chairman Sir Denning Pearson could point out in justification that while the government invested £33.6 million in helping to launch the Dart, Avon, Conway and Spey engines, the company itself had contributed no less than £90 million, a decision that proved fully justified when the total business for these engines was estimated at £1,260 million, 75 per cent for export.[14]

Adrian Lombard, a hard-driving and highly gifted engine designer. (Rolls-Royce)

While at first sight such earlier financial tactics seemed applicable to the RB211, by now its development costs were already three times greater than those of the Spey. Nonetheless, the company believed it had no alternative. As Sir Denning Pearson declared, 'Building a new engine would not guarantee we stayed in business. Not building one (and being denied major airline orders) would certainly guarantee we went out of business.'[15]

In the case of the RB211, it was not only a matter of cost comparisons, however important, but the bar was set even higher when the company lost Adrian Lombard to a sudden heart attack in July 1967. His death deprived the company of the man it most depended on to master the major teething troubles of a revolutionary engine four times as powerful as the Spey and then sell it in a hostile market to Lockheed. The hostility came from unashamed American preference for their own firms and more specifically through the imposition of a 10 per cent import duty on foreign products. This might have seemed reasonable to the US government that in 1970 spent some $3,800 million on aerospace products along with a further $3.1 billion towards its research and development. For Rolls-Royce it meant its engines had to be priced at least 15 per cent lower than those of its American competitors Pratt and Whitney and General Electric;' firms that enjoyed the additional advantage of operating in a large market that provided long production runs to enable them keep their prices low.[16]

The revolutionary RB211 engine that led to Rolls-Royce's financial disaster.
(Rolls-Royce)

To overcome such disadvantages, the RB211 had to be both cheaper and markedly superior in design. The taking on of American producers in this way was not Rolls-Royce's only route to success. There was, for instance, the European consortium of Britain, France and Germany that since 1965 had looked to Rolls-Royce to provide its twin-engined Airbus A300 with the RB207, big brother to the RB211. However, after landing a contract for the RB211 with the American Lockheed company, whether on very demanding terms or not, Rolls-Royce's design resources were fully committed and it no longer felt the same need to develop and sell the RB207, especially when during the same year it won a huge order for the RB199 engine to power the European multirole combat aircraft (MRCA) in a contract worth more than £600 million over the next fifteen years. As a result, it pulled out of Europe's civilian consortium and the Europeans turned to General Electric's CF6-50 engine for their A300 wide-bodied, twin-engined aircraft, with a somewhat smaller seating capacity than the Lockheed L-1011.[17]

The company's choice was influenced by the fact that, whereas Rolls-Royce had failed in its earlier attempts to get its engines on to either the Boeing 707 or 747, this time promised to be different, with the Americans acknowledging that the RB211 was two years ahead of any competitor. This conviction was supported by Rolls-Royce's offer to put it into service within four years. It was also amazingly powerful (55,000lb thrust) with massive stretch potential, lighter and cheaper to run, simpler, easier to maintain and quieter than existing turbofan engines. To achieve such clear advantages, Rolls-Royce relied on material advances by constructing the RB211's massive fan from Hyfil, an exceptionally strong and cheap material, made with strands of carbon fibre about a tenth of the diameter of a human hair, glued together with strong resin.[18] For what seemed a unique opportunity, from September 1966 Rolls-Royce had embarked on an energetic sales drive (costing some £400,000) aimed at both American manufacturers and their airlines.

For this it set prices at a low level – as favoured by Phil Gilbert – and then recklessly lowered them further. The campaign succeeded when, on 29 March 1968, a tripartite deal was struck involving Lockheed, Rolls-Royce and three American airlines, who together ordered 144 TriStars powered by the RB211. In Britain the press were ecstatic, with talk of Rolls-Royce gaining a total of £1 billion from future sales.

In a single bound Rolls-Royce appeared to have overcome all the obstacles with its largest project so far to gain access to the American market, although with such competitive costing everything depended on the accuracy of the company's calculations. This was especially so as Lockheed made Rolls-Royce sign a contract running to 483 pages, with no provision for the effects of inflation – accompanied by savage penalty clauses in the event of late delivery – for a contract that had been set exceptionally short time limits.

For the sums to come right Rolls-Royce not only banked on a totally benign situation with no major technical difficulties but factored in the advantages from follow-up contracts as well.

In reality, its estimates proved wildly inaccurate. Spending on the RB211 proved double that expected when the Hyfil used in a fan with a diameter almost double that of the Conway, and a fourfold increase in total air-flow, was found unable to withstand bird strikes and required substantial redesign. It had to be replaced with heavier and more costly titanium, the installation of which was bound to delay production and bring the firm closer to the timing of penalty clauses. Another major drain on funds was in the millions of pounds needed for the apparatus required to test the engine in high crosswinds.

The financial inaccuracies took a terrible toll. In its attempts to balance the books the company undertook savage economies, laying off 3,000 workers from aero-engine production along with a range of other cuts that even filtered down to the company magazine and canteen service, but they were nothing like enough. It was soon obvious that Rolls-Royce had either to renegotiate Lockheed's contract or obtain further massive loans from the British Government. Although it agreed to advance another £42 million and arranged additional bank loans for £18 million, by November 1970 it was clear that such initiatives were inadequate. It was estimated that the company was set to lose £110,000 on each engine, not counting the late-delivery penalties estimated at a further £50 million. As a result, on 4 February 1971 the UK government allowed Rolls-Royce to collapse into receivership, the very day the RB211 engine met its required thrust of 33,000lb for the first time.[19] In retrospect this was unlikely to have been allowed to happen in subsequent years with the City of London more able to structure necessary company reorganisations.[20]

Even so, the government realised that a firm of Rolls-Royce's reputation with its 80,000 workforce and equal numbers of sub-contractors could not be allowed to go under and the agreed – and humiliating – solution reached was to allow it to go bankrupt, thus ending its obligations to both Lockheed and the airlines, including the penalties for late delivery, and revive it in nationalised form. As Air Commodore Rod Banks commented, 'It was unthinkable that we could "rat" on the Rolls-Royce/Lockheed contract and hope to hold our heads up again in America.'[21] It certainly caused Lockheed itself to come under massive financial pressure from TWA and Eastern Airlines and likewise it was only rescued by a loan guarantee from the US Government.[22] On 4 February 1971 Rolls-Royce formally declared itself bankrupt and on 23 February the new nationalised company began operating and a fresh contract was signed between Rolls-Royce (1971) and Lockheed under which the price of each engine went up by £110,000 to £440,000 and penalties for late delivery were annulled.[23]

The shock and humiliation at the demise of the British firm that in the public's mind represented the best of the world's aero engines could not be exaggerated and it represented a massive a blow to British aviation as a whole, not least in the US.

The receivers split the motor-car and aero-engines divisions into two, with the motor division becoming Rolls-Royce Motors. By this time the aerospace company had already taken remedial action; a new managing director was appointed in place of Sir Denning Pearson, who accepted full responsibility for the financial risks run, with Stanley Hooker brought back from retirement to cure the RB211. Under his inspired leadership scores of small compressor leaks were stemmed, which brought about a transformation without requiring a radical engine redesign and the increased thrust enabled the firm to offer Lockheed an engine that produced 42,000lb thrust, notably better than the original design. Hooker took on additional responsibility for designing the RB211's second-generation engine, the RB211-524, thus setting the pattern for Rolls-Royce's regular and upgraded engine designs.

For the last four years of our period the company was under public owner-ship and would continue as such for the next thirteen years. It was not a time of spectacular success when, according to Frank Turner, the long-time director of the company's civil engines, 'it was constrained by the lugubrious process of Government in obtaining approval to do anything new when it was only able to react to the initiatives of our competitors and then when it was very late in the day'.[24]

For such reasons Turner argued that the first major initiative came two years later than it should have done and when the company had an engine to offer for installation in the improved version of the Boeing 747 it had already signed up with Pratt and Whitney and General Electric.

In any case, by 1971 70 per cent of the world's airframes were being made in the US and a majority of engine contracts were expected to go to American firms, where soft political support for native constructors acted powerfully against penetration from foreign producers, including Rolls-Royce.

Like the British aircraft industry as a whole, for British aero-engine manu-facturers, the years 1945–75 were ones of lowering expectations despite the amalgamation by 1966 of the one-time eight companies under the single banner of Rolls-Royce.[25]

While in 1975 Rolls-Royce was still technically up with the best, its production levels had dropped below that of other major companies such as America's General Electric, Pratt and Witney and France's Snecma. Even so, during the post-war period Britain possessed two towering aeroengine designers and internal aerodynamicists in Adrian Lombard and Stanley Hooker. The hard-driving Lombard was involved in the development of an ascending series of jet engines with the Derwent, Nene, the early Avon and Conway bypass engines, culminating in the iconic RB211, which 'Lom' banked on being accepted as the powerplant for a major American civil transport constructor. Significantly, it was after his sudden death that the latter programme would run into so many difficulties.

Sir Stanley Hooker, an outstanding talent. (Rolls-Royce)

The contributions of the academically gifted, highly personable and similarly dynamic Stanley Hooker were even greater, ranging from his recognition of Frank Whittle's jet engine and his part in Rolls-Royce's sponsorship of it, to his ultimate successes with the highly problematic Avon engine, his support for the thrust-vectoring Pegasus engine in the Harrier and his genius in realising the potential of the ultimately peerless Bristol Olympus for the supersonic Concorde.

With such a record it was entirely predictable that in 1971 he should be brought out of retirement when the RB211 engine ran into such major difficulties.

With Lombard's and Hooker's skills – together with their able support-ing staff – it seemed reasonable to expect British aero-engine technology to occupy a premier position in worldwide aviation post Second World War.

That their successes were not matched by widespread international sales owed much to the diminished scale and uncertain decisions made towards British defence requirements and with the insularity of British airlines in their orders for aircraft. Throughout the thirty-year period much-needed continuity and confidence was affected by economic crises, leading in one notable instance to Duncan Sandys' premature rejection of aircraft. At other times there were unrealistic ambitions that did not match Britain's impecunious position with, for instance, the government's unreal support for a leviathan Brabazon aircraft and the RAF's unjustified escalation of performance demands for TSR2.

Rolls-Royce's financial decisions were also open to justifiable criticism. Aviation authority Rod Banks believed that the financial risks taken by Rolls-Royce during the late 1960s were indefensible without obtaining other collaborative agreements.[25] While he was ultimately proved right the company did in fact take part in considerable collaboration. During the 1950s, out of the 1,376 Avon engines built for the Canberra, 403 were built by Martin in the US with forty-eight licensed to be built in Australia. During the same period the British Speys which powered the US A-7 aircraft were manufactured in collaboration with the Allison division of General Motors. In the case of Pegasus engines for the advanced Harriers ordered by the US Marine Corps, eighty-four were manufactured in Britain. Collaboration was also demonstrated with the Anglo-French Concorde programme during the 1950s and 1960s, although the engine involved was Bristol's Olympus.

Although the highest ambitions were seemingly out of reach, by 1975 Rolls-Royce's total aero-engine sales were still worth $1.3 billion, of which 50 per cent went for export and of that 50 per cent, $300 million was sold to North America.[26] America, however, would always be an ultra-competitive market and further participation in Europe and hopefully in the rest of the world was urgently required.

THE ROYAL AIRCRAFT ESTABLISHMENT: CONTINUING WORLD-CLASS FACILITIES, SHRINKING NATIONAL CAPABILITIES

In 2018, the Farnborough Air Sciences Trust, established to record the RAE's contributions to British aviation and to preserve its records and archives, published a lavishly illustrated account of the Establishment's past activities. This commenced with the statement that no other single location could claim such a unique technological contribution to the development of aviation as Farnborough, which 'became the centre of a national aeronautical research, development and test and evaluation effort that became world renowned for excellence in all aspects of aviation progress'.[1]

Mervyn Joseph Pius O'Gorman, Superintendent of HM Balloon Factory/Royal Aircraft Factory from 1909 until 1916. (Farnborough Air Sciences Trust)

It went on to draw attention to the outstanding work of the RAE's special-ist departments between the two world wars in providing expert advice on aircraft and weapons concepts, followed by their legacies towards the war effort from 1939 to 1945 and their continuing fundamental contributions during the post-war years towards current and future aviation projects, including super-sonic aircraft and space research.

At first sight, given the excellence and scale of the RAE's world-renowned achievements over the years, it seems misguided if not criminal for it to have suffered such transformational reductions to its functions during the late 1990s.

On fuller consideration, with the contraction of Britain's strategic respon-sibilities and the reduced scale of its military and civil aviation industry, some major rationalisation (rather than root-and-branch destruction) was only to be expected during the period after the Second World War. Hadn't the RAE's past history included both savage cuts and a contraction of its role when, imme-diately after the First World War, it ceased to be an aircraft producer and its numbers of employees fell from more than 5,050 in 1918 to 1,380 by 1920 – a reduction of no less than 73 per cent.[2] This had resulted in it coming to adopt its traditional role of research and evaluation through the establishment of departments of Aerodynamics, Engine Experimental, Physics and Instruments, Metallurgical, Mechanical Test, and Chemical and Fabrics.[3]

However, by 1922 the workforce was further reduced to 1,316 personnel, comprising 250 scientific and technical staff, including apprentices and 335 labourers.[4] This would mark a low point during the interwar years. Two years later a committee formed under Air Commodore F.C. Halahan to consider further reductions emphasised the RAE's importance as a full-scale aeronautical laboratory, which through its departments carried out widespread development work. Halahan also went on to point out the need for further facilities to investigate failures with an aircraft's specialist flying instruments and for wireless and photographic work, together with new responsibilities, including liaison with aviation contractors to carry out stress and safety tests on new types of aircraft, approve new aircraft designs and issue airworthiness certificates.

As a consequence, the RAE not only survived but during the interim visibly strengthened its position, when it became established practice for aircraft firms to evolve and develop their designs with the help of the accumulated experi-ence and facilities at Farnborough.[5]

This opened the way for the Establishment's work during the Second World War, where through the importance of its contributions towards the country's wartime successes it became one of the world's great aeronautical research and inspection establishments. An instance of this came with its contribution immediately before the war to the design of short-range, pilot-operated, radio-telephone equipment, which in the form of high-frequency wireless sets proved a game changer during the Battle of Britain and came to be used by all Allied air forces. Other important wartime contributions included work with pressure suits and flying clothing, wind tunnels, structural testing, aerial photography, engine developments, gun and bomb sights and enemy aircraft testing.

Pressure suits came to be developed in conjunction with the RAF Institute of Aviation Medicine for particular use in high-flying reconnaissance aircraft, while the RAE's wind tunnels, supplemented at the beginning of the war by its advanced 24ft facility, helped to evaluate all sorts of aircraft fittings and shapes, from bomber turrets to radiators and engine intakes, with the aim of reducing drag and improving the streamlining of airframes.[6 7] Its structural testing replicated typical in-service wear and tear on an aircraft, including the application of stressing forces many times greater than what might be experienced in a worst-case scenario in the air.[8]

Professor Lighthill and Tilly Shilling. (Farnborough Air Sciences Trust)

Early in the war the RAE's F24 camera became standard equipment, to be followed by the even more capable F52, which took just fifty-two days from initial design to completion.[9] Also, a notable breakthrough by the Engine Developments Department occurred when the RAE's Beatrice 'Tilly' Shilling cured the tendency of Merlin aero engines to suffer from flooding and reduced power by developing an ingenious and simple fuel-flow restrictor device. Yet another significant advance came with the Establishment's gyro mechanisms that, when used with aircraft gunsights, doubled the hit rate and came to be produced both in Britain and the US.

By the end of the war its inspection responsibilities had seen the RAE acquire a flying collection of more than sixty captured German aircraft. Under the leadership of Captain Eric 'Winkle' Brown its Aerodynamics Flight became recognised as the leading test flying unit in the world.[10]

Due to such wartime achievements, the RAE succeeded in establishing itself, in the words of Sir Stafford Cripps, 'as the nerve centre of our efforts in the air'.[11]

By now its core site straddling Farnborough Heath totalled 180 acres, which, when supplemented by the airfield and its adjoining land, rose to an amazing 1,196 acres, a third larger than the City of London.

After the Second World War, unlike the situation in 1918, while some scientists returned to complete their university courses, no measurable reduction in staff took place because Britain and its western allies faced renewed dangers from an expansionist Soviet Union. In December 1945 the RAE's total manpower (including its outstations) stood at 6,045, of whom 2,150 were scientists, with 1,150 draughtsmen and clerical staff, and 2,745 industrials.[12] Remarkably, fully twenty years later, this had actually increased to 8,500, made up of 1,500 scientists, 1,100 supporting technical staff and 4,800 industrial and admin grades, with research funding for the financial year 1975–76 revealing little change from the totals at the start of the decade.[13][14]

With the advent of the Cold War savage cuts such as those at the end of the First World War could never be expected, although the RAE's continuing high levels of manpower during the later 1960s and into the 1970s seems somewhat surprising.

One obvious reason for this was the state of the British aircraft industry at the end of the war. Although aircraft manufacturing formed Britain's largest single industrial sector, there was a strong belief that the industry was not as advanced as it should have been for the more complex types of aircraft, including interceptors flying up to supersonic speeds and the large, advanced planes needed to carry Britain's nuclear weapons.

Aero Flight and Stability Section 1948

Front Row, left to right:-

W E Gray, S Child, F/Lt J S R Muller-Rowland, W Stewart, F/Lt R V F Ellis, D E Morris, H Davies, S B Gates
M B Morgan, Lt Cdr E M Brown, D J Lyons, F/Lt G E C Genders, R R Duddy, F/Lt C J Lawrence, W J Charnley,
T G Hawkins, F Swift.

Second Row, left to right:-

H H B M Thomas, A W Thorpe, A S Taylor, J C Marchant, K W Smith, J G Walker, F M Ward, M Stedman, M Lovelace,
P K Pirrie, H J Ranks, I Watson, M Seed, J C Martin, E H Cox, J N Critchley, J P Smith, A Simpkins.

Third Row, left to right:-

H C B Mackey, G Sissingh, R C A Dando, P Brotherhood, R Maine, M Burle, D R Dennis, K Doetsch, W Pinsker,
H Schlichting, W Kahlert, R Woods, W W Curwell, P Sibbald, G H Thornton, A R Mettam, E H Fynn, J Zbrozek.

Fourth Row, left to right:-

R P Purkiss, P Fullam, A R Cawthorne, J C Morrall, W G A Port, A Slater, R J Ross, W Mangler, A R Bramwell,
D J Higton, R H Plascott, P L Bisgood, R Rose.

There was, in fact, a perception that so many of our wonderful (wartime) aircraft and their engines owed their origins to a few men of genius, with Peter Masefield, for instance, convinced that procurement practices were decidedly superior in America. [15] When the RAE's director W.S. Farren made a visit to Germany at the end of the war he discovered that its industrial facilities had 'a magnificence that beggars the imagination of anyone who has seen similar institutions in the UK'.

Farren's experience helped endorse the belief held earlier by the wartime coalition government that if industrial aircraft firms lacked the capital to bring their equipment up to state of the art, government research establishments should step in to provide the facilities. In practice this frequently meant the RAE, on whom they came to rely for support with their advanced projects and without whose help 'it would have been impossible for the firms to have completed the designs, testing and evaluation of the new post-war generation of high-speed aircraft … as they lacked the research equipment and wind tunnels required'.[16]

Such responsibilities undoubtedly brought additional involvement for the RAE; in 1956 its wind tunnels were upgraded to transonic with their chambers pressurised for the jet age. Its Structural Testing Department had to consider the effects of supersonic speeds and its Engine Development Department would become concerned with prolonged testing (at Pyestock) of Concorde's revolutionary Olympus and other engines.

The coming of the nuclear age brought new responsibilities, leading to the RAE's involvement with the design of early nuclear weapons and its evaluation of the bombers intended to carry them, with its experts expected to survey potential nuclear testing zones, while the foundation of its Space Department brought close involvement with industry for the construction of space launchers such as Blue Streak, Black Knight, Black Arrow and the sounding rocket Skylark. Decoys for ballistic missiles formed the subject of an April 1957 paper by the RAE's Guided Weapons Department, which found them to be just feasible but requiring major effort before becoming a major operational system.[17]

Significant new projects for Concorde and space research vehicles helped to justify the size of an historic and privileged organisation whose facilities covered the whole spectrum of aeronautical technology. The Establishment enjoyed other significant advantages, especially in the wide range of its research. Whereas the US was directly involved in a life or death contest with the Soviet Union that depended on it developing strategic systems more quickly and to superior specifications than its rival, Britain benefited from the US's nuclear shield with the RAE able to pursue projects for its scientific interests as well as their military ones.

Its scientists' degree of freedom at this time, however, could never compare with Farnborough's early years. Lord Cherwell, for instance, recalled his time as a young scientist during the First World War when he was posted to Farnborough and left very much to work on his own choice 'during happy go lucky days that he feared were over'.[18]

Even so, during the three decades following the Second World War and beyond, author Andrew Nathum could recall that Farnborough still had its own aerodynamic projects and style of research, the theoretical centre of which was the 'Aero' department, whose members led 'god-like separate existences and were to a very high degree self-directing'. Their work stayed at the highest levels partly due to the relative freedom they enjoyed, but he recalled them being 'in the fortunate position of never having to think about money for the things we were doing' and 'we never thought about the cost – we never asked'.[19]

In a publication about the RAE's outstation at Thurleigh (Bedford), which during the post-war years was responsible for flight research for V/STOL, helicopter aircraft and for blind-landing equipment, editor Michael Dobson considered what he believed was the best climate for successful research. He wrote that during the 1950s some senior managers took the view that it was their job to provide whatever resources were required in order to achieve a successful result, although many civil servants judged success by the size of their team and their budget.[20]

It was clear where Dobson stood: immensely proud of the department's world-class facility, he rejoiced in the fact that during its formative years the staff were not constrained to produce a precise set of results for a specific price (as had become the more recent tendency) for 'if a scientist employed to undertake innovative research is not allowed to explore, how can he discover other than by luck!'[21] On the other hand Dobson, was well aware of the over-large number of aero flight aircraft available for testing purposes, although he came to the convenient conclusion that the precise balance between research freedom and a precisely defined end aim is undefinable.[22]

By the 1970s changing attitudes and growing financial pressures were bound to affect the RAE's erstwhile freedoms of research. Due to the need for increased collaboration with other countries, questions were more likely to be asked about whether the establishment's amazingly wide activities, ranging from case studies on aeronautics to more specific ones on wind tunnels, propulsion facilities, flight simulators, guided weapons, structural materials and flight control systems, were actually bringing the returns expected.

In the thirty-year period of our concern responsibility for carrying out British aviation's advanced research, development and inspection functions continued to rely on the RAE. This in practical terms meant its directors, seven of whom held office up to 1975. They were:

W.G.A. Perring	1946–51
Sir Arnold Hall	1951–55
Sir George Gardner	1955–59
Sir James Lighthill	1959–64
Sir Robert Cockburn	1964–69
Sir Morien Morgan	1969–72
Rhys Price Probert	1973–80

In the British way, they differed markedly, not only in their approaches but in their length of tenure, which varied from three to seven years, and came at quite different stages of their careers. Whereas W.G.A Perring spent his whole career at Farnborough until his untimely death, Sir James Lighthill's first experience of the RAE came with his appointment as director. Both Sir James Lighthill and Sir Arnold Hall were appointed at early ages, Lighthill at 35 and Hall at 36, but Sir Robert Cockburn became director at 55 after holding senior posts at both the Ministry of Aviation and Ministry of Technology. While Sir Arnold Hall spent his subsequent career in commercial aviation, where he became Chairman of Hawker Siddeley Aviation (a position he held for nineteen years), Sir James Lighthill's was spent in academia, both at Cambridge and University College London.

In the case of the directors' educational patterns, W.G.A. Perring and Sir George Gardner started as engineering apprentices before undertaking their academic studies and Sir Robert Cockburn gained his academic qualifications 'the hard way' through an external London University degree – in contrast to Sir Arnold Hall, Sir James Lighthill, Sir Morien Morgan and Mr Rhys Probert, who took their initial degrees at Cambridge University. As for management styles, while Sir Arnold Hall was a notable delegator, W.G.A. Perring always preferred to keep the closest involvement with his individual staff.

What they all shared in common was marked and recognisable ability. Of the seven, only Perring and Probert failed to gain knighthoods for their services, which in Perring's case was almost certainly due to his sudden and unexpected death in office.

William George Arthur Perring (1946–51) had initally served with with the Royal Navy, where – following his time as an apprentice at Chatham Dockyard – his obvious ability had him admitted as a scholar to the Royal Naval College, Greenwich. There he gained a first-class professional certificate in naval architecture and was awarded two years, post-graduate research on the operation of ships.

In 1925 he changed direction when he joined the RAE as a junior scientific officer in its Aerodynamics Department, where in 1926–30 he carried out wind-tunnel research and helped in the construction of a flying-boat test tank. In 1937 he was responsible for the design and construction of the RAE's new high-speed wind tunnel, the most advanced of its type in Britain, which under his direction performed vital work during the war both in improving the performance of Allied aircraft and analysing that of the enemy ones. His practical scientific skills were evident, with his brilliant reconstruction of a German V2 rocket from parts recovered from a crashed prototype in Sweden, while his leadership strengths led him to be appointed as deputy to the RAE's Controller, Sir William Farren, before taking over from him in 1946.

At first sight Perring appeared no outstanding leader because his self-deprecating manner somewhat belied his keen intellect and exceptional ability at extracting the essentials from the reports produced at the RAE. However, as director his high dedication and close involvement in the RAE's wide-ranging responsibilities was unquestioned and led him to undertake a prodigious workload. Perring was prone to carry home sheaves of reports in a battered old suitcase that he customarily read into the night to leave the following day free for committee work and interchanges with individuals, including junior members of staff, which he valued highly.[23]

A practical achiever, apart from his pioneering work with wind tunnels his later legacies included the grouping of staff into specialist teams and the planning and establishment of a new world-class aircraft-testing facility at Bedford, which he considered essential to help provide 'the advanced equipment our aeronautical folk should have, in order to keep them in the first eleven class'.[24]

With the furious pace that Perring set himself, along with devoting the lion's share of his working day to his staff, his fatal heart attack proved all too likely.

William George Arthur Perring, director 1946–51. (Farnborough Air Sciences Trust)

Sir Arnold Alexander Hall (1951–55): Hall was an academic shooting star who gained a scholarship to Clare College, Cambridge, where he obtained first-class honours in the engineering tripos of 1935, 'winning with distinction the three chief prizes – for aeronautics, applied mechanics and heat engines'.[25] At Cambridge he collaborated with Frank Whittle on the early development of turbojet propulsion under Professor Sir Bennett Melvill Jones, as a result of which he and the normally 'prickly' Whittle became lifelong friends.

In 1938, following a two-year post-graduate appointment in aeronautics, he entered the RAE as a principal scientific officer, where he was soon fully involved in designing an advanced electronic gunsight and collaborating with Peter Masefield – a future leading figure in aviation – in bringing the Rolls-Royce Dart propeller turbine engines into service with the Vickers Viscount.

Between 1945 and 1951, Hall was Professor of Aviation at London University and head of the Department of Aeronautics at Imperial College, before returning to the RAE as its director. There his outstanding contribution was masterminding its examination of Comet airliners to establish the causes of their unexplained crashes, in the course of which he proved himself a calm and incisive leader, fully confident in his own ability, who required equally high standards from his fellow scientists. In conjunction with the RAE's materials expert, Percy Walker, Hall decided to conduct water tests on the plane, giving his engineers instructions 'to build a steel tank one hundred and twelve feet long, twenty feet wide and sixteen feet deep ... and ordering that it should be completed in six weeks'.[26]

After the airliner was placed in the tank its cabin was subjected to a succession of tests at up to 8¼lb pressure per square inch. At the equivalent of 5,500 hours flying time the cabin fractured with a crack in the skin at the lower rear corner of an escape hatch, confirming that structural failure was in fact to blame for the disasters. Hall's brilliant investigation described 'as the most remarkable piece of scientific detective work ever done' undoubtedly enhanced both the stature of the RAE and his own scientific powers and project leadership.

On leaving the RAE in 1963 he took up new posts within the aircraft industry. He joined Hawker Siddeley Aviation, becoming group managing director before moving on to become an influential chairman. When, for instance, the Labour government withdrew from the Airbus project he supported a wholly private venture on behalf of Hawker Siddeley for building the Airbus wings in order to uphold Britain's ability to continue playing a leading role in international aerospace projects.

Sir George Gardner (1955–59): Ulsterman Gardner attended school at Campbell College, Belfast, before becoming an engineering apprentice

Sir George Gardner, director 1955–59. (Farnborough Air Sciences Trust)

at Harland and Wolff's shipyard. In 1925 he was accepted by Queen's University in Belfast to read for a BSc degree in Engineering, which he obtained with first-class honours. His entry to the RAE in 1926 marked the commencement of a thirty-five-year career in aircraft research at government development organisations.

His involvement as a young scientist in the RAE's Instruments Department on experimental work associated with automatic pilot devices and target aeroplanes led to the construction of a highly successful pilotless target aeroplane – the Queen Bee – 500 of which were made.[27] At 39 he was promoted head of the department and in 1946 chosen to form and run the RAE's Controlled Weapons Section, from where he went on promotion to become Director of the Ministry of Aviation's Guided Weapons with the brief to help found a UK guided weapons and missiles industry.

He undertook a tour of industrial firms and introduced their executives to each other at a dinner in Manchester, as a result of which by 1949 they had dispatched teams (known as the forty-niners) to the RAE to learn about the subject and integrate with the GW team there.[28][29]

Sir James Lighthill, director 1959–64.
(Farnborough Air Sciences Trust)

In 1953 Gardner was appointed Director General of Guided Weapons at the Ministry of Supply, before in 1955 returning to Farnborough as its director. At Farnborough one of Gardner's notable initiatives was to convince the Ministry of Supply to back the RAE in a massive co-operative research programme with industry to explore the fundamentals of supersonic airliner design.[30] This led to the creation of the Supersonic Transport Aircraft Committee that under his successor, Morien Morgan, did so much to lay the foundations for work on Concorde.

On his retirement from Farnborough he took on further significant responsibilities. After acting as Controller of Aircraft at the Ministry of Aviation, like Hall he joined a private company, in his case John Brown Engineering, where he encouraged work on turbine developments before becoming company chairman from 1966 to 1972.

James Lighthill (1959–64): Lighthill was arguably the RAE's most brilliant director during our thirty-year period. In 1936 as a precocious child mathematician he won a scholarship to Winchester College, followed at just 15 years of age by a scholarship to Trinity College, Cambridge. Winchester prevented him from going to Cambridge until he was 17 but in 1943, following a two-year wartime course, he graduated with a first in part two and a distinction in part three of the Cambridge mathematical tripos.[31] Following this he was sent to the National Physical Laboratory at Teddington, where he studied supersonic flight, publishing his first paper on it before he was 20.

At the end of the war, when just 22 years of age, Lighthill became a senior lecturer at Manchester University before being elected to its Beyer Chair of Applied Mathematics, which he held until 1959. Over a nine-year period Lighthill produced academic papers ranging from applied mathematics to fluid dynamics, including one on the sound generated aerodynamically by highly turbulent flows in the wake of jet engines.

To general surprise, in 1959, he quit Manchester University aged 35 to become director at Farnborough. In typical fashion he began by making a critical examination of the reports emanating from it and learning the names and family background of all its 1,400 scientists and engineers, along with many others of its 8,000 staff. At Farnborough, Lighthill enjoyed the practical application of advanced scientific ideas from 'the aerodynamics of the slender wing for Concorde, on spacecraft and, with the Post Office, in developing the commercial use of television and communication satellites'.[32] He was also responsible for the creation of the RAE's Space Department and for promoting research on short-range air transport. In 1962 he already spoke enthusiastically about a manned craft taking off from Earth, being used and manoeuvred in space and then returned. Among his more futuristic projects was a hypersonic aircraft capable of flying to Australia in six hours. Its revolutionary design with wings shaped down to an inverted V was intended to make use of supersonic shockwaves to increase lift,[33] but this remarkable successor to Concorde was never taken up for both financial and environmental reasons.

After Farnborough, Lighthill became the Royal Society's Resident Professor at Imperial College, London, before returning to Trinity College, Cambridge, as Lucasian Professor of Mathematics, a chair he held until 1979, when he was succeeded by Stephen Hawking. From 1979 onwards Lighthill confirmed his administrative powers when, as Provost of University College, London, he restored its finances and extended its academic disciplines to include biotechnology.

Predictably the RAE much benefited from the leadership of such a brilliant man. His staff's appreciation was apparent when MP Tam Dalyell asked one of the senior members whether he liked having a director in his 30s. He replied that normally he and his colleagues would resent someone twenty years younger but since they were able to recognise scientific genius Lighthill was more than acceptable. 'He confirms us as one of the greatest – if not the greatest – aeronautical research establishments in the world; the US included.'[34]

However, with the major scientific developments currently taking place in the US it was an ascendancy that was unlikely to continue and while director Lighthill himself became aware that many of the cherished ambitions of the talented scientists at Farnborough and the innovations he had so enthusiastically supported were not likely to be attainable.

Speaking at Lighthill's funeral, Professor Julian Hunt recognised the extent of his frustration:

> Disappointingly for him the 1960s was a period when the UK had to scale down its ever more costly aerospace and other technological ambitions to a level that its very slowly-growing economy could afford. Yet at the same time the UK was not ready to participate fully in European-wide projects with the notable exception of Concorde. It has been suggested that this is why after the RAE and the government decisions of the 1960s, James barely spoke about aerospace even, I gather, in his family.[35]

Sir Robert Cockburn (1964–69): In contrast to his predecessor, Cockburn completed twenty-seven years of notable scientific service before becoming the RAE's director.

Sir Robert Cockburn, director 1964–69. (Farnborough Air Sciences Trust)

While his circumstances were unquestionably more humble than Lighthill's, Cockburn's early ability was soon apparent. Following secondary school he studied for an external BSc degree at London University, which he gained with first-class honours. After teaching science at West Ham Municipal College during 1930–37 he joined the RAE as a researcher in communications and was awarded his doctorate.

At the RAE his wartime contributions quickly proved significant, particularly those concerned with the vital VHF short-range radio communications first used by RAF fighters in the Battle of Britain.[36] Cockburn went on to head the team of scientists and engineers developing radio countermeasures to the Luftwaffe raids who successfully jammed the radio beams by which the German bombers were directed to British cities. His team was then commissioned to counter the German radar's ability to detect British bombers: one of the principal weapons adopted for this purpose was the dropping of metallic strips, a small bundle of which cut to the right length could cause a radio echo as big as that from a four-engined bomber.[37] Under the British code name 'window' and the American 'chaff' it became a principal item of electronic warfare.

Cockburn's electronic skills were again in evidence when in June 1946 his signals depicted a phantom armada crossing the Channel from Dover to Calais in order to eclipse the genuine signals associated with the actual crossings to Normandy.

Following the Second World War, Cockburn worked at Harwell on countermeasures against the atomic bomb and in 1956 he was made Controller of Guided Weapons and Electronics at the Ministry of Aviation before becoming its chief scientist during 1959–64. On becoming Director of the RAE Cockburn brought wide-ranging knowledge about British aviation, including the workings of the Ministry of Aviation at the highest levels.

In 1972 he chaired a conference on 'Computers – System and Technology', where in his opening address he justly acknowledged that, 'He had had some experience ... in radio communications, radar, atomic energy and in various aspects of aviation,' but then proceeded in notably cautious fashion to conclude that, 'The real danger is not that computers will become more like us but that we will become more like computers.'[38]

After Lighthill, it might have been thought that a director with a rather more conservative approach and a wider knowledge about the workings of the Ministry of Defence was required. Significantly, the RAE's own magazine's comments on Cockburn's achievements, as director, included the comment that:

He has led the Establishment through one of its most difficult periods in which the role of the Establishment has changed from pure research and application of scientific knowledge to aerospace research, to one of diversification in which many other engineering and scientific projects have been undertaken.[39]

The strong impression given was that under Cockburn the RAE was having to extend its training commitments rather than initiating the novel and knowledge-seeking projects that the previous director believed constituted its lifeblood and enabled it to preserve its unique position.

Morien Morgan (1969–73): Like Cockburn, Morgan became director at the RAE following a lifetime in aviation. In fact it was his last appointment before retirement, although during his previous service at Farnborough he had been engaged on a project that unquestionably dominated his professional life.

In 1931 Morgan's schoolboy ability resulted in his admittance to St Catharine's College, Cambridge. There he gained a second in the mathematical tripos and a first class in the 1934 mechanical sciences tripos, where he specialised in aeronautics, winning the prestigious John Bernard Seely prize. So keen was Morgan to make a career in aeronautics that during his vacations he worked on the shop floor at Vickers and, following a short unhappy experience as an apprentice at Mather and Platt Ltd, in 1935 he readily accepted a post at the RAE as a junior scientific officer. There in 1941 he met and married local girl Sylvia Axford, which helped him cement his relationship with Farnborough, where he was to serve in different appointments for a total of twenty-four years. He began in its Aero Flight Department, where he was concerned with an aircraft's flying qualities (a job he loved), followed by a post in its newly established Guided Weapons Department. In 1954 Morgan became Deputy Director of the RAE's aircraft section before leaving it five years later to spend a year as a scientific adviser to the Air Ministry. After a decade in the Ministry of Aviation's Headquarters, during which he became Controller of Aircraft then Controller of Guided Weapons and Electronics, he finally returned to the RAE as director.

Together with his unquestionable professional abilities, Morgan was known for his friendliness and advanced 'people qualities', characteristics that were clearly evident in his carefully crafted message on his retirement:

I hope I have done the RAE a bit of good. You have certainly done me a lot of good. Whether from the shops, the scientists and engineers, the drawing offices, the laboratories, the airfields, the outstations, the ranges, the Serving

Officers attached, the admin side, the supporting services – from all of these I have received nothing but the utmost co-operation, friendship and loyalty. Things have understandably not been uniformly smooth – what with cuts, industrial and staff worries, reorganisation at HQ, rationalisation and what have you, but with all this, the RAE seems to be sailing through in fairly good shape …[40]

Throughout his career Morgan was an unashamed proponent of Farnborough, where he was always inclined to look at the positives. In his early days he was blissfully happy in the aero flight section where, despite his short sight, he obtained his flying licence. Like Ted Busk twenty-five years earlier, his scientific approach towards aircraft handling enabled him to extend the knowledge of stability and control with aircraft used in the Second World War.

However, much his most important contribution, prior to becoming director, was as Chairman of the Supersonic Transport Aircraft Committee, where he laid the foundations for the design and building of Concorde. Sir Arnold Hall, who was director during Morgan's early term on the project, revealed the difficulties he met with as project leader. Hall commented that, 'Morgan was always characterised by very strong enthusiasm for aeronautics in general and what he was doing in particular,' and continued:[41]

He became enthusiastically attached to the project throughout the rest of his career. Concorde critics have from time to time taken the view that he allowed his enthusiasm to overrun assessment on issues affecting the economic viability of the project. Be this as it may, he undoubtedly exerted considerable influence in the various 'battles' political and technical, which were argued around this aeroplane, in which he had the greatest faith.[42]

A 2018 publication on Concorde strongly corroborates Morgan's identification with the aeroplane, maintaining that he became 'one of the driving forces behind the SST (the Supersonic Transport Concept)'.[43]

While major scientific contributions by the RAE towards Concorde included those on its revolutionary wing led by brilliant German scientist Dietrich Küchemann along with the vital roles played by its wind tunnels and the Pyestock engine division towards the plane's overall development, Morgan's part as its apologist was most likely to bring criticisms. His impassioned addresses to the Royal Aeronautical Society in 1960 and 1972 about the utility of an aircraft that, however beautiful and technologically brilliant, excited such serious objections, do appear somewhat excessive. In 1960, for instance, he predicted that 'there will come safe, convenient and economic, long distance supersonic travel on a scale we still do not appreciate'.[44] Twelve years later, after so many setbacks, he was still predicting that, 'it is likely that supersonic transport aircraft – once introduced – will penetrate subsequently into the routing patterns of global aviation'.[45]

In fairness to Morgan, while his committee established a pattern of large-scale co-operation on research and development tasks between the aircraft industry and the relevant government departments that would become the norm, it was never designated to solve the financial problems of Concorde, nor could it remove the attendant environmental problems of noise, sonic boom and massive fuel consumption – although it certainly should have been fully aware of them.

The astute Arnold Hall was ever conscious of the pitfalls facing supersonic flight but Morgan's unfettered belief in supersonic air travel being 'both inevitable and necessary' might conceivably have tempted some of those less convinced than himself to wonder whether 'the most influential and grandest' of British aviation's R&D facilities should have devoted so many of its resources into furthering such aircraft.[46 47]

Rhys Price Probert, director 1973–80. (Farnborough Air Sciences Trust)

Some might also have legitimately wondered what part Morgan played in the appointment of his successor, Rhys Probert – a fellow Welshman from the same Cambridge College – a coincidence that Morgan referred to humorously, if inconclusively, in his farewell address to the RAE staff.

Rhys Price Probert (1973–80): Whatever the circumstances, the new director unquestionably deserved his appointment, one that he held for longer than any of his predecessors. After graduating in 1942 from Cambridge, Probert joined the RAE's Gas Turbine Department, where he stayed for fifteen years. During this time, as a man with an analytical and propulsion background, he went to America to help the US Navy, which was starting to develop guided missiles.[48] He also spent a year studying applied physics at America's Johns Hopkins University, before becoming Deputy Director at Pyestock with responsibility for Concorde and Tornado engines. By 1963 Probert was Director-General of Scientific Research at the Ministry of Aviation, where he led negotiations with France on an Anglo-French helicopter package, subsequently being promoted to Deputy Controller of Aircraft (RAF) with responsibility for a number of aircraft design and collaborative programmes.

In contrast to Morgan's especial relationship with Concorde, when Probert became director of the RAE he had already contributed to the whole gamut of aircraft and space activity, both civilian and military, as well as guided weapons.[49] As director he attempted to underline the RAE's continuing importance by attempting to transform it into an Air Systems Establishment with an important role in all aspects of civil and military aeronautics, 'assessing total aircraft/weapon system performance within an environment (while) appreciative of the practical problems of airframe avionics and missiles sub-systems', by which he hoped to create fresh opportunities for its staff.[50]

Unlike most other directors, Probert had no prior interest in aviation before being directed into the gas-turbine field during the Second World War and he continued to be a keen reader of history and classical literature throughout his life.[51] This gave him a measure of detachment and when asked about his hopes for the RAE he responded somewhat non-committally, acknowledging that, 'It is an institution of long standing with a record of contributions of all kinds. It has very useful traditions, which to a degree are self-sustaining.'[52]

Even so, when confronted by critical observations he showed himself quite prepared to deflect them by making major changes to the RAE's internal structure.

In Probert the RAE acquired someone who, while laid back and somewhat aloof, proved a shrewd and careful leader who sought to emphasise the

Establishment's widespread scientific services, through which he earned its staff's respect rather than the undoubted affection paid to his rash but more charismatic predecessor Morien Morgan.

Over the thirty-year period of our concern, due to their distinction and deep knowledge of both the Air Ministry's and civil service's workings, the RAE's directors played an influential role in helping their Establishment retain its predominant position.

Some proved particularly able proponents but none could be accused of incompetency. For instance, whatever criticisms Lighthill attracted with some of his soaring (and somewhat unrealistic) concepts, he made ample amends through his unquestioned scientific eminence. The impressive Arnold Hall oversaw one of the most successful aviation enquiries of all time, while the highly committed and the relatively incautious Morgan, who strayed into territory where Professor Hawthorne, for one, believed the RAE was in danger of losing its ability to help others and its credibility as an adviser, was succeeded by the cool and habitually analytical Probert. [53]

As a body they were unquestionably men imbued in the tradition that the most advanced levels of aviation research should be conducted at Farnborough and supported by government funds, rather than leaving it in the hands of a lesser-considered commercial aviation industry.

Whatever the directors' unquestioned impact and influence, between 1945 and 1975, external events played a fundamental role in the British aviation industry, including its laboratories and research establishments. By the late 1960s, following Nikita Khrushchev's fall from power, the Soviets showed themselves willing to begin Strategic Arms Limitation Talks (SALT), and such easing of tensions, along with some contraction in British defence responsibilities, were bound to bring new questions about the size and cost of its armed services, including their research facilities.

Even so, Leonid Brezhnev's hawkish interpretation of détente during Richard Nixon's presidency, where Brezhnev pressed for the Soviets to have an increasingly free hand in their foreign policy-making, led to Nixon's successor – Gerald Ford – reminding the West that the Cold War was in fact continuing by banning the word détente from the official diplomatic lexicon. [54]

With America's R&D laboratories tending to peak at some 7,000 staff some trimming of a larger RAE seemed likely – but there were as yet no major challenges to its existence. [55] If future RAE directors were to prove of similar calibre to those over the past thirty years it seemed reasonable to expect the Establishment to preserve its traditional structure.

An aerial photograph taken in 1979 of the RAE's extensive facilities. (Farnborough Air Sciences Trust)

What could never have been foreseen were the massive Soviet economic weaknesses exposed by the challenges from belligerent American President Ronald Reagan, along with the transformational attitudes to the rest of the world by new Russian premier Mikhail Gorbachev, culminating in their summit meeting at Geneva in 1985 that ended the Cold War. This was sure to bring change to Western defence establishments, including those in Britain, where Reagan enjoyed the ready support of Margaret Thatcher, who since 1979 had led one of the most anti-statist administrations since the war with its attacks on the boundaries of the state, including research and development spending on British military aviation. In typical fashion, she ordered the latter's costs to be halved, when those for the nation's nuclear deterrent remained ring-fenced.

Such developments conspired to form a perfect storm where the RAE was concerned and not only change the pattern of post-war defence research but to bring about even more fundamental threats to its traditional edifice than at the end of the First World War. Equally important at this time, there were no strong political defenders in sight.

SUMMARY

Before attempting to review what I have ultimately come to see as a harrowing and ill-fated, if not heartbreaking, period for British aviation, I decided to weigh my reactions against others; in this case four prominent and contemporary commentators: Arthur Reed, Derek Wood, Keith Hayward and Peter Hearne. In the case of the first two, I found a common belief that British aviation had in fact been betrayed by successive national governments. In his 1973 book *Britain's Aircraft Industry: What Went Right? What Went Wrong?* Reed – air correspondent of *The Times* – concluded that the achievements of the British aircraft industry were marred by a series of shuddering starts and stops as a consequence of its tumultuous and largely unhappy relationships with successive governments, and that 'as a pawn in the hands of the politicians it has never been given a real chance to flourish – or to die through its own efforts …'[1]

For him aerospace was the unsacred cow whose short-term future had been sacrificed to assuage the consciences of political parties or sections of political parties, to fit in with alterations of strategic policy and to help the government of the day to be seen to be doing something about the latest of the series of deep economic and financial crises that had shaken Britain since the war.

Two years later another book appeared, written this time by Derek Wood, Editor of *Jane's Defence Weekly*, entitled *Project Cancelled: The Disaster of Britain's Abandoned Aircraft Projects,* which was equally critical of different political administrations. In a closely argued work, Wood maintained that:

Since the Second World War Britain had become notorious as the nation which spends time and money embarking on advanced aviation projects and then destroys them by withdrawing support at the eleventh hour.

In terms of 1974 money he maintained that more than £1 billion had been spent over twenty-nine years on projects cancelled for political, economic or so-called strategic reasons.[2] His detailed examination of individual projects up to 1972 led him to believe that 'Study of the Years from the Second World War until now reveals an incredible mixture of wrong decisions, poor choices of specifications and continuous vacillations on the part of successive Ministers and Service Chiefs.'[3]

The two accounts accorded with my direst conclusions, but however powerful and persuasive I found it difficult to accept that ministers and their scientific advisers could have been so opposed to the aviation industry, unless, of course, they believed it to have a monopoly of scientific manpower and capital requirements that somehow constituted a threat to the true interests of the state.

My third commentator was Professor Keith Hayward, who after some thirty-five years writing about British post-war aviation decided in March 2015 to produce an extended article to give a more coherent overview of government policy towards the civil aviation sector up to the mid-1960s.[4] With Hayward there was no conspiracy theory, although he too came to hold governments responsible for the adverse developments, if primarily through failing to capitalise on innovative leadership present in the industry.

He began by looking at the initiatives of the Brabazon Committee, which aimed to lead British civil aviation into making a healthy recovery in world markets. Hayward believed that although early opportunities were lost, due to the country's airlines having to rely on inadequately converted bombers or American aeroplanes, with the US manufacturers' understandable reluctance to abandon their massive financial commitments in propeller aircraft, the UK possessed an undoubted ace in the jet engine, which either as a pure jet or a geared turbojet promised a massive leap forward in the range and payload of civil aircraft. Instead, the Brabazon transatlantic aircraft was designed to be powered originally with conventional piston engines, with the result that the huge aeroplane named after the committee's chairman proved obsolete at its launch. This was in contrast to the British success stories coming through the privately supported turboprop Vickers Viscount and the jet-powered de Havilland Comet. Hayward believed that it was by not going all out for jet propulsion that the British aircraft industry failed to achieve financial success, a belief confirmed by Exchequer grants of £40.65 million during 1945–51 bringing just £12.35 million of sales, a situation he believed was not helped by the Labour government's reluctance to move to much-needed rationalisation.[5]

Hayward proved no less critical of the incoming Conservative administration of 1951 that, while fully aware of aviation's weaknesses in both capital and technical ability, favoured a system of private industrial investment for future projects in the expectation the airlines would buy British and that Viscounts, Britannias and Comet airliners would provide the basis for a self-sustaining export-led civil sector. He revealed how such plans unravelled through the aircraft industry's own shortcomings, with the Comet's undoubted lead being destroyed by material weaknesses, while another major setback for the Conservatives' investment model came when the Vickers V1000 military transport aircraft and its civil equivalent the VC7 – which was expected to be bought by BOAC – encountered the airline's growing reluctance, which led to the VC7's cancellation in July 1955. This worsened when, despite BOAC's earlier plans to buy the Britannia and the Comet 4, the airline turned to the Boeing 707 for its North Atlantic routes.

A further instance where the government's financial projections were foiled by the aircraft industry was when permission was granted for BOAC to buy fifteen Boeing 707s on the condition that it ordered a British-built aircraft for its other routes. In practice the only company that could take on the contract for an aeroplane with the 'hot and high' performance needed for BOAC's Empire routes was Vickers, and in any case its projected VC10 required further development before being touted for the international North Atlantic run. In the event, Vickers came close to ruin by seriously underestimating the aircraft's costs and banking on considerable exports to bail them out. When the government tried to help Vickers by bringing pressure on BOAC to place a large order it brought about a major financial crisis for the airline that led it to dismiss its senior management and to carry out radical financial restructuring.

Hayward instanced a further attempt by the government at private venture initiatives with the Trident short-haul aircraft intended for BEA. Unfortunately, when faced with the likelihood of an economic downturn BEA panicked and ordered a smaller plane, a decision that in the adverse financial climate of the time, de Havilland felt unable to oppose, despite its only too likely effects on the aircraft's worldwide prospects. As a result, the larger Boeing 727, launched in 1959 with provision for thirty more passengers, ran away with the market and instead of receiving funding through private ventures, British aviation required support from public funds.

Unlike the first two commentators, the picture drawn by Hayward was not one of aerospace as the unsacred cow but of successive governments struggling against adverse domestic and international trends where fewer military orders and a comparatively small civil market proved unable to match American competitors and where the industry shared in some of the shortcomings.

This latter belief was also held by the fourth commentator, distinguished aerodynamicist and aviation executive Peter Hearne.[6] Hearne's criticisms were directed both at the industry and nationalised airlines for their aeronautical projects 'veering between large and sometimes unachievable and disappointingly small in respect of our international competitors as much as governments'.[7] He was particularly concerned with the undue size proposed for some of the aircraft, in particular the Saunders-Roe Princess flying boat (and its land equivalent the Brabazon). He made play of the flying boat's span of 220ft, wing area of 5,000 square ft and intended weight of 330,000lb, designed to carry just 105 passengers, who enjoyed the enormous privilege of having thirteen toilets between them.

As Hearne caustically observed. 'The Flying boat really was an air yacht whose wartime usefulness in using relatively unprepared bases had now evaporated,' but he was little better disposed toward the Brabazon, with its 100 passengers, pointing out that the Americans had normal-sized aircraft that could cross the Atlantic with one stop (or exceptionally two) and make reasonable-length journeys to the Middle and Far East with a range in excess of 2,600 nautical miles.[8] The British Tudor, Hermes and the early Britannia aircraft did not possess such a range, which in the case of the Britannia he put down to Bristol's dismissal in 1942 of its notable engine designer Roy Fedden, although America, of course, always had a greater need for long-distance aircraft for both its internal and external transport links rather than Europe's shorter routes and Britain's 'stopping train' Empire journeys.

Like Hayward, Hearne strongly believed in the superiority of jets over piston or turboprop engines, where he believed up to 36 per cent extra revenue could be earned, although in the case of the Comet this advantage was reduced by its initial small Ghost engine and limited 1,700-mile range.[9] Hearne was also enthusiastic for the projected Vickers V1000/VC7 with its ability to fly 100 passengers from London to New York with Rolls-Royce Conway engines and he held BOAC directly responsible for the misplaced conviction that the future of long-range transport lay in the turboprop (Britannia) rather than the large jet because of its lower operating costs rather than the money it could earn. Such obsession with cost killed off the V1000, which 'like the contemporary Boeing 707 and DC8 was the right size and it mattered very much indeed when it was axed'.[10] Hearne believed the V1000's higher cruising speed over the turboprop would have offered greater flexibility of scheduling and with it the UK could have picked up

20 per cent of the early long-range jet market. It was a conviction shared by Sir George Edwards, who saw its cancellation as 'the biggest blunder that put us behind [the Americans] all the time'.[11]

In the case of the military TSR2, Hearne also believed that, while it showed every sign of being a technical and operational success, it was far too big – and hence too expensive. Hearne blamed the RAF for what was a self-inflicted wound with their demands for a plane that started as a Canberra replacement and ended up as a supersonic V-bomber.

For Hearne such counterproductive decisions from within the industry as a whole sowed the seeds of self-destruction before the 1965 financial crisis led them to germinate alarmingly. Governments did not escape his anger, either, specifically the 1965 Plowden Committee with its craven aim of seeking co-operation as a way of protecting the industry against competition. As he expressed it:

> Of the three or four competent aircraft design and manufacturing countries, the UK is the only one who seeks co-operation, believing that other parties will flock to join them as men of goodwill and common interest. What a hope! Our competitors … are rubbing their hands and watching us slowly self-destructing what was once one of the two or three most innovative and potentially profitable aircraft industries in the world.[12]

However far I might concur with the serious shortcomings identified by my chosen correspondents in the decision-making of both governments and the aircraft industry, I believe that further major factors bore down on the British state during the early post-war years.

Pre-eminent was the expense overload caused by a combination of unforeseen strategic threats, like the outbreak of the Korean War and the 1956 Soviet invasion of Hungary, in addition to the large and protracted commitments caused by the return of the massive British Empire into its constituent states. These coincided with heavy over-expenditure during the Second World War and the subsequent ambitious social schemes leading to sporadic balance-of-payments crises and agonising disputations about central support for aviation.

Less definable but also significant was the change of mood in Britain at the end of the 1939–45 war. While during it an exceptional level of mutual co-operation and purpose existed between British government departments and industry, this slackened over the post-war years, descending at times to a state of near civil war between the Treasury (sometimes abetted by the Board of Trade) and the RAF and aircraft industry.

Evidence of this blinkered, if not bloody-minded, thinking had been apparent to Peter Masefield during the war's later stages when he visited aircraft factories across the country and found that in many instances there was little or no interest in post-war initiatives, whereas in the US, aviation editor Reginald Cleveland, for instance, believed that in spite of the tremendous demands for production and modification of aircraft for war, development work on planes and helicopters should be carried on at the same time, due to their new utility for peace with but minor modifications.[13]

In contrast, within the UK a sense of misplaced self-confidence and the wish to 'return to normal after the war' served to encourage its aircraft manufacturers to continue with their time-honoured methods of production and for aviation to remain a fragmented industry with its twenty-seven aircraft firms, of vastly different size and strength, and eight engine manufacturers. Proud owners and their staff, many of whom had been together since the early 1920s, opposed much-needed amalgamations, with Frederick Handley Page, for instance, finding it impossible to unite with another firm and choosing liquidation instead.

Such procrastination undoubtedly proved costly for both the strength and competitiveness of the industry. In 1955 there were the same number of design firms as at the end of the war, which resulted in an unnecessary number of aircraft cancellations – sometimes at the design stage. Even more serious, aversion to change occurred against a climate of escalating costs and lengthening gestation times. Contemporary aeroplane projects were due to take up to ten years, the equivalent of two full parliamentary terms, during which the ministers responsible were sure to have changed. Above all, this took place against shrinking order books and the need to manage a high-technology operation against a relative handful of initial production aircraft. By 1960, for instance, numbers of military aircraft orders were down from the 2,000 of 1955 to 510, with just 41 per cent of the 1955 weight.

Across the Atlantic there were no comparable problems, with military sales increasing due to the US's position as the world's leading superpower and its large and ever-expanding civil market. The more benign situation in the US tended to encourage other advances. Peter Hearne for instance, drew attention to the superior system of US project management during the 1960s, which he believed owed something to production successes and enabled the American Government to leave its defence contractors to produce a well-rounded technical solution with only a light supervisory touch. In contrast, the trouble-seeking chiefs of UK defence procurement, in their search for economies, seemed to relish 'telling the world how inefficient and ineffective UK Defence contractors are and how MoD are going to give them a bloody nose'.[14]

Whatever its other advantages, in the US there were no comparable feelings with some in Britain who felt that at the end of a long and draining war they could justifiably take their feet off the throttle. The US entered the Second World War relatively late and during it its industrial production had made exciting and permanent strides, with widespread adoption of sophisticated mass production techniques. Peter Hearne, for one, believed that in Britain the sense of some need for relaxation after 1945 was widespread and included those concerned with the key political and technical direction of British aviation, who did not always balance their intelligence and creativity with judgement and common sense.[15]

He believed one instance occurred with the Sandys doctrine of 1957, where undue emphasis on guided weapons and the wholesale cutting of military aircraft led to confidence in British military aircraft being shattered. Even more grievous during 1965 was the Labour government's wholesale cancellation of the three key British military aviation projects, the P.1154 vertical take-off fighter, HS.681 V/STOL transport and, most notably, the TSR2 strike and reconnaissance aircraft, along with Denis Healey's panic purchases of US aircraft leading to a situation where Britain was no longer able to pursue any major national aircraft project.

As if this were not enough, the destructive political decisions were paralleled by technical and economic lapses of judgement within the aircraft industry. Notable was the de Havilland Company's disastrous overconfidence in the wafer-thin gauge of metal for the cabin envelope of its Comet, along with its square window design, which lost Britain a unique opportunity to dominate the civil air market, together with Rolls-Royce's later willingness to ignore economic facts with its RB211 engine.

The seriousness of the underlying problems were well known to certain leading individuals at the time. When addressing the Society of Engineers in 1954, Roy Fedden had declared that:

> The position in British Aviation at the moment and for the next few years ahead is critical, and what we require is a realistic regeneration, the dropping of this new brand of complacency and the building up of a government team which can insist upon a fair share of adequate aeronautical research money being spent amongst those who deserve it and who will make the best use of it.[16]

While Fedden's advocacy of an improved system of allocating research funds was long-standing, no one could doubt his engineering skills, legendary drive and monumental loyalty towards the industry. Unfortunately, Fedden was a man who attracted fierce loyalty and opposition in equal measure.

Another outstanding engineer who was not hampered by Fedden's confrontational reputation but was equally conscious of serious contemporary failings was Professor R.V. Jones, who in his Thomas Hawksley Lecture of 1974 to his fellow IMechE engineers brought their attention to the fact that despite Britain's share of basic inventions such as the steam turbine and jet engine, the country had 'notably failed in mechanical detail and in precision engineering and machine tools' during the Second World War compared with American and German engineering.[17]

Although he believed that mechanical engineering was still the biggest of British export industries, 'inferiority of this kind has become increasingly apparent in recent years, where the value of our exports per pound weight has increased at a lower rate than most of our principal competitors'.[18]

Jones ended his lecture with the fear, shared by Peter Masefield during his 1944 visits to aviation firms, that in some respects industry seemed to have lost its way and that 'what is both ultimately and immediately needed to encourage creativity in our engineers is a revival of a sense of purpose in our country generally. Its greatness was founded on humanity, discipline and initiative – and a good deal of the initiative came from its engineers.'[19]

Whatever the problems experienced by the British aviation industry between 1945 and 1975 due to the Brabazon Committee's unreal aspirations, the allegedly misguided interventions of successive British governments together with the industry's own difficulties over producing the required aircraft on budget and to a competitive timescale, together with the presence of a malaise – real or imagined – affecting the country as a whole, by far the most important element was American competition. The world's most vigorous and ambitious superpower had already established a dominant position in civil aviation through its airliners and went on to seize the initiative in the military field with its jet fighters. In the face of such dynamism backed by far superior resources, despite its undoubted achievements, many of British aviation's most notable initiatives were trumped (or assimilated), while its deficiencies were cruelly exposed to deny the country participation in major independent aircraft programmes and render it progressively less able to take a leading role in multinational projects.

NOTES

CHAPTER 1

1   *Air Enthusiast*, No. 26, H.A. Taylor, 'Brabazon, The Work of the Committees', p.72.
2   *Air-Britain Archive*, Winter Issue, 4 December 2011, Michael West, 'Imperial and British Airways go to war', pp.181–86.
3   Halford-Macleod, Guy, *Born of Adversity: Britain's Airlines, 1919–1963*, p.39.
4   *Air-Britain Archive*, pp.200, 201.
5   *Born of Adversity*, p.42.
6   Sampson, Anthony, *Empires of the Sky*, 1984, p.58.
7   House of Commons Debates, 17 December 1942, Vol. 385, p.2121.
8   *Born of Adversity*, p.49.
9   Bray, Winston, *The History of BOAC 1939–1974*, c. 1983, p.36.
10 *Aeronautics* Vol. 28, March 1952, S. Scott Hall, 'Our New Airliners, The 11 Results of the New British Formula for Developing Civil Aircraft', p.28.
11 *Propliner*, No. 77, Winter 1998, Peter Berry, 'The Brabazon Propliners', p.10.
12 Masefield, Sir Peter, with Gunston, Bill, *Flight Path: The Autobiography of Sir Peter Masefield*, 2002, p.82.
13 Ibid., p.82.
14 Masefield, p.95.
15 Phipp, Mike, *The Brabazon Committee and British Airliners 1945–60*, 2007, p.31.
16 War Office Paper. 537, 3 December 1943, Post-war Civil aviation, Secret Memorandum by the Lord Privy Seal to the War Cabinet.
17 Proceedings of the First National US Clinic of Domestic Aviation Planning, 1943, p.205.
18 Andrews, C.F. and Morgan, E. B., *Vickers Aircraft since 1908*, 1988, p.406.
19 Phipp, p.81.
20 Gardner, Robert, *From Bouncing Bombs to Concorde: The Authorised Biography of Aviation Pioneer Sir George Edwards*, 2006, p.65.
21 Phipp, Mike, p.81.
22 *Journal of the RAeS*, LXIII 1959, John L.P. Brodie, 'Frank Bernard Halford, 1894–1955', p.201.
23 Marcus Aurelius, *Meditations*, 1960, p.63.

CHAPTER 2

1   *Air Transport* (Editor Peter J. Lyth) 1996, ix. By 1990 the total world air traffic amounted to a fifth of the world's population.

2   Ministry of Civil Aviation on British Air Services, Command Paper 6712, HMSO, December 1945, 3, Section 27.

3   Phipp, pp.50, 51.

4   *Propliner*, p.9.

5   Phipp, p.51.

6   Ministry of Civil Aviation on British Air Services, , p.7, Sections 27, 28.

7   Masefield, p.205.

8   Ibid., p.208.

9   Ibid.

10   National Aerospace Library, Fedden Mission Report, June 1943, Copy No. 31, Review of the Civil Aviation Position in America, Chapter 1, pp.3–4.

11   Kaplan, Philip, *Big Wings: The Largest Aeroplanes Ever Built*, 2005, p.115.

12   *Aeroplane* (monthly) September 1999, Bill, Gunston 'The Behemoth from Bristol', p.54.

13   Civil Aviation, Report of the Ministry of Civil Aviation for 1948, 9 HMSO, 1950, p.21.

14   Robertson, F.H., British Civil Transport, unpublished paper of 1956, p.15.

15   Barnes C.H., *Bristol Aircraft*, 1964, p.358.

16   *Propliner*, p.13.

17   Hayward, Keith, *The British Aircraft Industry*, 1989, p.55.

18   *Aeronautics*, March 1953, Scott Hall, 'Our new airliners – first results of the new British formula for developing civil aircraft', pp.26–38.

19   Masefield, p.208.

20   *Air Transport*, p.xx.

21   Robertson, p.8.

22   Ibid., p.24.

23   *Journal of Aeronautical History*, Paper No. 2018/04, 4 March 2018, Prof. Keith Hayward, 'Government and British Civil Aerospace 1945–64', p.102.

24   *Air Transport*, p.85.

25   Ibid., p.86.

26   Minutes of SBAC, 27 October 1943, p.6.

27   Minutes of SBAC, 14 March 1945, p.100.

28   Minutes of SBAC, 11 June 1947, p.269.

29   Ibid., p.270.

30   *Journal of Transport, Economics and Policy*, Vol. 1, No. 2, May 1967, Brooks, Peter W., 'Development of Air Transport', pp.10, 11.

31   *The Times*, obituary of J.T.C. Moore-Brabazon, 18 May 1966. The American airman Samuel Franklin Cody had already flown at Farnborough in October 1908.

32   Moore-Brabazon, John, *The Brabazon Story*, 1956, p.11.

33   *Oxford Dictionary of National Biography*, 2004–16, Article 32018.

34   Moore-Brabazon, p.161.

35   *The Times*, 12 September 1962.

36   *Air and Space*, May 2012, Stephan Wilkinson, 'Bristol Brabazon – Design by Committee', p.56.

37   Brabazon gave the Romanes lecture at Oxford on 'Forty Years of Flight' on
     17 May 1949.
38   *Journal of the Royal Aeronautical Society,* LXIX 1965, p.5.
39   *Daily Mail*, 3 November 1951.
40   Hewat, Timothy and Waterton, W.A., *The Comet Riddle*, 1955, pp.144–46.
41   *Journal of the RAeS* XLVI, 1942, Wilbur Wright Memorial Lecture by Hon. Lord
     Brabazon of Tara, 28 May 1942, p.256.
42   Ibid., p.253.
43   Secret Cabinet Paper (46)217 of 23 July 1946, Civil Aircraft Requirements, p.12.
44   *Air Britain,* June 2011, Derek King, 'The Brabazon Committee', p.95.

CHAPTER 3

1   Reed Arthur, *Britain's Aircraft Industry: What Went right? What Went Wrong?*, 1973,
     p.27.
2   Taylor, Douglas R., *Boxkite to Jet: The Remarkable Career of Frank B. Halford*,
     1999, p.116.
3   Armitage, Michael, *The Royal Air Force*, 1999, p.186.
4   Wood, Derek, *Project Cancelled: The Disaster of Britain's Abandoned Aircraft Projects*,
     1986, p.21.
5   The Supply of Military Aircraft, HMSO, February 1955, p.4.
6   Gunston, Bill, *Plane Speaking: A Personal View of Aviation History*, 1991, p.163.
7   Ibid., p.164.
8   Ibid., p.165.
9   Wood p.7.
10   Ibid.
11   Ibid., p.31.
12   Peden, G.C., *Treasury and British Public Policy*, p.458.
13   Second Report from the Select Committee on Estimates concerning the Supply
     of Military Aircraft, HMSO, 19/12/1956, p.xxxiii.
14   Ibid.
15   Ibid., pp.xv, xxxiv.
16   Ibid., p.vii, para 14.
17   Ibid., p.xxx, para 118.
18   Minutes of Evidence, para 203, p.4.
19   Ibid., p.xxv, para 99.
20   Mason, Francis K., *Hawker Hunter: Biography of a Thoroughbred*, 1985, p.22.
21   Mason Francis K., *Hawker Aircraft since 1920*, 1991, p.376.
22   Mason, *Biography of a Thoroughbred*, p.40.
23   Ibid., p.19.
24   Jackson, Robert, *Hawker Hunter*, 1982, p.74.
25   Beamont, Roland and Arthur Reed, *English Electric Canberra*, 1984, p.7.
26   Jackson, Robert, *Canberra: The Operational Record*, 1988, p.2.
27   Ibid., p.14.
28   Ibid., p.22.
29   *Aviation Week,* Vol. 51, 19 September 1949, p.13.

30   Armitage, Michael, *The Royal Air Force*, p.258.
31   *Aeroplane*, Vol. LXXXIII, 5 September 1952, Leading Article, p.339.
32   Davies, Glyn, *From Lysander to Lightning: Teddy Petter, Aircraft Designer*, 2014, p.29.
33   *The Times*, Edward Petter, Obituary 27 May 1968.
34   Davies, p.37.
35   Unpublished biography of Teddy Petter, Aircraft Designer, compiled by Robert Page, Roy Fowler and Adrian Page, November 1991, p.47.
36   Ibid., p.61.
37   Ransom, Stephen and Fairclough, Robert, *English Electric Aircraft and their Predecessors*, 1987, p.236.
38   Unpublished biography of Teddy Petter, p.204.
39   Ibid., p.267.
40   Ibid., p.268.

CHAPTER 4

1   Brookes, Andrew, *V-Force: The History of Britain's Airborne Deterrent*, 1982, p.18.
2   Gardner, Charles, *British Aircraft Corporation*, 1981, p.18.
3   Brookes, p.19. In fact the wind tunnel at Farnborough was upgraded to transonic by 1951 and from 1950 onwards a series of advanced tunnels were constructed at the National Physical Laboratory.
4   Hubbard, Kenneth and Simmons, Michael, *Dropping Britain's First Hydrogen Bomb: The Story of Operation Grapple*, 1957–58, 1985, pp.140–41.
5   Mason, Francis K., *The British Bomber since 1914*, 1994, p.379.
6   Ibid., p.380.
7   Armitage, p.209.
8   Brookes, pp.45, 46.
9   Dancey, Peter G., *The Avro Vulcan, a History*, 2007, p.106.
10   Mason, *The British Bomber Since 1914*, p.385.
11   Ibid., p.386.
12   Ibid.
13   Blackman, Tony with O' Keefe Garry, *Victor Boys: True Stories from Forty Memorable Years of the Last V-bomber*, 2012, p.17.
14   de Saint-Exupéry, Antoine, *Night Flight*, 1939, p.17.

CHAPTER 5

1   Jackson, A.J., *De Havilland's Aircraft since 1909*, 1987, p.468.
2   Simons, Graham M., *Comet: The World's First Jet Airliner*, 2013, p.17.
3   Darling, Kevin, *De Havilland Comet*, 2005, p.17.
4   Dempster, Derek D., *The Tale of the Comet*, 1959, p.67.
5   Simons, p.50.
6   Darling, p.24.
7   Simons, p.40.
8   Darling,, p.25.
9   Ibid.

10   Dempster, pp.85–87.
11   Ibid., p.94.
12   Hewat, p.46.
13   Dempster, p.103.
14   Simons, p.132.
15   ibid, p.133.
16   Dempster, p.106.
17   Reed, p.38.
18   Dempster, p.143.
19   Hewat, pp.121–122.
20   Ibid., p.123.
21   Dempster, p.183.
22   Report of the Court of Inquiry into the accidents to Comet G-ALYP on
     10 January 1954 and Comet G-ALYY on 8 April 1954, HMSO, 1955, para 115.
23   Ibid., para 117.
24   Ibid., para 118.
25   Ibid., para 120.
26   Ibid., para 122.
27   Ibid., para 127.
28   Ibid., para 162.
29   Darling, p.85.
30   Hennessy, Peter, *Never Again*, 1992, p.429.
31   National Aerospace Library, Oral Recordings, Interview of D.P. Davies by
     R. Giesler, July 1992.

CHAPTER 6

1   Peden G.C., *Arms, Economics and British Strategy from Dreadnoughts to Hydrogen
     Bombs*, 2007, p.259.
2   *Air Power Review*, Vol. 20, No. 1, Spring 2017, Bill Pyke, Air Chief Marshal,
     'Sir John Slessor, The Unsung British Cold War Strategist', p.68.
3   Peden, p.275.
4   Defence White Paper, Outline of Future Policy, HMSO, March 1957, para 1.
5   Ibid., para 2.
6   Ibid., para 3.
7   Ludlow, N. Piers. 'Sandys, (Edwin) Duncan, Baron Duncan-Sandys (1908–1987),
     politician' *Oxford Dictionary of National Biography*, 3 January 2008, Oxford
     University Press, Date of access 21 March 2017, www.oxforddnb.com/
     view/10.1093/ref:odnb/9780198614128.001.0001/odnb-9780198614128-e-39858
8   1957 Defence White Paper, para 7(e).
9   *Oxford DNB*, OUP 2004, Article 39858.
10   1957 Defence White Paper, para 23(c).
11   *Diplomacy and Statecraft,* 2013, David French, 'Duncan Sandys and the Projection of
     British Power after Suez', p.4.
12   Ibid., p.45.
13   *Interavia*, Vol. xii No. 9, 1957, E. Baur, Britain's Aircraft Industry in 1957, p.875.
14   Hayward, pp.68–69.

15 Ibid., p.71.
16 *The Aviation Historian*, Iss. No. 19, 2017, Keith Hayward, '60 years On, Duncan Sandys and the 1957 Defence White Paper,' p.15.
17 Ibid., p.19.
18 Ibid., p.20.
19 Gardner, Robert, *From Bouncing Bombs to Concorde*, pp.141–42.
20 Ibid.
21 Gardner, Charles, *British Aircraft Corporation, A History*, 1981, p.20.
22 Ibid.
23 Reed, p.9.
24 Wood, p.5.
25 MacMillan, Harold, *The Macmillan Diaries, The Cabinet Years 1950–57*, 2003, p.600.
26 Rowan, Sir Leslie, *Arms and Economies: The Changing Challenge*, 1960, p.15.
27 Sandbrook, Dominic, *Never Had It So Good: A History of Britain from Suez to the Beatles*, 2005, p.226.
28 *Journal of Strategic Studies*, Wyn Rees, The 1957 Sandys White Paper, New Priorities in British Defence Policy, p.226.
29 *The Aviation Historian*, Iss. No. 19, 2017, p.20.
30 Ibid.

CHAPTER 7

1   RAeS Symposium, The History of the UK Strategic Deterrent, 17 March 1999, John C. Garnett, Reflections on the British Deterrent, paras 1.1–1.2.
2   Armitage, p.212.
3   Boyes, John, *Project Emily, Thor IRBM and the RAF*, 2008, p.139.
4   RAeS Symposium, The History of the UK Strategic Deterrent, 17 March 1999, D. Wright and R.L. Dommett, Introduction to Blue Streak, pp.8, 9.
5   Ibid., pp.8, 11.
6   Karp A., *Ballistic Missile Proliferation: The Politics and the Technics*, 1996, p.77.
7   RAeS Symposium, The History of the UK Strategic Deterrent, 17 March 1999, Ben Cole, The Cancellation of Blue Streak, p.1.
8   Ibid.
9   Hill, C.N., *A Vertical Empire: History of the British Rocketry Programme*, 2012, p.25.
10 Prospero, Proceedings from the British Rocket Oral History Conferences at CharterHouse, Number 2, Spring 2005, p.32.
11 RAeS Symposium, The History of the UK Strategic Deterrent, 17 March 1999, R.H. Francis, The Development of Blue Steel, p.1.
12 Ibid., pp.5, 6.
13 Ibid., paras 4.4–4.5.
14 RAeS Symposium, The History of the UK Strategic Deterrent, 17 March 1999, John E. Allen, Blue Steel and its Developments, p.4.
15 Hill C.N., *A Vertical Empire*, p.91.
16 RAeS Symposium, John E. Allen, p.47.
17 RAeS Symposium, The History of the UK Strategic Deterrent, 17 March 1999, John Bone, Submarine-Based Deterrent: Polaris, pp.9.
18 Grove, Eric J., *Vanguard to Trident: British Naval Policy Since World War II*, 1987, p.237.

19 Macmillan, Harold, *At the End of the Day*, p.363.
20 Armitage, p.204.
21 Wood, Appendix 5.
22 *RUSI Journal*, Vo. 108, 1969, Sir Kenneth Cross, 'Bomber Command's Thor Missile Force', p.131.
23 Hill, p.117.
24 Ibid., p.122.
25 Ibid., p.123.
26 Ibid., p.135.
27 Ibid., p.223.
28 Prospero functioned fully until 1973 and remained in radio contact until 1996. Recently it has been contacted again in deep space by a team from UC London, following help from the National Aerospace Library on its commanding codes.
29 Baxter A.D., A History of Rocketry, Cayley Memorial Lecture to Brough Branch of the RAeS on 25 March 1964, p.21. (Professor Baxter was Chief Executive Rockets and Nuclear Power at the Air Ministry in 1957 and President of the RAeS in 1966–67.)
30 Hastings, Stephen, *The Murder of TSR2*, 1966, p.191.
31 Millard, Douglas, *An Overview of United Kingdom Space Activity, 1957–1987*, 2005, p.3.
32 Hill, p.216.
33 Gainor, Chris, *To a Distant Day: The Rocket Pioneers*, 2008, p.54.

CHAPTER 8

1   Jackson, A.J., *De Havilland Aircraft since 1909*, 1987, p.464.
2   Wood, p.84.
3   Wilson, Keith, *VC10: Owners' Workshop Manual*, 2016, p.11.
4   Andrews, pp.465–66.
5   Its robust design prevented any similar problems of cabin decompression suffered by the Comet.
6   Higham, Robin, *The Complete History of BOAC*, 2013, p.210.
7   *The Aviation Historian*, Iss. No. 18, January 2017, Keith Hayward, 'Between the Devil and the Deep Blue Sea', p.13.
8   ibid, p.14.
9   Cole, Lance, *VC10: Icon of the Skies, Boeing and a Jet Age Battle*, 2017, p.209.
10 *The Putnam International Review*, May 1989, Dr Norman Barfield, 'VC10, Engineering Pedigree of a Thoroughbred', p.28.
11 *Air Britain Aviation World*, June 2012, John P. McCrickard, 'Vickers VC10 – Commercial Failure – or Success?', p.90.
12 *The Aviation Historian*, Iss. No. 16, July 2016, Keith Hayward, 'Trident, Britain's Fork in the Road', p.17.
13 McKim, Dr Frank, *Trident, A History*, 2008, p.17.
14 Wood, p.87.
15 *The Aviation Historian*, Iss. No. 16, July 2016, p.10.
16 Ibid., p.16.
17 McKim, p.140.

18 Skinner, Stephen, *The BAC One-Eleven, The Whole Story*, 2002, p.12.
19 *Aeroplane* (Monthly), November 2012, Martyn Chorlton, 'British Aircraft Corporation One-Eleven', p.71.
20 Ibid., p.76.
21 A modified 1-11, the series 475, was produced with a strengthened undercarriage and other adaptations for flying in and out of similar airports under more extreme conditions.
22 Bowers, Peter M., *Boeing Aircraft since 1916*, 1989, p.423.
23 McKim, p.84.
24 Skinner, p.167.
25 Report of a 1969 Working Party of the RAeS into 'Effectiveness in R & D', Part One, p.3.
26 Skinner, p.167.
27 *The Putnam International Review*, p.28.

CHAPTER 9

1   Mason, Francis K., *Harrier*, 1986, p.6.
2   Fozard J.W., Harri-ing Sir Isaac Vertically, Secrets of Engineering Elegance to Jumping Jets, Proceedings of the Royal Institution, Pamphlet Vol. 58, p.243.
3   Mason, *Harrier*, p.23.
4   Davies, Peter E., and Thornborough, Antony M., *The Harrier Story*, 1996, p.13.
5   Mason, *Hawker Aircraft since 1920*, p.82.
6   There has been some debate about the order of the telephone calls but the essence of the story is clear enough.
7   Mason, *Harrier*, p.27.
8   *Aerospace*, Vol. 2, April 1975, Sir Stanley Hooker, 'From Merlin to Pegasus. From Hurricane to Harrier', p.18.
9   Buttler, Tony, *Hawker P.1127, Kestrel and Harrier: Developing the World's first Jet V/STOL Combat Aircraft*, 2017, pp.26–27.
10 *Aerospace*, p.19.
11 Davies, p.22.
12 Mason, *Harrier*, p.54.
13 March, Peter R., *The Harrier Story*, 2007, p.14.
14 Subsequent permission was given for a further ten.
15 *Hermes* was a helicopter-only carrier, subsequently converted for use by Harriers.
16 Mason, *Harrier*, p.147.
17 Ibid., p.115.
18 Mason, *Hawker Aircraft since 1920*, pp.92–93.
19 Fozard, p.228.
20 ibid, p.283.
21 *The Aviation Historian*, Iss. No. 10, 15 January 2015, Lon Wordeen, 'Bird of Prey, The AV8A in US Marine Corps Service', p.55.
22 *Aviation*, August 2015, Tom Kaminski, 'Harrier Fights On', p.56.
23 Myles Bruce, *Jump Jet: The Revolutionary V/STOL Fighter*, 1986, p.10.

CHAPTER 10

1   Dockrill, Saki, *Britain's Retreat from East of Suez: The Choice between Europe and the World*, 2002, p.81.
2   Royal Air Force Historical Society, *TSR2 with Hindsight*, 1988, p.188.
3   Ibid., p.72.
4   McLelland, Tim, *TSR2: Britain's Lost Cold War Strike Aircraft*, 2010, p.24.
5   Ibid., p.29.
6   Burke, Damien, *TSR2: Britain's Lost Bomber*, 2010, p.91.
7   Ibid., p.108.
8   Ibid., p.141.
9   Ibid., p.266.
10 Sir Frank Cooper, *TSR2 and Whitehall*, 1988, p.40.
11 *Journal of Strategic Studies*, Vol. 20, No. 4 (December 1997) Sean Straw and John W. Young, 'The Wilson Government and the Demise of TSR2', October 1964–April 1965.
12 *The Times*, 24 September 1964.
13 Ibid., 5 January 1965.
14 Ibid., 11 January 1965.
15 Ibid., 12 January 1965.
16 Ibid., 15 January 1965.
17 *Journal of Strategic Studies*, pp.12–13.
18 Ibid., p.35.
19 *The Times*, 7 April 1965.
20 Salisbury, M.W., The Significance of TSR2, RAeS lecture at Weybridge, 18 October 1989.
21 Williams, Dr Geoffrey, Gregory, Frank and Simpson, John, *Crises in Procurement: A Case Study of the TSR2*, 1969, p.7.
22 Hastings Stephen, *The Murder of TSR2*, 1966, p.164.
23 Healey Denis, *The Time of My Life*, 1989, p.54.
24 *Journal of Strategic Studies*, p.37.
25 Ibid., p.38.
26 Cockerel, Michael, *Denis Healey: The Best Premier Labour Never Had*, BBC2 programme on Wednesday, 7 October 2015.
27 Ibid.
28 *Aviation News*, January 2017, Dr Kevin Wright, TSR2, 'The Greatest Aircraft the RAF Never Flew?', p.19.
29 *Journal of the RUSI*, Vol. CXV, March 1970, No. 657, D. Keith Lucas, The Case Study of the TSR2: A Critique, p.42.
30 Healey, p.273.
31 Ibid., p.277.

CHAPTER 11

1   *Journal of the RAeS* LXXV, November 1971, Lecture by I. Sikorsky, Sixty Years of Flying (read by his son Sergei), p.765. Although by 1971 a single RAF squadron was equipped with the V/STOL Harrier it was still a largely unproven weapon system.

2   Uttley, Matthew, *Westland and the British Helicopter Industry 1945–60: Licensed Production versus Indigenous Innovation*, 2001, p.1.
3   Pitcairn, Harold F., Juan de la Cierva, Pamphlet of 9 January 1939, p.3.
4   *Journal of the RAeS*, Vol. 70, 1966, Raoul Hafner, British Rotorcraft, pp.235, 236.
5   Spencer, Jay P., *Whirlybirds: A History of the US Helicopter Pioneers*, 1998, p.12.
6   Dowling, Wing Commander John, *RAF Helicopters: The First Twenty Years*, 1992, p.5.
7   Uttley, p.27.
8   Spencer, p.27.
9   Ibid., p.45.
10 National Aerospace Library, Unpublished Articles and Lectures by Reginald A.C. Brie, October 1966, p.90.
11 Ibid., p.45.
12 Ibid., p.59.
13 Uttley, p.33.
14 Ibid., p.40.
15 Ibid., p.43.
16 Ibid., p.46.
17 Ibid.
18 Dowling, p.99.
19 Uttley, p.102.
20 James, Derek, N., *Westland Aircraft since 1915*, 1991, p.333.
21 Armitage, p.243, A description of the Whirlwind's mechanical limitations is found in Dowling, Wing Commander John, *RAF helicopters: The First Twenty years*, 1992.
22 *Journal of the RAeS*, Vol. 70 Part I, January 1966, R. Hafner, 'British Rotorcraft', p.241.
23 National Aerospace Library, Unpublished Monograph by R.C.B. Ashworth, 1979, (8 pages) p.1.
24 *RAF Rotorcraft History*, RAF Publication, 2007, p.22.
25 *Fairey Aviation: The Archive Photographs Series*, compiled by John W.R. Taylor, 1997, p.124.
26 Gibbings, David, *Fairey Rotodyne*, 2009, p.82.
27 Spencer, p.390.
28 Uttley, p.147.
29 Ibid., p.152.
30 James, p.57.
31 Ibid., p.401.
32 Schofield, Jim, *Developing British Military Helicopters: The Memoirs of a Helicopter Designer*, 2009, pp.71, 72.
33 Farrar-Hockley, General Sir Antony, *The Army in the Air: The History of the Army Air Corps*, 1994, p.205.
34 Ibid., p.213.
35 Prouty, Raymond, W,. *Military Helicopter Design Technology*, 1989, pp.10–11.
36 First Report of the Interdepartmental Helicopter Committee, September 1950, p.14.
37 Bell Helicopter Corporation, *Yesterday, Today and Tomorrow*, c.1959, p.17.
38 *Journal of the RAeS*, Vol. 70, p.242.
39 Gardner, Richard and Longstaff, Reginald, *British Service Helicopters*, 1985, p.182.

CHAPTER 12

1   Report of The Committee of Inquiry into the Aircraft Industry appointed by the Minister of Aviation under the Chairmanship of Lord Plowden 1964–65, HMSO 1965, Chapter 41, Summary of Recommendations No.(i), p.95.
2   Ibid., Nos. (vi), (ii), p.95.
3   Ibid., Nos. (xx), (xxii), p.97.
4   Ibid., No. (XXIV).
5   Sir George had been a senior scientist at the RAE for thirty-five years, initially as a head of department, before becoming its director in 1955. After becoming chairman of John Brown Engineering Ltd he was subsequently president of the RAeS in 1965–66.
6   RAeS Discussion on the Plowden Report, p.4.
7   Ibid., p.3.
8   Ibid., p.5. Peter Masefield was Britain's first ever civil air attaché in Washington who later helped develop BEA into a substantial and profitable air carrier and who in 1955 became managing director of Bristol Aircraft.
9   RAeS Discussion on the Plowden Report, p.13.
10 Ibid., p.42.
11 Ibid., p.31.
12 Ibid., p.50.
13 Ibid., p.32.
14 Plowden Committee, Chapter 8, Government Policy and Results – Civil, para 112.
15 Ibid.
16 The Mach number was the way of relating an aircraft's velocity to the speed of sound. Mach 1 was about 760mph at sea level and Concorde's design speed of Mach 2 was some 1,430mph at 60,000ft.
17 RAeS Publication, April 2009, Concorde, The Supersonic Achievement: Hayward, Professor Keith, Concorde a Historical Overview, p.8.
18 Britain assented to the 'e' in 1967.
19 Owen, Kenneth, *Concorde: Story of a Supersonic Pioneer*, 2001, p.35.
20 Ibid.
21 Ibid., p.62.
22 Ibid., p.63.
23 Ibid., p.75.
24 Following his successes with Concorde Gedge went on to become director of manufacturing at the British Aircraft Corporation.
25 Owen, p.125.
26 Costello, John and Hughes, Terry, *Concorde: The International Race for Supersonic Passenger Transport*, 1976, p.145.
27 Davies, R.E.G., *Fallacies and Fantasies of Air Transport History*, 1994, p.119.
28 Costello, pp.143–44.
29 A full-length account of the struggle can be found in Owen, Kenneth, *Concorde and the Americans: International Politics of the Supersonic Transport*, 1997, pp.49–134.
30 Davies, *Fallacies*, p.110.
31 Owen, p.155.
32 Summary of the Report of the Supersonic Transport Aircraft Committee, p.282.

33 Broadbent, E.G. Unpublished Biographical Memoir of Morien Bedford Morgan, p.391.

34 Davies, *Fallacies*, p.107.

35 *Flight*, Vol. 96, 1969, 'Concorde Costs Probed,' July/Dec, p.565.

36 *Air Transport World*, January 1986, Vol. 23, No. 1, James P. Woolsey, 'British Airways Concorde now considered "flagship of the fleet"', pp.40–41.

CHAPTER 13

1 Gunston, Bill, *Rolls-Royce Aero Engines*, 1989, p.103. Frank Halford never received the adulation given to the other designers such as Frank Whittle and Stanley Hooker but his work on the Goblin and Ghost jet engines was truly ground-breaking.

2 Ibid.

3 Golly, John, *Whittle, The True Story*, 1987, p.54.

4 Harvey-Bailey, Alec, *Rolls-Royce: Hives, The Quiet Tiger*, 1986, p.61.

5 Gunston, *Rolls-Royce*, p.108.

6 Ibid., p.65.

7 Ibid., p.112.

8 National Aerospace Library, Original specification produced by Roy Fedden for the Cotswold Aircraft company and its Propeller Gas Turbine.

9 Gray, Robert, *Rolls on the Rocks: The History of Rolls-Royce*, 1971, p.74.

10 Pugh, Peter, *The Magic of a Name: The Rolls-Royce Story, Part Two: The Power Behind the Jets*, 2001, p.58.

11 Banks, Air Commodore F.R., *I Kept No Diary: 60 years with Marine Diesels, Automobile and Aero Engines*, 1983, pp.248–49.

12 Hooker, Sir Stanley, *Not Much of an Engineer*, 1984, p.154.

13 Pugh, p.69.

14 Gray, Robert, *Rolls on the Rocks*, 1971, p.76.

15 Ibid.

16 Ibid., p.77.

17 Garvin, Robert V., *Starting Something Big: The Commercial Emergence of GE Aircraft Engines*, 1998, p.58.

18 Ibid., p.84.

19 Turner, Frank, Rolls-Royce in Perspective Past Present and Future, R.J. Mitchell Memorial Lecture, 1991, p.23.

20 Ibid.

21 Banks, Air Commodore, op. cit., p.212.

22 The Magic of the Name, op. cit., p.110.

23 Garvin, Robert V., op. cit., p.47.

24 Frank Turner, op. cit., p.25.

25 Banks, p.252.

26 Address to the Newcomen Society of North America, The Achievement of Excellence, The Story of Rolls-Royce, p.30.

CHAPTER 14

1   Gardner, Richard, and Rood, Dr Graham, *RAE 100: The Royal Aircraft Establishment Legacy since 1918*, 2010, p.3.
2   Ibid., p.7.
3   Fifty Years at Farnborough, HMSO 1955, p.10.
4   Gardner, p.11.
5   Fifty Years at Farnborough, p.10.
6   Gardner, p.13.
7   Ibid., p.15.
8   Ibid., p.21.
9   Ibid., p.25.
10 Ibid., p.55.
11 Fifty Years of Farnborough, p.15.
12 National Aerospace Library, *RAE Five Year Plan*, typewritten document on the development of the RAE, p.1.
13 Nicolson, L.F., The Work of the Royal Aircraft Establishment, the RAE, 12th Mitchell Memorial Lecture of 24 February 1965, p.6.
14 National Aerospace Library, RAE Annual Review 1974, EPR(C)/R, RAE Copy No. 79.
15 Publication by Farnborough Air Sciences Trust in 2002 entitled 'Enough has been bulldozed, Save Farnborough, the Cradle of British Aviation'; Andrew Nahum, Farnborough in the Cold War, p.13.
16 Ibid.
17 Jones, Matthew, *The Official History of the UK Strategic Nuclear Deterrent, Vol. 1*, 2017, p.68.
18 Fifty Years at Farnborough, p.26.
19 Weber, Johanna and Warrer, C.H.E., quoted by Andrew Nahum, 'World War to Cold War, Formative Episodes in the Development of the British Aircraft Industry 1943–1965'. Thesis submitted for the degree of PhD., The London School of Economics and Political Science, March 2002, p.183. (Accessed on ethesis.lse.ac.uk/3568)
20 Dobson, Michael D., ed., *Wings over Thurleigh: An Aeronautical Research Heritage 1954 to 1994*, 2001, p.234.
21 Ibid., p.238.
22 Ibid.
23 *Oxford DNB*, Bradley, John K., William George Arthur Perring, doi.org/10.1093/ref. odnb/35484, p.3
24 Morgan, Sir Morien, Perring – the Man, RAE Memorandum of February 1976, p.67.
25 *Oxford DNB*, Masefield, Peter G., Sir Alexander Hall doi.org/10.1093/ref. odnb/73646, p.1.
26 Dempster, p.149.
27 *The Times*, 29 August 1975.
28 Adams A.R., *Good Company*, 1976, p.6.
29 ibid, pp.19–20.
30 *The Times*, 1 September 1975, Article by Sir Morien Morgan on Sir George Gardner.

31 *Oxford DNB*, Pedley, T.J., Sir Michael James Lighthill, Biographical Memoirs of the
    Fellows of the Royal Society 2001, Vol. 47, p.336.
32 *The Independent*, 22 July 1998, Crighton, D.G., Obituary on Sir James Lighthill.
33 *Daily Telegraph*, 20 July 1998, Obituary on Sir James Lighthill.
34 *The Independent*, 22 July 1998, Dalyell, Tam, on Sir James Lighthill.
35 University College London, Recollections of Sir James Lighthill 1924–1998, by
    Hunt, Professor Julian. Address given at Sir James Lighthill's Funeral on 27 July 1998.
36 RAeS publication, The Fifty-Ninth Wilbur and Orville Wright Memorial Lecture
    and Presentation of Awards, 3 December 1970, p.8.
37 *The Independent*, 31 March 1994, Jones, Professor R.V., Obituary of Sir Robert
    Cockburn.
38 *Radio and Electronic Engineer*, Vol. 42, Iss. 12, 1972, Robert Cockburn, pp.554, 561.
39 *RAE News*, Journal of the Royal Aircraft Establishment, Vol. 22, No. 7, July 1969,
    p.5.
40 *RAE News*, Journal of the Royal Aircraft Establishment, Vol. 25, No. 12,
    December 1972, farewell from the director, p.6.
41 Broadbent, E.G., Biographical Memoir of Morien Bedford Morgan, Biogr. Mems
    Fell. R. Soc. November 1980, p.390.
42 Ibid., p.391.
43 Buttler, Tony, with Carbonel, Jean Christophe, *Building Concorde from Drawing Board
    to Mach 2*, 2018, p.11.
44 *Journal of the RAeS*, Vol. 64, June 1960, Morgan, Sir M.B., Supersonic Aircraft –
    Promise and Problems, p.326.
45 *Journal of the RAeS*, Vol. LXXVI, May 1972, Morgan, Sir M.B., A New Shape in
    the Sky, p.326.
46 *The Times*, Thursday, 6 April 1978, Obituary on Sir Morien Morgan.
47 Director Morien Morgan became renowned for the number and quality of
    Farnborough's rose beds.
48 *Aerospace* June/July 1979, Aerospace talks to R.P. Probert, p.14.
49 *The Times*, 16 August 1980, Robinson, H.G.R., Obituary of Mr Rhys Price
    Probert.
50 Ibid.
51 *Aerospace* June/July 1979, Aerospace talks to R.P. Probert, p.14, 15.
52 Ibid., p.15.
53 66th Wilbur and Orville Wright Memorial Lecture at the RAeS on 1 December
    1977, Hawthorne, Professor Sir William, Aircraft Propulsion from the Back Room,
    p.17.
54 Reynolds David, *Summits: Six Meetings that Shaped the Twentieth Century*, 2007,
    p.261.
55 The Management of Research Institutions, A Look at Government Laboratories,
    NASA Publication SP-481, 1984, p.69.

SUMMARY

1   Reed, p.1.
2   Wood, preface, p.5.

3   Ibid.
4   *Journal of Aeronautical History*, Paper 2018/04, Hayward, Keith, 'Government and British Aerospace 1945–64'.
5   Ibid., p.102.
6   Hearne, Peter, The Right Size Matters. Lecture to the RAeS on Wednesday, 28 April 2004.
7   Ibid., p.1.
8   Ibid., p.2.
9   Ibid., p.6.
10   Ibid., p.8.
11   Reed, p.4.
12   Hearne, p.17.
13   *The Aviation Annual of 1946*, Cleveland, Reginald M. New United States Planes, p.171.
14   Hearne, p.15.
15   Ibid., p.9.
16   Fedden, Roy, Lecture to the Society of Engineers, London, May 1954, p.237.
17   The Institution of Mechanical Engineers, Jones, Professor R.V., The Sixty First Thomas Hawkesley Lecture, 'Engineering Creativity', p.587.
18   Ibid., pp.587–88.
19   Ibid., p.595.

SELECT BIBLIOGRAPHY

PAPERS AND MISCELLANEOUS OFFICIAL PUBLICATIONS

Address to the Newcomen Society of North America, The Achievement of Excellence, The Story of Rolls-Royce, 1977.

Cabinet Paper (46) 217, 23 July 1946 [Secret], Civil Aircraft Requirements.

Sir Sydney Camm, Lecture at Hamilton Place by Austin, Sir Roger, FRAeS 24 May 1995.

Crisis in Procurement, A Case Study on TSR2 by Williams, Dr Geoffrey Gregory, Frank and Simpson, John, RU51 Journal 1969.

Fedden, Roy, Original specification for the Cotswold Aircraft Company and its Propeller Gas Turbine (National Aerospace Library)

Gottinger Monograph, German Research and Development on Rotary-Wing Aircraft (1938–1945), Edited by Berend G. Van der Wall, 2015.

Hansard: Parliamentary Debates on Air Estimates 1946–77.

Hansard, Parliamentary Debates on Civil Aviation, Vols I & II, 1945–46, 1947–50.

Interview of D.P. Davies by Giesler, July 1992, (National Aerospace Library, Oral Recordings).

Memoirs of Sir Frederick Page, Unpublished Typescript, National Aerospace Library, 1997.

Ministry of Civil Aviation on British Air Services, Command Paper 6712, HMSO December 1945.

Minutes of The Society of British Aerial Constructors.
27 October 1943.
14 March 1945.
11 June 1947.

Oxford DNB 3 January 2008, Ludlow, Piers N., Sandys (Edwin) Duncan, Baron Duncan Sandys (1908–87).

Pamphlet of 9 January 1939, Pitcairn, Harold F., 'Juan de la Cierva'.

Paper by Lord Douglas of Kirtleside (chairman of British European Airways) on The Aircraft Industry – A National Asset, The Operators Point of View, Published on 16 April 1959.

Prospero, Proceedings from the British Rocket Oral History Conferences at Charterhouse, No. 2, Spring 2005, p.32.

RAeS, Weybridge Branch Lecture, 18 October 1989, Salisbury, M.W. , The Significance of TSR2.
RAeS, Yeovil Branch Diamond Jubilee, 31st Henson and Stringfellow Memorial Lecture of 1986, Rogers, V.A.B, 40 years of Helicopter Engineering (Machines and Men).
RAeS Paper, April 1909, Hayward, Keith, Concorde: The Supersonic Achievement.
RAeS Publication, RAF Rotorcraft History, 2007, p.22.
RAeS Symposium, The History of the UK Strategic Deterrent, 17 March 1999.
Recommendations of the Brabazon Committee for Post-War British Transport Aircraft, 1942–1944, compiled by Berry, Peter, February 2011.
Review by the Aeronautical Research Council for the Years 1949–1954, HMSO 1955.
The Royal Air Force Historical Society, TSR2 with Hindsight, 1988, p.188.
Unpublished History of Westland Helicopters Ltd., A History of British Rotorcraft 1866–1965, compiled by Brie, Reggie, National Aerospace Library, August 1968.

REPORTS

Report of the Committee of Inquiry into the Aircraft Industry appointed by the Minister of Aviation under the Chairmanship of Lord Plowden, 1964–65, HMSO 1965.
Report of the Court of Inquiry into the Accidents to Comet G-ALYP on 10 January 1954 and Comet G-ALYY on 8 April 1954, HMSO 1955.
Report of the Fedden Mission, June 1943, Copy No. 31, Review of the Civil Aviation Position in America.
Reports of the Ministry of Civil Aviation 1946 and 1947, HMSO 1948.
Reports of the Ministry of Civil Aviation for 1948 and 1949, HMSO 1950.

MAGAZINES

Aeronautics, March 1953, Scott-Hall, S., 'Our new airliners – first results of the new British formula for developing civil aircraft', pp.28–33.
Aeroplane Monthly, July–December 2012, Chorlton, Michael, 'One-Eleven Origins: The Bare Bones of the "Bus-Stop" Jet's Rocky Road to Certification, Half a Century of Service', pp.68–78.
Aerospace, Vols 1/11, July 1974, Probert, R.P. (director of the Royal Aeronautical Establishment), 'On the Role of the RAE in European Collaboration', pp.12–17.
Aerospace, Vol. IX, No. 10, December 1982, Mashman, Joseph, 'Development and Early Introduction of the Helicopter', pp.12–17.
Aerospace, May 1983, Kirkpatrick, Dr D.L. and Pugh, P.O., 'Towards the Starship Enterprise – Are the Current Trends in Defence Unit Costs Inexorable?', pp.16–23.
Air and Space, May 2012, Wilkinson, Stephan, 'Bristol Brabazon: Design by Committee', pp.56–57.
Air Britain Archive, Winter Issue, December 1911, West, Michael, 'Imperial and British Airways go to War', pp.181–186.
Air Britain, Aviation World Spring Issue, March 2011, 'The Brabazon Committee', pp.94, 95.
Air Britain, Aviation World, Summer Issue, June 2011, King, Derek, 'The Brabazon Committee', pp.94–96.

Air Britain, Aviation World, Summer Issue, June 2012, McCrickard, John P., 'Vickers VC10 – Commercial Failure – or Success', p.90.

Air Power Review, Vol. 20, No. 1, Spring 2017, Pyke, Air Chief Marshall, and Slessor, Sir John, 'The Unsung British Cold War Strategist', p.68.

Air Transport World, January 1986, Vol. 23, No. 1, Woolsey, James P., 'British Airways Concorde now considered the "Flagship of the Fleet"', pp.40–41.

Australian Aviation, 2002, Wilson, Stewart, 'British Airliners since 1945, Part 1', pp.45–49.

Aviation News, January 2017, Wright, Dr Kevin, 'TSR2: The Greatest Aircraft the RAF Never Flew,' p.19.

Diplomacy and Statecraft, 2013, French, David, 'Duncan Sandys and the Projection of British Power after Suez', p.44.

Flight International, 1969 Supplement, Concorde, 'The Background Story – Described by the Engineers'.

Interavia, Vol. XII, No. 9, 1957, Baur, E., 'Britain's Aircraft Industry in 1957', p.875.

Journal of Aeronautical History, Paper of 4 March 2018, Hayward, Professor Keith, 'Government and British Civil Aerospace', 1945–64, pp.100–36.

Journal of the RAeS, LVI 1952, Roberts, G.N., 'On Civil Aviation in the Second Elizabethan Era', pp.849–853.

Journal of the RAeS, LXV 1961, The First Cierva Memorial Lecture, Bennett, J.A.J., 'The Era of the Autogiro', pp.649–60.

Journal of the RAeS, LXVI 1964, Lord Douglas of Kirtleside, 'The Progress of European Air Transport 1946–61 – with particular reference to BEA', pp.141–62.

Journal of the RAeS, LXXV 1971, Eleventh Cierva Memorial Lecture, Sikorsky, Igor I., 'Sixty Years of Flying', pp.761–68.

Journal of the RAeS, LXXX 1976, Armstrong, F.W., 'The Aero Engine and its progress – Fifty years after Griffith', pp.499–520.

Journal of the RAeS, November 1962, Pardue, G.K.C., 'Space Flight Projects Based on Blue Streak', pp.690–98.

Journal of the RAeS, Vol. 70, Part 1, January 1966, Hafner, R., 'British Rotorcraft', p.241.

Journal of the RAeS, Vol. LI, 1947, Cochrane, Air Marshal the Hon. Sir Ralph, 'Development of Air Transport During the War', pp.384–417.

Journal of the RAeS, Vol. LXII, January–December 1958, 46th Wilbur Wright Memorial Lecture, Gardner, W.H. (Director Royal Aircraft Establishment), 'Automatic Flight – The British Story', pp.476–96.

Journal of the RUSI, Vol. CXV, March 1970, No. 657, Lucas, Dr Keith, 'The Case Study of the TSR2', p.42.

Journal of Strategic Studies, Rees, Wyn, 'The 1957 Sandys White Paper, New Priorities in British Defence Policy', p.226.

Propliner, No. 77, Winter 1998, Berry, Peter, 'The Brabazon Propliners', p.10.

Propliner, No. 79, Summer 1999, Berry, Peter, 'The Brabazon Propliners: Article on the variety of aircraft types proposed for construction by the wartime Brabazon Committee', pp.37–42.

Royal Air Force Historical Society Journal, 31 May 2004, 'Recollections of a Secretary of State for Defence – The R. Hon The Lord Healey', pp.4–16.

Royal Air Force Historical Society Journal, 'TSR2 with Hindsight', 1998.

RUSI Journal, Vol. 108, 1969, Cross, Sir Kenneth, 'Bomber Command's Thor Missile Force'.

The Aviation Historian, Iss. No. 16, July 2016, Hayward, Keith, 'Trident: Britain's Fork in the Road', pp.10–19.

The Aviation Historian, Iss, No. 18, January 2017, Hayward, Keith, 'Between the Devil and the Deep Blue Sea', p.13.

The Aviation Historian, Iss. No. 19, 2017, Hayward, Keith, '60 Years On – Duncan Sandys and the 1957 Defence White Paper', pp.11–20.

The Putnam Aeronautical Review, Iss. No. 1, May 1989, Barfield, Dr Norman, 'VC10, Engineering Pedigree of a Thoroughbred', pp.18–32.

The Putnam Aeronautical Review, Iss. No. 1, May 1989, Edwards, Sir, George, 'VC10, Personal Overview and Perspective', pp.3–6.

The Putnam Aeronautical Review, Iss. No. 1, May 1989, Finnimore, J.R., 'VC10, A Niche in History'; pp.13–14.

The Putnam Aeronautical Review, Iss. No. 1, May 1989, Stroud, John, 'VC10, Operational Analysis', pp.15–17.

The Putnam Aeronautical Review, Iss. No. 1, May 1989, Wheeler, Barry, C., 'VC10, In RAF Service Today', pp.7–12.

BOOKS

Andrews, C.F. and Morgan E B., *Vickers Aircraft since 1908*, 1988.

Armitage, Michael, *The Royal Air Force*, 1999.

Aurelius, Marcus, *Meditations*, Penguin 1964.

Bailey, H.W.F., *50 Years of Bristol Engines*, unpublished book produced in July 1970 (National Aerospace Library).

Balfour, Harold, *Wings over Westminster*, 1973.

Banks, Air Commodore, F. R., *I Kept No Diary: 60 years with Marine Diesels, Automobile and Aero Engines*, 1983.

Barnes, C. H., *Bristol Aircraft*, 1966.

Barnett-Jones, Frank, *TSR2: Phoenix or Folly?*, 1994.

Beamont, Roland and Reed, Arthur, *English Electric Canberra*, 1984.

Bell Helicopter Corporation, *Yesterday, Today and Tomorrow*, c.1959

Birtles, Philip, *The Avro Vulcan: Britain's Cold War Warrior*, 2007.

Blackman, Tony with O' Keefe, Garry, *Victor Boys: True Stories from Forty Memorable Years of the Last V-bomber*, 2012.

Blackman, Tony with Wright, Anthony, *Valiant Boys: True Stories from the Operators of the UK's First Four Jet Bombers*, 2014.

Bowers, Peter M., *Boeing Aircraft Since 1916*, 1989.

Boyes, John, *Project Emily: Thor IRBM and the RAF*, 2008.

Brand, Robin H., *Britain's First Space Rocket: The Story of the Skylark*, 2014.

Braybrook, Roy, *Hunter: A Personal View of the Ultimate Hawker Fighter*, 1987.

Brie, Reginald, *The Autogiro and How to Fly It*, 1935.

Broadbent, E. G., *Unpublished Biographical Memoir of Morien Bedford Morgan*, National Aerospace Library.

Brookes, Andrew, *V-Force: The History of Britain's Airborne Deterrent*, 1982.

Buckley, John, and Beaver, Paul, *The Royal Air Force, The First One Hundred Years*, 2018.

Burke, Damien, *TSR2: Britain's Lost Bomber*, 2010.

Buttler, Tony, *British Secret Projects: Jet Bombers since 1949*, 2003.

Buttler, Tony, *Hawker P.1127, Kestrel and Harrier: Developing the World's First Jet V/STOL Combat Aircraft*, 2017.

Chichester, Michael and Wilkinson, John, *The Uncertain Ally: British Defence Policy 1960–1990*, 1982.

Chisholm, Anne and Davie, Michael, *Beaverbrook: A Life*, 1993.

Cockrane, Dorothy, Von Hardesty and Lee, Russell, *The Aviation Careers of Igor Sikorsky*, 1989.

Cole, Lance, *VC10: Icon of the Skies, Boeing and a Jet Age Battle*, 2017.

Comfort, Nicholas, *Surrender, How British Industry Gave up the Ghost: 1952–2012*, 2012.

Costello, John and Hughes, Terry, *Concorde: The International Race for Supersonic Passenger Transport*, 1975.

Dancey, Peter G., *The Avro Vulcan: A History*, 2007.

Darling, Kev, *De Havilland Comet*, 2005.

Davies, Glyn, *From Lysander to Lightning: Teddy Petter, Aircraft Designer*, 2014.

Davies, Peter E., and Thornborough, Anthony M., *The Harrier Story*, 1996.

Davies R.E.G., *Fallacies and Fantasies of Air Transport History*, 1994.

Davis, John, *The Concorde Affair*, 1969.

De Saint-Exupéry, Antoine, *Night Flight*, 1939.

Delve, Ken, Green, Peter and Clemons, John, *English Electric Canberra*, 1992.

Dempster, Derek D., *The Tale of the Comet*, 1958.

Dockrill, Saki, *Britain's Retreat from East of Suez: The Choice between Europe and the World*, 2002.

Dowling, Wing Commander John, *RAF Helicopters: The First Twenty Years*, 1992.

Edgerton, David, *England and the Aeroplane: An Essay on a Militant and Technological Nation*, 1991.

Evans, Andy, *BAE/McDonnell Douglas Harrier*, 1998.

Farrar-Hockley, General Sir Antony, *The Army in the Air: The History of the Army Air Corps*, 1994.

Farrer, David, *The Sky's the Limit: The Story of Beaverbrook at MAP*, 1943.

Fedden, Sir Roy, *Britain's Air Survival: An Appraisement and Strategy for Success*, 1957.

Forbat, John, *TSR2: Precision Attack to Tornado*, 2006.

Foyle, Christopher and Marriott, Leo, *Pioneers to Partners: British Aircraft since 1945*, 2009.

Gardner, Charles, *British Aircraft Corporation*, 1981.

Gardner, Richard and Longstaff, Reginald, *British Service Helicopters*, 1985.

Gardner, Robert, *From Bouncing Bombs to Concorde: The Authorised Biography of Aviation Pioneer Sir George Edwards*, 2006.

Garvin, Robert V., *Starting Something Big: The Commercial Emergence of GE Aircraft Engines*, 1998.

Gethin, Michael J., *Sky Guardians: Britain's Air Defence, 1918–1993*, 1993.

Gibbings, David, *Fairey Rotodyne*, 2009.

Gibbings, David, *A Quiet Country Town: A Celebration of 100 years of Westland at Yeovil*, 2015.

Golly, John, *Whittle: The True Story*, 1987.

Gray, Robert, *Rolls on the Rocks: The History of Rolls-Royce*, 1971.

Grove, Eric J., *Vanguard & Trident: British Naval Policy Since World War II*, 1987.

Gunston, Bill, *Rolls-Royce Aero Engines*, 1989.

Gunston, Bill, *Fedden: The Life of Sir Roy Fedden*, 1998.

Gunston, Bill, *Plane Speaking: A Personal View of Aviation History*, 1991.

Gunston, Bill, *The Development of Jet and Turbine Aero Engines*, 2002.

Halford-Macleod, Guy, *Born of Adversity: Britain's Airlines 1919–1963*, 2014.

Halfpenny, Bruce Barrymore, *English Electric Canberra: The History and Development of a Classic Jet*, 2005.

Harker, Ronald W., *The Engines that were Rolls-Royce*, 1979.

Harkins, Hugh, *Tornado, Air Defence Variant: Protecting Britain's Skies*, 1995.

Harvey-Bailey, Alec, *Rolls-Royce: Hives, The Quiet Tiger*, 1986.

Hastings, Stephen, *The Murder of TSR2*, 1966.

Hayward, Keith, *Government and British Civil Aerospace: A Case Study in Post-War Technology Policy*, 1983.

Hayward, Keith, *The British Aircraft Industry*, 1989.

Healey, Denis, *The Time of My Life*, 1989.

Hennessy, Peter, *Having It So Good: Britain in the Fifties*, 2007.

Hewat, Timothy and Waterlow, W.A., *The Comet Riddle*, 1955.

Higham, Robin, *Speedbird: The Complete History of BOAC*, 2013.

Hill, C.N., *A Vertical Empire: History of the British Rocketry Programme*, 2012.

Hollingsworth, Mike and Owen, Gorden Campbell, *FireFlash to SkyFlash: A History of Air to Air Missile Firings in the Royal Air Force, 1952 to 2002*, 2004.

Hooker, Sir Stanley, *Not Much of an Engineer: An Autobiography*, 1984.

Howard, Bill, *Evolution of British Jet Engines 1926–1966*, 2016.

Hubbard, Kenneth and Simmons, Michael, *Dropping Britain's First Hydrogen Bomb: The Story of Operation Grapple 1957–58*, 1985.

Jackson, A. J., *de Havilland's Aircraft since 1909*, 1987.

Jackson, Robert, *Hawker Hunter*, 1982.

Jackson, Robert, *Avro Vulcan*, 1984.

Jackson, Robert, *Canberra: The Operational Record*, 1988.

James, Derek N., *Westland Aircraft since 1915*, 1991.

Kaplan, Philip, *Big Wings: The Largest Aeroplanes Ever Built*, 2005.

Karp, A., *Ballistic Missile Proliferation: The Policies and the Technics*, 1996.

Kay, Anthony L., *Turbojet History and Development 1930–1961, Vol. 1: Great Britain and Germany*, 2007.

Lucas, Paul, *TSR2: Lost Tomorrows of an Eagle*, 2009.

McKim, Dr Frank, *Trident: A History*, 2008.

McLelland, Tim, *TSR2: Britain's Lost Cold War Strike Aircraft*, 2010.

MacMillan, Harold, *The Macmillan Diaries, The Cabinet Years 1950–57*, 2003.

Masefield, Sir Peter with Gunston, Bill, *Flight Path: The Autobiography of Sir Peter Masefield*, 2002.

Mason, Francis K., *Hawker Hunter*, 1985.

Mason, Francis K., *Harrier*, 1986.

Mason, Francis K., *Hawker Aircraft since 1920*, 1991.

Mason, Francis K., *The British Bomber Since 1914*, 1994.

Massey, Harrie, and Robins, M.O., *History of British Space Science*, 1986.

Millard, Douglas, *An Overview of United Kingdom Space Activity, 1957–1987*, 2005.

Morton, Peter, *Fire Across the Desert: Woomera and the Anglo Australian Joint Project, 1946–80*, 1989.

Munson, Kenneth, *Pictorial History of BOAC and Imperial Airways*, 1970.

Myles, Bruce, *Jump Jet: The Revolutionary V/STOL Fighter*, 1986.

Neale, M.C., *The Memoirs of George Purvis Bulman: An Account of Partnership, Industry, Government and The Aero Engine*, 2002.

Orlebar, Christopher, *The Concorde Story*, 2004.

Owen, Kenneth, *Concorde and the Americas: International Policies of the Supersonic Transport*, 1997.

Owen, Kenneth, *Concorde: Story of a Supersonic Pioneer*, 2001.

Pakenham, Lord, *Born to Believe: An Autobiography*, 1953.

Peden, G.C., *Treasury and British Public Policy*, 2000.

Peden, G.C., *Arms, Economics and British Strategy: From Dreadnoughts to Hydrogen Bombs*, 2007.

Petter, Teddy, *A Biography: Triumph and Disasters*, Compiled by Robert Page, Roy Fowler and Adrian Page, 1991.

Phipp, Mike, *The Brabazon Committee and British Airliners 1945–1960*, 2007.

Porter Andrew, *Transatlantic Betrayal: The RB 211 and the Demise of Rolls-Royce Ltd*, 2013.

Price, Dr Alfred, *Panavia Tornado: Spearhead of NATO*, 1988.

Prouty, Raymond W., *Military Helicopter Design Technology*, 1989.

Pugh, Peter, *The Magic of a Name: The Rolls-Royce Story, Part II: The Power Behind the Jets*, 2001.

Ransom, Stephen and Fairclough, Robert, *English Electric Aircraft and their Predecessors*, 1987.

Reed, Arthur, *Britain's Aircraft Industry: What Went Right? What Went Wrong?*, 1973.

Rivas, Brian, *De Havilland Comet: Owners' Workshop Manual*, 2016.

Ross, Tony, *75 Eventful Years: A Tribute to the Royal Air Force, 1918–1993*, 1993.

Rowan, Sir Leslie, *Arms and Economies: The Changing Challenge*, 1960.

Sampson, Anthony, *Empires of the Sky: The Politics, Contests and Cartels of World Airlines*, 1986.

Sandbrook, Dominic, *Never Had It So Good: A History of Britain from Suez to the Beatles*, 2005.

Simons, Graham M., *Concorde Conspiracy: The Battle for American Skies, 1962–77*, 2012.

Simons, Graham M., *Comet! The World's First Jet Airliner*, 2013.

Skinner, Stephen, *BAC One-Eleven: The Whole Story*, 2002.

Skinner, Stephen, *British Aircraft Corporation: A History*, 2012.

Spenser, Jay P., *Whirlybirds: A History of the US Helicopter Pioneers*, 1998.

Stroud, John, *European Transport Aircraft since 1910*, 1966.

Thomas, Shirley, *Men of Space*, 1968.

Trimble, William F., (Editor), *From Airships to Airbus: The History of Civil and Commercial Aviation, Vol. 2: Pioneers and Operations*, 1995.

Turner, Frank, *Rolls-Royce in Perspective: Past, Present and Future*, 1991.

Uttley, Matthew, *Westland and the British Helicopter Industry, 1945–1960*, 2001.

Verhovels, Sam Howe, *Jet Age: The Comet, the 707 and the Race to Shrink the World*, 2010.

Whittle, Sir Frank, *Jet: The Story of a Pioneer*, 1953.

Williams, Dr Geoffrey, Gregory, Frank, and Simpson John, *Crisis in Procurement: A Case Study of the TSR2*, 1969.

Williams, Ray, *Comet and Nimrod*, 2000.

Wilson, Keith, *Vickers/BAC VC10: Owner's Workshop Manual – Insights into the Design, Construction, Operation and Maintenance of the VC10 in Civil and Military Service*, 2016.

Wood, Derek, *Project Cancelled: The Disaster of Britain's Abandoned Aircraft Projects*, 1986.

Woodley, Charles, *BOAC: An Illustrated History*, 2004.

Woodley, Charles, *Golden Age: British Civil Aviation 1945–1965*, 1992.

Woodley, Charles, *History of British European Airways, 1946–1974*, 2006.

Wynn, Humphrey, *RAF Nuclear Deterrent Forces*, 1994.

INDEX

You may also be interested in …

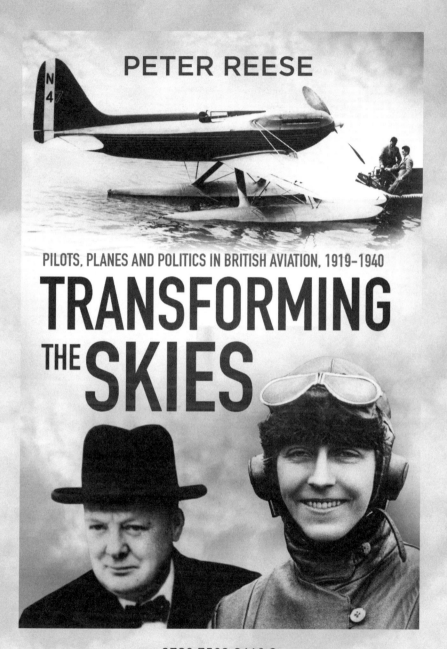

PETER REESE

PILOTS, PLANES AND POLITICS IN BRITISH AVIATION, 1919–1940

TRANSFORMING
THE SKIES

9780 7509 8410 2

KEITH MCCLOSKEY

UNSOLVED AVIATION MYSTERIES

FIVE STRANGE TALES OF AIR AND SEA

9780 7509 9258 9

DON'T LET
THEM BAG
THE NINES

THE FIRST WORLD WAR MEMOIR
OF A DE HAVILLAND PILOT –
CAPTAIN F. WILLIAMS MC DFC

FOREWORD BY PATRICK BISHOP

9780 7509 9131 5

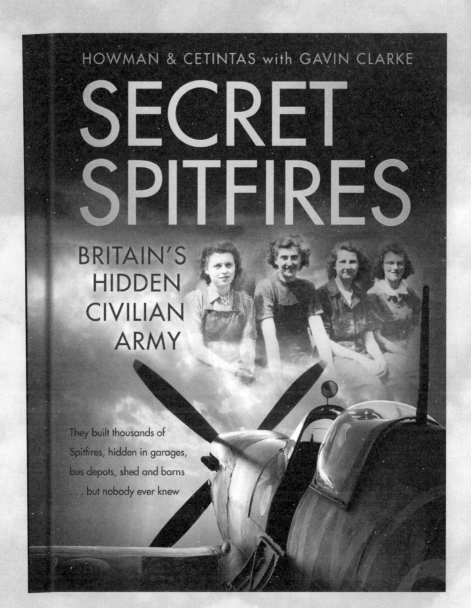

HOWMAN & CETINTAS with GAVIN CLARKE

SECRET SPITFIRES

BRITAIN'S HIDDEN CIVILIAN ARMY

They built thousands of
Spitfires, hidden in garages,
bus depots, shed and barns
. . . but nobody ever knew

9780 7509 9199 5

The History Press

The destination for history
www.thehistorypress.co.uk